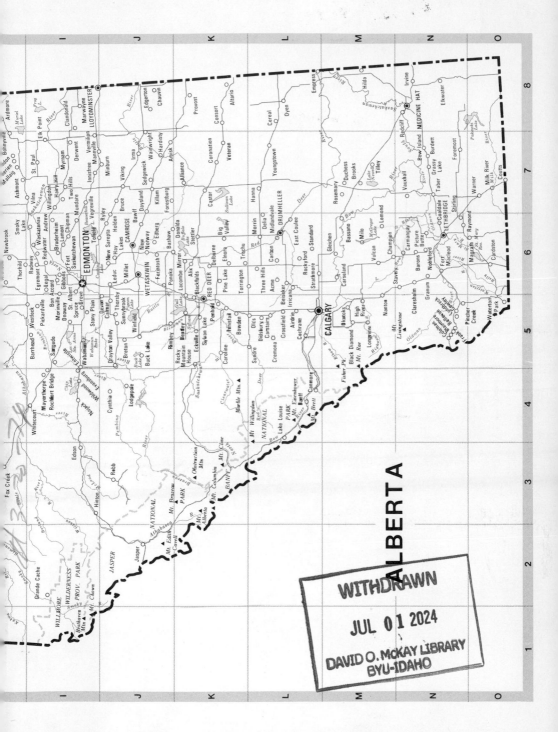

ALBERTA

H. R. H. Princess Louise Caroline Alberta (1848-1939). Fourth Daughter of Queen Victoria.

(Alberta Provincial Library)

OVER 2,000 PLACE-NAMES OF ALBERTA

By

ERIC J. HOLMGREN

and

PATRICIA M. HOLMGREN

WESTERN PRODUCER BOOK SERVICE

SASKATOON

1973

ISBN 0-919306-37-3

first edition 1972
second edition 1973

WESTERN PRODUCER BOOK SERVICE
SASKATOON
Printed and Bound in Canada
by Modern Press

To our Native People who gave us the first Alberta Place-Names and to those pathfinders and pioneers who came from other climes bringing names,

And to our son, DAVID, and his generation of Albertans,

This book is appropriately dedicated.

FOREWORD

The pursuit of place-names takes the student to the very roots of local history and can be both pleasant and useful, but the stories behind the numerous names on the map are for more than those who are engaged in academic pursuits. For residents, tourists and others, some knowledge of the origin of place-names is capable of greatly enriching life's day-to-day adventures in the country and particularly in the area.

Some people have engaged in this particular study as a hobby. It can be fun. It is something in which anybody can engage and the benefits may be varied. It will bear repeating that to know how places on the map received their names is to know much more about local history and local traditions.

On the fresh soil of Western Canada there was an unusual amount of earthy romance attached to names. Apart from a few attempts to name railroad stations in alphabetical order, there was no particular pattern in the name choices. Some names were adopted from foreign lands; some were chosen to honour pioneer personalities; many had amusing or subtle origins and many more of the most attractive names were from the Native Indian tongues. The student may wish there were more of these beautiful names of Indian origin. Still other names may have been selected for no particular reason except that they sounded well or were the first to come to mind when decisions had to be made in the rush and hurry of a rapidly developing area. But regardless of meaning, the circumstances leading to their adoption are worth noting. What do those commonly used names mean and how did they happen to be chosen?

Many writers and hobbyists over the years discovered pleasure in the study of place-names and left fragmentary records or short articles on the subject. Their contributions were useful. But now a comprehensive work is making its appearance to be available as a valuable contribution to Canadiana in book form. Based on exhaustive study, the new book will occupy an important place on home, school and library shelves and be welcomed by students of the Canadian story.

On my own behalf I offer congratulations to the authors and on behalf of all who will find the new work useful and enjoyable, I say "thanks."

Grant MacEwan
Lieutenant Governor of Alberta.

June, 1972

ACKNOWLEDGMENTS

This work could not have been completed without the help of many people. Particularly do we wish to extend our grateful thanks to the Geographic Board of Alberta and to the Canadian Permanent Committee on Geographical Names for their support. To the Surveys Branch of the Alberta Department of Highways and Transport; to C. W. Youngs, Director of Surveys; to W. H. Bogdan, chief cartographer who made many helpful suggestions; also to Jack Marsh of the mapping staff. To Barbara Smith who checked some of the manuscript and to her husband "Tobe" who aided in the correct placing of features for the end paper "grid". To the Hudson's Bay Company, Edmonton for their interest and help. To Dr. J. Godfrey of the Research Council of Alberta for information on geologists after whom a number of lakes were named. To the Provincial Archives of Alberta; to the Glenbow-Alberta Institute, Calgary and to the Archives of the Canadian Rockies, Banff, for their assistance. To the many secretary-treasurers of the villages and towns who kindly supplied information on the origins of the names of their municipalities. To Government of Alberta Photographic Services. With this revised edition due acknowledgment must be made to the Library of the Mountain Region of the Canadian National Railways at Edmonton for further information on many names; to Mr. J. G. Coté of the Canadian National in Montreal; to Mr. K. R. Perry, General Manager, Northern Alberta Railways Company; to Dr. E. O. Drouin, O.M.I. of the Oblate Archives, Edmonton; to Reverend Dr. Peter Ream of Fort Saskatchewan; to the Archives of the University of Alberta and to the Archives of the United Church of Canada, Alberta Conference, Edmonton. Finally, we must thank those members of the Historical Society of Alberta who supplied useful information and gave encouragment and to our many friends who helped in any way, no matter how small. To each and every one our sincere thanks.

E.J.H.
P.M.H.

THE HERITAGE OF ALBERTA PLACE-NAMES

One of the surest ways to read the history of any given area is through its place-names for in them are recorded the comings and goings of successive waves of people. The origins may be elusive for some but sooner or later they yield their secrets. So it is with Alberta, for although the Province entered history only in 1754, a rich collection of place-names was to be created.

The first inhabitants, the Indians, gave their names to lakes, rivers, hills, creeks and mountains. The greatest traditions here are from the Cree, Stoney and Blackfoot who were by far the most dominant groups in the area. For untold centuries they gave their names and many have survived to this day although attempts to put them into the script of the European languages are frequently crude effronteries for the often musical sounds of the names themselves. Thus "Saskatchewan" meaning swift water comes from *Kissaskatchewan,* a descriptive name. Wetaskiwin is from *wi-ta-ski-oo-cha-ka-tin-ow,* meaning hill of peace, commemorating a treaty between the Cree and the proud Blackfoot to the south. "Wabamun" is mirror which brings to mind the often calm appearance of that lake. Etzikom is a Blackfoot word meaning "coulee" and Etzikom Coulee therefore means "Coulee Coulee" which is not so strange as it may seem since the English are guilty of this same thing. Witness the Avon River. The word "avon" means "river" in Anglo-Saxon and therefore Avon River (of which there are three in England and one in Ontario) means, "river river."

Other Indian names are still preserved: Chipweyan meaning pointed skins. Assiniboine in both the mountain and village of Fort Assiniboine; Michichi meaning hand — from the Hand Hills — *michichi ispatinan;* Nisku meaning wild goose (appropriate now with an airport nearby). The credit for the preservation of these names must go to Father Lacombe, the pioneer missionary who compiled his *Dictionnaire de la Langue Cris* and to Joseph Burr Tyrrell of the Geological Survey of Canada who listed many Indian names in both Cree and Stoney. These and others who set down lists of these names have eased the task of those who followed in determining what the name exactly means as well as the correct spelling and, wherever possible the pronunciation. It must not be forgotten that the spelling as set down are approximations for the gutteral sounds and glottal stops of these aboriginal languages which often elude the Anglo-Saxon and French tongues.

The fur traders came next, approaching from the east. In 1754 Anthony Henday journeyed from York Fort to a point somewhere near present day Innisfail where from a low hill he viewed the Rockies, the first white man to do so. Henday was in too great a hurry to leave any names and his diary is scrappy—or rather that portion of it which has come down to us. In any event he had a specific mission to accomplish.

It remained for those who came later to record and leave names: Peter Fidler, Peter Pond, William Tomison, Alexander Mackenzie and David Thompson to name but a few. They travelled slowly and recorded carefully what they saw and they gave names. Some were Indian such as Chipweyan; others had a distinctly English ring about them: Manchester House, Buckingham House, Fort Augustus, Jasper's House. This was the period of intense rivalry between the North West Company and the Hudson's Bay Company with its "leap frogging" from place to place. One of the most indefatigable of these post builders was William Tomison of the Hudson's Bay Company. Many of the posts he built have disappeared and their names survive only in old journals and on historic site markers. The name of one post he founded, has survived with consequences he could not have foreseen. The name of that post was Edmonton House.*

The fur trade era was not devoid of achievement. The fur traders in their explorations in search of furs located and mapped the Saskatchewan River system, the northern branch of which formed a convenient highway into the interior. They also found a feasible route across the mountains—the express route over Athabasca Pass to the Columbia—a route that was to remain in use until the coming of the railway. Many names such as Roche Miette, Roche à Perdrix, Roche Ronde, Lac la Biche attest to the voyageurs who supplied the power to move furs and supplies along this route.

Hard on the heels of the fur traders came the missionaries. At first they were not welcomed and then were simply tolerated. The Oblates such as Albert Lacombe, Hippolyte Leduc and Emile Petitot not only established missions but left the French accent on lakes and other features. The active missionary period from 1840 onward saw the emergence of names such as Lac Ste. Anne, Lac la Nonne, St. Albert, St. Paul des Metis, all attesting to the work of these men. While on the subject of French names Bourgeau of the Palliser Expedition named Lac des Arcs and reference is often seen to Lac des Isles or Lac des Islets, now known as Lake Isle; it is a mystery why such an euphonous name as Lac des Isles disappeared.

Co-incidental with the Oblates were the first Methodist missionaries of whom the best known was Robert Terrill Rundle whose name is preserved on a mountain near Banff. The MacDougalls followed with Morley and Victoria, later changed to Pakan.

It was at this time that a few hardy souls other than missionaries and Company servants ventured into what amounted to the great preserve of the Hudson's Bay Company. The best known is Paul Kane, the artist, who while he did not bestow any names faithfully noted them. Others such as the Earl of Southesk, Viscount Milton and Dr. Cheadle who came later, actually gave names to features as well as noting them and many of these have remained to the present.

These men like the missionaries were not exactly welcomed with open arms and had to pay for their stay in Company territory. The Company stoutly defended its right to the area, basing its claim upon its two hundred year old charter. When an inquiry was held in London to investigate this,

---

*Historic site names are not included (except where the trading post grew into a permanent habitation) as they are not in the Gazetteer of Canada.

the only witnesses who knew the area were employees of the Company. Sir George Simpson, the determined Governor and arch opponent of any form of settlement, expounded at length on the doubtful value of settlement of the area to the inquiry but even he must have realized that the *status quo* could not have been preserved for long.

Events in Canada were marching toward Confederation and the Imperial Government was concerned about the prairie heartland, a concern that may well have been justified by the statements of the Honourable Company and by the noisy utterances of certain expansionist elements active in the United States at that time. In any event an expedition was sent out to examine the territory and to report upon it. Its leader was Captain John Palliser and his expedition spent four seasons studying the hinterland. In 1863 there appeared his celebrated report, a highly readable document. In it Palliser and his assistant Dr. James Hector (later Sir James Hector), as well as Bourgeau, the botanist to the expedition and Lieutenant Blakiston recorded faithfully the many features that they named. Names like Mount Balfour, Pyramid Mountain, Mount Hardisty, were given by Hector while Blakiston named the Livingstone Range and several features near the Waterton Lakes area and Bourgeau named Lac des Arcs and Wind Mountain. Hector also carefully noted stories lying behind such names as Snake-Indian River and Snaring River. The contribution of Palliser and his men toward place-names in Alberta is outstanding and Palliser deserves more recognition in the Province than he has received.

Four years after the publication of Palliser's report, the British North America Act created the Dominion of Canada. Then, in 1869 the Ancient and Honourable Hudson's Bay Company surrendered to Canada its title to what are now the three prairie provinces and the North-West Territories were formed shortly thereafter. Into the southern part of this sparsely settled land came the whisky traders from Montana, giving the Indians a few cups of bad whisky for buffalo robes. These men established their posts: Whoop-Up, Slide Out and Stand Off—the name of the last survives as a locality to this day, commemorating an incident when a group of traders managed to "stand off" a U.S. sheriff who had followed them from Montana.

To assert the Canadian claim to the newly formed North-West Territories and to stamp out the whisky trade, the North-West Mounted Police was established in 1873 and the following year there occured the famous march. The story of the Force in Alberta is well known. The names that they gave to their posts have survived: Fort Macleod, Calgary, Fort Saskatchewan and one of their officers gave his name to a hamlet, Walsh.

Even when law and order were established in the West the land had still to be made ready for the settlers. Treaties were concluded with the Indians but most important of all the land had to be surveyed to insure equitable distribution. There then began and continued for some two decades what was one of the greatest feats of measurement—the Dominion Land Surveys. These entailed accurate measurement of all lands in the prairie regions down to sections of one square mile. The surveyors in their task of preparing the land for the settlers accurately recorded everything, gave names occasionally, and placed existing named features upon the map for everyone to see. The land was then ready for the oncoming tide of settlement whereby a settler could take out a homestead of 160 acres and ultimately gain title to it.

When the surveys of lands began so did the explorations and surveys for the Pacific Railway as it was first called. Men such as Sandford Fleming carefully surveyed the possible routes and like their land survey colleagues carefully noted existing names and added new ones. The actual building of the Canadian Pacific brought forth a proliferation of stations and the names of these for the most part have survived. Many commemorate shareholders, engineers and other railway officials, as does Banff. Later as the C.P.R. branch lines spread out and the Grand Trunk Pacific and Canadian Northern were built more new names (not always of railway officials) appeared.

While the land surveyors were at work, their counterparts of the Geological Survey of Canada were also active, probing the record of the rocks to determine the potential of as yet unknown mineral resources. In the course of their meticulous search, they not only named features such as mountains, lakes and creeks, but like the land surveyors they carefully recorded Indian names. Prominent among them were G. M. Dawson, the hunchback famous for his extensive travels in the rugged areas of B.C. and J. B. Tyrrell, later to gain prominence in his avocation as a historian. It was Tyrrell who, as has previously been noted, set down the Stoney and Cree names (with their English translation) for all well-known features in a list that is invaluable in preserving these names. Tyrrell and Dawson at times carefully set out the origins of names as for example, Tyrell's explanation of the name "Hand Hills" (*michichi ispatinan*).

From the completion of the C.P.R. until the outbreak of World War I a tremendous tide of settlers flowed into Alberta. It did not however begin all at once. Even before the railway arrived, ranchers had been gradually entering the southern area of the Province where they established tremendous "spreads" such as the Bar U, Quorn and Oxley ranches. These people, the last of the old West left behind names such as Stavely, Waldie Creek and others. The era of the big ranch was brief, however, as settlers began to fill up even this part of the land taking up their homesteads on quarter sections which thanks to the surveys were now ready for them. The greatest number came from the British Isles and brought with them names reminding them of the land they had left: Hythe, Didsbury, Innisfail, Lloydminster, Kitscoty and many others. They came with other groups: Americans, Scandinavians, Ukrainians (Galicians), Germans and not a few Canadians from eastern Canada. It was in this era that the pattern of settlement in Alberta took shape. Many towns grew, flourished briefly and then sank into obscurity and now only their names remain to remind us of an optimistic day; others flourished and remain with us. Alliance, Valhalla, Vilna, Wostok, remain as a reminder of the ethnic pattern of the Province.

It was at this time that a different kind of exploration had been attracting attention. Climbers had begun to explore the Rockies and to climb the then unnamed peaks. The opening of Rocky Mountains National Park (now Banff) in 1885 and Jasper at a later date gave impetus to this. Adventurers such as Hugh Stutfield, J. N. Collie, Walter Wilcox, Mary Schäffer, A. P. Coleman and others climbed the peaks and gave many of them names. While some of these names, after alpinists of other lands may be open to question, there is no denying that the climbers did much in their written accounts to draw attention to the tourist potential of the parks. Columbia Icefield, Mount Columbia, Mount Temple, Mount Alberta, Snow Dome and scores now known to thousands of tourists, all date from this time. Lakes and rivers never before seen by man were discovered: Moraine Lake, Fortress Lake, Sunwapta Falls—the list is endless. Then from 1913 to 1920 the Alberta-British Columbia boundary was carefully surveyed; new names and origins of names were added and the surveyors noted the names of many mountains and passes and placed them accurately upon the map.

Alberta, like the rest of Canada was still very much a colony of Britain and the concept of the British Empire, "the empire upon which the sun never sets" was still very strong. In 1911 the year of the Coronation of George V and Queen Mary a number of settlements were named: Coronation, Consort, Loyalist, Throne, Veteran. The link seemed further strengthened when at the start of World War I hundreds flocked to the colours to fight for their country. To them Britain had to stand. World War I may have depopulated sections of Canada but its end saw a large number of names added to the map—particularly mountains. There were the generals—Haig, Foch, Allenby, Kitchener—and admirals: Jellicoe, Beatty, Evan-Thomas. The Battle of Jutland had attracted much attention and names of battleships that took part in this engagement were given to mountains: Inflexible, Warspite, Invincible—some of them quite appropriate. Near Jasper the Victoria Cross Ranges were set aside for those who won that award. Mount Edith Cavell recalled the tragedy of a British nurse. Finally there were the names of many who distinguished themselves upon the field of battle.

World War II and its aftermath saw a lessening of the almost indiscriminate naming of mountains after high military officers and battles but a number of features were named for those who fell in that conflict. In most instances an effort was made to name a feature in the area from which the man came although this was not always possible.

Like other provinces, Alberta has its share of features named for the prominent citizens. Mount Bulyea recalls George Hedley Vicars Bulyea (1859-1926), the first Lieutenant Governor of the Province. Mount Rutherford honours Alexander Cameron Rutherford, the first premier. Winston Churchill had a range named for him in recognition of his services in World War II. Hector Lake is after Sir James Hector of the Palliser Expedition. The missionaries and the churches were not forgotten: Mount Machray for Archbishop Robert Machray, the well-known Anglican metropolitan of Rupertsland; Lacombe after the well-known Oblate missionary, Albert Lacombe; Grouard after Bishop Grouard; Mount McQueen after Dr. D. G. McQueen longtime Presbyterian minister in Edmonton; Mount William Booth after the founder of the Salvation Army. Royalty too was remembered. The Province was named for Princess Louise Caroline Alberta, fourth daughter of Queen Victoria—who also gave her name to Lake Louise. King Edward VII and his consort Queen Alexandra have mountains named for them. Even the pharaohs of ancient Egypt came in with Mount Chephren being named for Chephren or Khafre.

This then, in brief is the story of the place-names of Alberta. It is a colourful part of the larger whole that is the history of the Province for it tells us much of the Indians, the fur traders, missionaries, surveyors, settlers, railwaymen, climbers and others who came this way. Many are the stories that may be told of place-names. Kicking Horse Pass comes from the story of Dr. James Hector being kicked by a horse. Gladys, formerly a post office, now a locality was named for one Gladys Harkness whose husband in 1890 frequently brought out mail from High River for his neighbours before a post office was established. At first this was a courtesy but when a post office was established it was named Gladys as settlers had been saying "Let's go to Gladys' for the mail." What could be more logical? Or Pibroch—when there was an argument over a suitable name one settler suggested Pibroch as that was the name of his cat! It is not known whether the meowing of the animal resembled the bagpipes.

There are still many unnamed features in Alberta and they cannot all be named at once. Future generations will come along to place names upon them and so continue this preservation of the ongoing history of the Province.

The responsibility for naming new features and for verifying existing names is vested with the Geographic Board of Alberta which works in close conjunction with the Canadian Permanent Committee on Geographical Names. In its work the Board seeks the advice of all who are interested in place-names. Every effort is made to preserve the heritage of Alberta's place-names and to guard against what was—it must be admitted—in many instances the all too careless abandon in giving names that formerly existed. Naming is now governed by carefully laid down rules to insure that names are fitting to Alberta and to Canada. This has not always been the case and too many names (particularly those of mountains) are of individuals who are forgotten today.

Unlike many books which are written and then complete, this is an on going project and here is where you, the reader can help. Perhaps you know of the origin of a name not included here. Or you may know of further information on names we have included. There are some 7,000 place-names in Alberta; we have included only one third of them. We would like to find the origin of many more. So if you know anything of the origin of a name or can give us further information on names already included please drop us a line. Any information be it serious or anecdotal is welcome. Just address your letter to the authors, care of the publisher.

E.J.H.
P.M.H.

DEFINITIONS

In the listing of inhabited places we have made use of the following terms as defined by the Alberta Department of Municipal Affairs:

City
An incorporated place having 10,000 or more inhabitants.

County
A rural municipality set up to place municipal and school administration under one elected authority.

Hamlet
An unincorporated place usually containing not less than eight separate dwellings and one business outlet such as a general store.

Locality
An unincorporated place usually with at least eight dwellings but no business outlet. Or it may be an area with a scattered population. Many names in this work fall into this latter category; the name may be still used locally. A locality may or may not have a post office.

Municipal District
A rural municipality wherein municipal and school administrations are under two separate authorities.

Post Office
A place so designated by the Canada Post Office.

Settlement
Any legal land sub-division so designated as a settlement.

Station
A number point on a railroad as defined by a railway company to where freight is dispatched or tariff calculated.

Summer Village
The same as for village but having at least 50 separate dwellings, i.e. summer cottages.

Town
An incorporated place having from 1,000—10,000 inhabitants.

Village
An incorporated place containing not less than 75 separate buildings continuously occupied as dwellings.

Indian Reserve
An area of land set aside for Native People and administered by the Federal Government.

Note: Where possible the date that the name became official is given in brackets following the derivation.

ERRATA

ACHESON, locality: 'Tisdal' should read 'Tisdale.'

ANNETTE, lakes: 'wife of the then manager' should read 'mother of the then manager.'

DEBOLT, hamlet, creek: add 'See supplement'.

DEVILS THUMB, THE, mountain: add 'Named by Allen, 1891.'

FORT, hills and creek: (0-7 should read (D-7).

HORSESHOE, ridge: read 'Descriptive. Southeast of Mount Livingstone. (1959).'

NOBLEFORD, village: read 'Charles Noble' (d. 1957). . . .

STOLBERG, locality: read 'Probably after Stollberg, Saxony, Germany; originally C.N.R. Station.'

TURNER VALLEY, village and valley: read 'After Robert and James Turner from Edinburgh,' early settlers. . . .

WADLIN, lake: read 'After L. N. Wadlin (1884-1954),' D.L.S. . . .

WASEL, locality: add 'See supplement.'

WESTON, lake: add (1859).

ABBREVIATIONS

A.F.C.	Air Force Cross
A.G.W.R.	Alberta and Great Waterways Railway
A.L.S.	Alberta Land Surveyor
B.A.	Bachelor of Arts
B.C.L.S.	British Columbia Land Surveyor
C.B.	Companion Order of the Bath
C.E.	Civil Engineer
C.E.F.	Canadian Expeditionary Force (World War I)
C.M.G.	Companion of the Order of St. Michael and St. George
C.N.R.	Canadian National Railway, also Canadian Northern Railway
C.P.R.	Canadian Pacific Railway
C.S.M.	Company Sergeant Major
D.C.M.	Distinguished Conduct Medal
D.D.	Doctor of Divinity
D.F.C.	Distinguished Flying Cross
D.F.M.	Distinguished Flying Medal
D.L.S.	Dominion Land Surveyor
D.S.C.	Distinguished Service Cross
D.S.O.	Distinguished Service Order
D.T.S.	Dominion Topographical Surveyor
E.D. & B.C.R.	Edmonton, Dunvegan and British Columbia Railway
F.R.G.S.	Fellow of the Royal Geographical Society
F.R.S.	Fellow of the Royal Society (London)
F.R.S.C.	Fellow of the Royal Society of Canada

G.C.M.G.	Grand Cross of St. Michael and St. George
G.T.P.R.	Grand Trunk Pacific Railway
H.M.S.	His/Her Majesty's Ship
Hon.	Honourable
I.S.O.	Imperial Service Order
K.C.	King's Counsel
K.C.B.	Knight Commander Order of the Bath
K.C.M.G.	Knight Commander Order of St. Michael and St. George
K.C.V.O.	Knight Commander Victorian Order
Kt.	Knight
K.T.	Knight of the Order of the Thistle
Lieut. Col.	Lieutenant Colonel
LL.D.	Doctor of Laws (Honoris Causa)
M.D.	Doctor of Medicine
M.I.D.	Mentioned in Despatches
M.L.A.	Member of the Legislative Assembly
M.M.	Military Medal
M.P.	Member of Parliament
N.A.R.	Northern Alberta Railways
N.W.M.P.	North-West Mounted Police
O.M.I.	Order of Mary Immaculate
Pte.	Private
Q.C.	Queen's Counsel
q.v.	qui vide (which see)
R.C.A.F.	Royal Canadian Air Force
R.N.	Royal Navy
Rt. Hon.	Right Honourable

ABBOT, pass (9,588 feet) (L-3)
After Philip Stanley Abbot, member of the Appalachian Mountain Club, who met his death on the slopes of Mount Lefroy, 1896. Abbot and his companions were climbing and had unroped on a slope of rotten rock. Abbot was looking for a route down when he suddenly slipped and fell, landing on the slope below. Although conscious when his companions reached him, he soon died from the effects of the fall.

ABEE, hamlet (H-6)
After A. B. Donley, manager, Northwest Lumber Company, Edmonton. (1914).

ABERDEEN, mount (10,340 feet) (L-4)
Named in 1897 after Lord Aberdeen, then Governor General of Canada. John Campbell Gordon, First Marquis of Aberdeen and Temair (1847-1934) was Governor General from September, 1893 to November, 1898. While in office, he travelled extensively throughout Canada, owning a fruit ranch on the Coldstream River near Vernon, B.C. The travels are recorded in the journals of his wife Ishbell (née Marjoribanks) and reveal a keen perception of Canadian life at this time. The journal was published by the Champlain Society in 1960.

ABRAHAM, lake (K-4)
This lake, formed behind the Bighorn Dam, is named for Silas Abraham and the Abraham family, Stoney Indians who have lived in the area for many years. The name was chosen by school students in a contest. (1972)

ACADIA VALLEY, hamlet (L-8)
Settled by Nova Scotians. During the French regime, Acadia included what is now Nova Scotia and New Brunswick. (1911)

ACHESON, locality (I-5)
After A. Acheson Tisdal, one time assistant to the general manager, Canadian National Railway, Winnipeg.

ACME, village (L-6)
Greek word meaning "summit"; point of perfection. When named Acme was the most northerly point on the Canadian Pacific Railway branch line northeast of Calgary; Tapscott Post Office prior to 1909.

ADEN, locality (O-7)
After Aden, Arabia; the first postmaster, H. E. Anderson had been a sailor, and Aden was his last port of call. (1913).

ADOLPHUS, lake (I-2)
This lake, at the headwaters of the Smoky River, was named by A.P. Coleman after Adolphus Moberly, an Iroquois who guided Coleman and his party to Mount Robson in 1908. Coleman writes: "He was . . . a striking figure of powerful physique and tireless muscles, and thoroughly master of everything necessary for the hunter in the mountains." Later, after the party had arrived at the head of Mount Robson watershed, they came upon "a pretty lake which we named after Adolphus."

AEOLUS, mountain (8,672 feet) (J-2)
In Greek mythology, the God of the winds; the survey party who named the peak reached it on a windy day. (1916)

AETNA, creek and hamlet (O-6)
The creek flows into the St. Mary River. Named after the Mormon ecclesiastical district of Aetna, which was named, 1890, after Mount Etna (Aetna) volcano, Sicily. (1900)

AGGIE, locality (G-3)
After a relative of W. R. Smith, former general manager of the Edmonton, Dunvegan and British Columbia Railway. (1915)

AGNES, lake (L-4)
After Susan Agnes, Baroness Macdonald of Earnscliffe (wife of Sir John A. Macdonald) who visited the lake in 1886.

AIGUILLE, peak (9,840 feet) (K-3)
A needle like peak; from the French "aiguille" meaning needle.

AIRDRIE, village (L-5)
After Airdrie, Scotland. According to the official tourist guide of Airdrie, Scotland, the Alberta village got its name as follows: "There is an Airdrie in Canada founded in 1889 between Edmonton and Calgary, and we have it on good authority that this settlement was named by William MacKenzie, a Scot by birth and a contracting engineer by profession—after one situated a few miles northeast of Glasgow, in a quarry and mining section." The origins of the name Airdrie are lost in history but have been the subject of considerable argument. One theory suggests that the name comes from the atmospheric conditions "air-dry." This is suggested by one James Knox who wrote a history of Airdrie, Scotland as a trick of imagination. He further dismisses another theory that the origin of the name is Celtic and means "high level" for although Airdrie may "stand high" it has no level part. Also a third interpretation that the name means "high pasture run" is unlikely. Historians of the town are now satisfied that the true meaning of the town is "The King's Height." A British historian Chalmers accepts this view and considers that the rising ground upon which the modern Scottish town now stands was the scene of the Battle of Arderyth fought in 577 between the forces of Aeddan, King of Kintire and Rydderich the Bountiful, King of Strathelid. This has, however been questioned. Whenever the Battle of Arderyth was fought it was a decisive one for it secured the independence of Strathclwydas a kingdom for some 400 years and if the foregoing is accepted, according to S. W. Wilk in this book *One Day's Journey* we can be proud of the fact that the name 'Airdrie' had its origin in antiquity. (1893)

AIRWAYS, locality (K-7)
On proposed Canadian National Railway line from Alliance, Alberta to Unity, Saskatchewan; surveyed from the air by Colonal Birdseye, the grade was made but no steel ever laid.

AKAMINA, pass (5,835 feet) (O-5)
The name seems to be Indian meaning "bench land." It was applied to a joint astronomical station occupied in 1861 by the British-American

2

Boundary Commission and is referred to in their report as "Akamina Camp and Astronomical Station."

ALBERTA, province and mount (11,874 feet)   (K-3)
After H.R.H. Princess Louise Caroline Alberta (1848-1939), fourth daughter of Queen Victoria; she was the wife of the Marquis of Lorne who was Governor General of Canada from 1878-1883. The name first appears in a sonnet he wrote entitled *On the New Province of Alberta*:

"In token of the love which thou has shown
For this wide land of freedom, I have named
A province vast and for its beauty famed,
By thy dear name to be hereafter known.
Alberta shall it be. Her fountains thrown
From Alps unto three oceans, to all men
Shall vaunt her loveliness e'en now; and when
Each little hamlet to a city grown,
And numberless as blades of prairie grass
Or the thick leaves in distant forest bower
Great peoples hear the giant currents pass,
Still shall the waters, bringing wealth and power
Speak the loved name—the land of silver springs
Worthy the daughter of our English kings."

Alberta was created a provisional district in 1882 and in 1905 the Province was established by Act of Parliament. Mount Alberta was named in 1889.

ALBRIGHT, locality, lake and creek   (G-1)
After W. D. Albright (1881-1946), pioneer agriculturist of the Peace River district. He was associated with the Federal Experimental Station at Beaverlodge and demonstrated the value of the area in the field of agriculture. (1947)

ALCOMDALE, locality   (I-5)
After Dr. Alcombreck of Edmonton, owner of land in the vicinity. (1913)

ALCOVE, mountain (9,200 feet)   (J-2)
In a recess; descriptive.

ALDER FLATS, hamlet   (J-5)
Descriptive.

ALDERSON, mount (8,833 ft.), lake, creek (O-5) and locality (M-7)
After Lieutenant General E. A. H. Alderson, K.C.B., who commanded the Canadian Expeditionary Force in France, 1915-1916. Locality formerly known as Carlstadt. (1915)

ALDERSYDE, hamlet   (M-5)
Name suggested by a Scottish settler; after *Aldersyde* by Annie S. Swan; a story of the Scottish border country.

ALEXANDER, Indian Reserve   (I-5)
After the Cree Chief Alexander Arcand (1845-1913); when the Reserve was formed in 1882, he and his band moved to it from Lac la Nonne.

ALEXANDRA, mount (11,214 feet), river and glacier (K-3)
North Saskatchewan River; mountain named, 1902, after Queen Alexandra (1844-1925), consort of King Edward VII.

ALEXO, locality (K-4)
After Alexo Coal Co., Ltd., which in turn was named after Alex. Kelso, discoverer of the mine there. (1923)

ALHAMBRA, hamlet (K-5)
After the ancient palace and fortress of the Moorish kings of Granada; Horseguards was the post office name until 1916.

ALICE, lake (L-3)
Head of Dolomite stream, northeast of Bow Lake; named in 1898 by Reverend H. P. Nichols after his wife.

ALIX, village and lake (K-6)
After Mrs. Alexia (Alix for short) Westhead whose husband was one of the pioneer ranchers in the area. Their home was a scene of hospitality and many celebrations. (1905)

ALLAN, mount (9,150 feet) (L-4)
After Dr. J. A. Allan (1884-1955), one time Professor of Geology, University of Alberta, who surveyed provincial coal resources. (1948

ALLEN, mount (10,520 feet) (L-4)
Sixth of the Ten Peaks, (q.v.), named after S. E. S. Allen, a pioneer climber in the Rockies. (1924)

ALLENBY, mount (9,500 feet), creek and pass. (L-4)
After Field Marshal Viscount Allenby (1861-1936), Commander of the British Army in Palestine during the First World War. (1918)

ALLERSTON, locality (O-7)
After Jacob Allers, early settler; changed in 1914, from Doran, which was named after the son of the postmaster.

ALLIANCE, village (K-7)
Formerly Galahad Post Office it was named after Alliance, Ohio which in turn was formed by the uniting of four communities in 1854. (1916)

ALLISON, peak (8,671 feet) and creek (N-5)
After Douglas Allison, formerly in the Royal North-West Mounted Police; he settled on this creek.

ALNESS, locality (L-7)
Presumably after Alness, Rosshire, Scotland.

ALNUS, peak (9,753 feet) (K-2)
Alders (Latin *alnus*) grow on the mountain sides. (1921)

ALTARIO, hamlet (K-8)
Combination of Alberta and Ontario; probably after homes of the early settlers; Wilhelmina Post Office until 1919.

AMBER, mountain (8,341 feet) (J-2)
The summit is covered with amber-coloured shale. (1916)

AMBER, river   (B-2)
From the colour of the water.

AMERY, mount (10,943 feet)   (K-3)
After L. S. Amery (1873-1955), British statesman. He held many
political posts; Secretary for India; extensive traveller and avid mountain climber. He climbed the mountain in 1929.

AMETHYST, lakes   (J-2)
Cautley in his report on the Survey of the Alberta-British Columbia
border (1917-1921) notes that "the Amethyst Lakes, both a beautiful
blue, add colour to the scene."

AMISK, village   (J-7)
Cree word for "beaver"; became a village in 1956.

ANCONA, locality   (K-4)
Ancona is a town in Italy and there is a place of the same name in
Illinois, U.S.A. Formerly Pollock. (1914)

ANDERSON, creek   (K-5)
Flows into the Blindman River; named after James Sangster Anderson,
of Craigmyle, killed in World War II. (1950)

ANDERSON, peak (8,700 feet)   (O-5)
After Captain S. Anderson, R.E., Chief Astronomer of the second British
Boundary Commission (49th parallel, Lake of the Woods to the
Rockies) and also a member of the first British Boundary Commission
(Strait of Georgia to the Rockies), 1858-1862.

ANDREW, village   (I-6)
After Andrew Whitford, farmer; named in 1902.

ANDROMEDA, mount (11,000 feet)   (K-3)
Andromeda—from Greek Mythology—who was the wife of Perseus;
named by well-known climber, Rex Gibson. (1959)

ANGLE LAKE, locality   (I-7)
At the angle of a lake. (1911)

ANGLE, peak (8,844 feet)   (J-2)
Situated at a sharp turn in the ridge. (1916)

ANGEL, glacier   (J-2)
Mount Edith Cavell (q.v.) from fancied resemblance to an angel.

ANKERTON, locality   (J-6)
After Anker H. Laurityen, Scandinavian grandfather of an early post-
master; formerly Campbelton. (1916)

ANNETTE, lakes (Lake Louise area—L-4; Jasper)   (J-2)
That at Lake Louise named by Wilcox. 1896. after Mrs. Astley, wife
of the then manager of the Lake Louise chalet. Annette Lake, Jasper, is
after the wife of Col. C. Maynard Rogers, former superintendent of the
Park.

ANSELMO, locality   (I-4)
After Anselmo, Nebraska, former home of the postmaster. (1913)

5

ANTHOZOAN, mount (9,060 feet)   (L-4)
From coral (anthozoan) reefs in the Devonian limestone of the mountain. (1925)

ANTHRACITE, hamlet   (L-4)
Semi-anthracite was mined here from 1885 by the Canadian Anthracite
Company until the mine was closed in 1897.

ANTLER, hill   (K-5)
Translation of Cree *was-ka-suk-is-kun ka-so-pit* meaning "pile of elk
horns"; in Stoney *pa-chi-di ha-ba-jo-bi* (Tyrrell). "Antler Mt." on
Palliser map, 1863.

ANTOINE, lake   (H-6)
After one Antoine Desjarlais, who trapped on the lake, 1814; formerly
an employee of the North West Company.

ANTONIO, locality   (N-7)
From the character in Shakespeare's *Merchant of Venice*.

ANTROSS, locality   (J-5)
Combination of the names Anthony and Ross; sawmills were operated
in the vicinity by the Ross Board Lumber Company and the Anthony
Lumber Company. (1926)

ANZAC, hamlet   (F-7)
From the abbreviated name familiarly given to the Australian-New
Zealand Corps in World War I, 1914-1918 and derived from the initial
letters. (1917)

AQUILA, mountain (9,269 feet)   (J-2)
An eagle (*aquila*) was seen on the peak when it was named. (1916)

ARCADIA, locality   (G-4)
A region of rural quiet. (1914)

ARCS, LAC DES, lake   (L-4)
Arc is Fench for "bow"—descriptive—lake formed by the expansion
of the Bow River; named by Bourgeau, 1858.

ARCTOMYS, peak (9,162 feet)   (I-2)
After whistling marmots (*arctomys columbianus*) seen in the valley.

ARDENODE, locality   (L-6)
After a place in Ireland; formerly Hawick. (1914)

ARDLEY, locality   (K-6)
Changed from Coalbanks, 1912, possibly after Ardley, Oxfordshire,
England. There was also a Calgary pioneer family by this name.

ARDMORE, hamlet   (H-8)
After the school district which was erected before the hamlet. It may
have been named after Ardmore, Pennsylvania which in turn was named
after Ardmore, Ireland.

ARDROSSAN, hamlet   (I-6)
After Ardrossan, Ayrshire, Scotland; suggested by a Miss Edmiston.
(1910)

ARÊTE, mount (9,810 feet) (J-3)
Descriptive name meaning "edge".

ARETHUSA, mount (9,000 feet) (M-5)
After the famous British light cruiser, sunk by a mine, February 11, 1916.

ARGENTIA BEACH, summer village (J-5)
Originally named "Silver Bay"; changed to Argentia Beach to avoid confusion with Silver Beach on Pigeon Lake. The name is derived from Latin argentum, silver.

ARIES, peak (9,000 feet) (K-3)
Rocky Mountain rams (aries) were seen on the mountain when it was named.

ARMADA, locality (M-6)
Spanish word meaning "fleet" or "squadron." (1914)

ARMSTRONG, mount (9,161 feet) (M-5)
After D. J. Armstrong of the Surveyor General's staff, Ottawa. Killed in action, April 12, 1917.

ARNICA, lake (L-4)
So named as arnica flowers border the lake and provide a charming frame when blooming. (1959)

ARRIS, mountain (8,875 feet) (J-2)
Synonymous with arête—descriptive; arris—a sharp edge. (1916)

ARROWWOOD, village (M-6)
From its situation on East Arrowwood creek, a tributary of the Bow River. Blackfoot—hents-ziks-kway—Arrowwood (place where wood obtained for arrows).

ASHLAR, ridge (J-2)
Fiddle River; a smooth wall, hence a fancied resemblance to ashlar masonry. (1916)

ASHMONT, hamlet (H-7)
After a suburb of Boston, Massachusetts, former home of the postmaster, L. W. Babcock. (1911)

ASPEN BEACH, summer village (K-5)
The reference is to the poplar (aspen) trees on Gull Lake; post office changed from Wiesville in 1916.

ASSINEAU, river and locality (G-4)
Cree Indian word meaning "nobody".

ASSINIBOINE, mount (11,870 feet) and pass (7,152 feet) (M-4)
After the Assiniboine (Stoney) Indians, who hunted in the Rockies from the 49th parallel to the watershed between the North Saskatchewan and the Athabasca; the name means "those who cook by placing hot stones in water."

ASTORIA, river and pass (7,600 feet) (J-2)
After the Astoria fur traders who travelled east through Athabasca

Pass, 1814. Named after Fort Astoria, established in 1811 at the mouth of the Columbia River by the American Fur Company under John Jacob Astor I, from which Astoria takes its name. (1917)

ASTOTIN, creek and lake (I-6)
Probably from the Cree *asteyotin* (Lacombe), "it ceases to blow," i.e. a reference to the often quiet appearance of this lake.

ATHABASCA, lake (B-7)-(C-7), river (K-3)-(C-7), falls (J-2), glacier, mount (11,452 feet) K-3) and pass (K-2)
The name "Athabasca" is derived from the Cree Indian and means "where there are reeds"; this refers to the marshy delta of the river where it empties into Lake Athabasca. The lake appears on Peter Pond's map of 1790 as "Great Araubaska" while the Arrowsmith map of 1801 refers to it as "Lake of the Hills" with the Athabasca River shown as "Elk" River. The Arrowsmith map of 1802 shows "Athapescow" Lake and "Athapescow" or "Elk" River.

Athabasca Pass was for many years the main route by which the fur traders crossed the Continental Divide after having ascended the Athabasca and Whirlpool Rivers. From the pass they descended via the Wood River to Boat Encampment at the Big Bend of the Columbia River whence they journeyed down to the Pacific Coast. It was the geographer David Thompson who in the autumn of 1810 accompanied by Thomas, an Iroquois Indian, travelled up the valleys of the Athabasca and Whirlpool Rivers and crossed the water-shed to the Columbia.

The name appears something of a misnomer and can only be explained by the fact that the largest section of the fur trade route on the eastern slope of the Rockies lay up the Athabasca River before branching off at the confluence of the Athabasca and Whirlpool Rivers.

Athabasca Glacier and Mount Athabasca take their names from their proximity to the headwaters of the Athabasca River while Athabasca Falls are on the river itself and are a well-known tourist attraction.

ATHABASCA, town (H-6)
The town of Athabasca located on the Athabasca River some 90 miles north of Edmonton was, until 1904 known as Athabasca Landing; the Indian (Cree) name was *caupawin* meaning "landing." In 1884 the Hudson's Bay Company established a trading post there as a distribution centre and goods were shipped overland from Edmonton and freighted down the river for the north. During the era of the Klondike Gold Rush and the decades of settlement immediately following this was an important route to the north with cargoes being sent downstream by steamboat or scow for the MacKenzie River or upstream by steamer through Lesser Slave Lake for the Peace River area and Athabasca Landing was the central transfer point. With the completion of the Alberta and Great Waterways Railway and the Edmonton, Dunvegan and British Columbia Railway (both now the Northern Alberta Railways) Athabasca's importance as a shipping point waned.

Athabasca was formerly spelt with a "k"; the spelling was changed to the present form in 1945.

ATIMOSWE, creek (I-7)
Indian for "dog-rump" which name appears on Palliser map, 1863. Flows into the North Saskatchewan River.

ATLEE, locality (M-8)
After W. Atlee James, former assistant chief engineer of the Canadian Pacific Railway. (1914)

AUBURNDALE, locality (J-7)
After Auburndale. Massachusetts, former home of the first postmaster, L. W. Crowe. (1907)

AUDET, lake (D-7)
After Flight Lieutenant R. J. Audet, D.F.C., Lethbridge, killed in World War II. (1950)

AURORA, mountain (9,150 feet) (M-4)
After a light cruiser engaged in the North Sea Battle, January 24th, 1915. (1917)

AVALON, locality (O-7)
Named after the Isle of Avalon, Somerset, England, an area associated with the legend of King Arthur.

AVENS, mount (9,500 feet) (L-4)
After the wild flower. (1911)

AVION, ridge (7,997 feet) (O-5)
French word meaning an airplanc. (1915)

AYLMER, mount (10,375 feet) (L-4)
North of Lake Minnewanka; named 1890, after his native town, Aylmer, Quebec, by J. J. McArthur, D.L.S.

— B —

BABEL, mount (10,175 feet) and creek (L-4)
South of the Tower of Babel (q.v.) which was named in 1899.

BACKUS, mount (5,954 feet) (N-5)
After a homesteader who lived nearby.

BAD HEART, river (G-2)
Translation of the Cree Indian name *maatsiti.*

BAILEY, lake (A-7)
In honour of Sir Edward B. Bailey, renowned Scottish geologist of the early twentieth century period; his main fields of study were in metamorphic-igneous petrology.

BAIN, locality (O-8)
Named for James Bain, section foreman at Bredenbury, Saskatchewan. He won the D.C.M. and M.M. in World War I. (1922)

BAKER, lake and creek (L-4)
After a prospector who worked in the vicinity in 1882 or 1883.

BAKER, mount (10,451 feet)   (L-3)
After one G. P. Baker, a member of the Appalachian Mountain Club, Boston. (1898)

BALCARRES, mount (9,506 feet)   (J-3)
Named by Southesk after Sir Coutts Lindsay, Balcarres, Scotland. See also Lindsay, mount. (1925)

BALFOUR, mount (10,741 feet), glacier and pass (8,200 feet)   (L-3)
Named by Dr. James Hector (afterwards Sir James Hector) surgeon to the Palliser Expedition and its second in command, after John Hutton Balfour (1808-1884), Scottish botanist. Although Hector studied medicine at the University of Edinburgh, he seized the opportunity to study botany under Balfour which proved of considerable value on the expedition. Under the date of September 8, 1859, when he was in the Howse Pass area and, viewing the mountains, he notes: "that, which the previous summer I named Mount Balfour from this side presented two peaks one of which resembles a lofty irregular obelisk." Hector had named the mountain in 1858 and observed it again the following year.

BALINHARD, mountain (10,741 feet) and creek   (J-3)
After one of the titles of the Earl of Southesk, Baron Balinhard. See also Southesk, mountain.

BALL, mount (10,869 feet), pass (7,300 feet) and range   (L-4)
Named by Hector in 1858 after John Ball (1818-1889), Under-Secretary of State for the Colonies, 1855-1857. A friend of Palliser, Ball helped secure government support for the expedition and was of great help in organizing it. He was a student of mathematics, meteorology, botany, glaciers and mountains, and was first president of the Alpine Club of Great Britain. He was M.P. for County Carlaw from 1852-1857.

BALZAC, locality   (L-5)
After Honoré de Balzac (1799-1850), noted French novelist. (1910)

BANDED, peak (9,629 feet)   (M-5)
Descriptive. (1896)

BANFF, town and national park   (L-4)
After Banffshire, Scotland, birthplace of Lord Mount Stephen (1829-1921). George Stephen was born at Dufftown, Banffshire, Scotland. After coming to Canada he became a director of the Bank of Montreal. In 1873 he became a member of the syndicate which undertook the construction of the C.P.R. and to which he lent the prestige of the Bank of Montreal. He became a baronet in 1886 and was raised to the peerage in 1891; in 1905 he received the Grand Cross of the Victorian Order. In later life he engaged in many philanthropic causes.

One interesting story has it that a Winnipeg citizen, Harry Sandison, suggested the name Banff for the resort. Like Stephen he was born in Banffshire, Scotland, and duly emigrated to Canada. Shortly after his arrival in Winnipeg he stayed with one Dr. James Stewart, a retired Hudson's Bay Company employee. One of Stewart's friends was John H. MacTavish also a former Hudson's Bay man who then became land commissioner for the C.P.R. It appeared that MacTavish was shortly going to Montreal to attend a meeting with George Stephen, Donald Smith (later Lord Strathcona) and W. C. Van Horne concerning the building of a resort in the mountains at a watering place on the Bow River. On hearing of this Sandison said to MacTavish: "I know a good name for that place. You tell them to call it 'Banff' and when you spring the word 'Banff' just watch the faces of George Stephen and Donald Smith because they both come from near Banff."

At the meeting in Montreal, George Stephen and Donald Smith were seated near William Van Horne when MacTavish made the proposal. Donald Smith looked at Stephen and went over to him and whispered something in his ear. They both appeared quite excited and Van Horne for once was non-plussed, wondering what it was all about. Donald Smith explained that he knew Banff very well and Stephen affirmed that he, too, had been born very close to it. Van Horne's immediate comment was: "I like that name Banff" and Banff it was. No date for this meeting is given according to the *Banff Crag and Canyon*.

BAPTISTE, lake   (H-6)
After Baptiste Majeau, an early settler in the area.

BARBER, lake   (C-7)
After H. G. Barber, D.L.S.

BARBETTE, mountain (10,080 feet) and glacier   (K-3)
Descriptive. From a fancied resemblance to a barbette which is a stationary or rotating gun platform used with heavy naval or coastal defence guns. There are two high platform-like peaks rising from the surrounding mountains.

BARDO, locality   (I-6)
Named by Norwegians after a village in northern Norway. From 1898 to 1904, the post office name was Northern.

BARE, range   (L-4)
Descriptive. Red Deer River area.

BARIL, peak (9,837 feet) (M-5) and lake   (C-7)
After M. C. L. Baril of the Surveyor General's staff, Ottawa, who was killed in action on November 9, 1915.

BARLOW, mount (10,320 feet)   (K-3)
After Dr. A. E. Barlow, geologist, Associate Professor of Geology, McGill University. Dr. Barlow and his wife were lost on the *Empress of Ireland*, May, 1914.

BARNARD, mount (10,955 feet)   (K-3)
After Sir Frank Barnard, K.C.M.G., (1856-1936), Lieutenant Governor of British Columbia, 1914-1919.

BARNEGAT, locality   (H-7)
After Barnegat Bay, New Jersey, which was named by Henry Hudson. The name is from the Dutch *barende gat* to indicate a break in the barrier islands where surf was breaking; literally "foaming passage."

11

BARNWELL, hamlet (N-7)
Founded in 1902 by four Mormon pioneers, it was originally called Woodpecker after Woodpecker Island in the Oldman River to the north. Later the name was changed to Barnwell after one R. Barnwell, then general tie agent for the C.P.R. at Winnipeg.

BARRE, RIVIÈRE-QUI, river (I-5)
In Cree *ma-ta-hi-to si-pi-sis* signifying Present Creek, (Tyrrell); the current name was given by lumbermen who could not use the river for driving their logs; literally the "river that bars."

BARREYRE, lake (H-8)
After Alphonse Barreyre, a squatter who settled nearby. (1908)

BARRHEAD, town and county (I-5)
After Barrhead, Scotland, birthplace of James McGuire, an early settler. (1914)

BARRICADE, mountain (10,300 feet) (I-1)
From a ridge on it resembling a barricade. (1924)

BARRIER, mountain (9,718 feet) (L-4)
Descriptive; it forms a ridge which extends northwest from Panther River to Red Deer River.

BARWELL, mount (6,000 feet) (M-5)
After C. S. W. Barwell, D.L.S., assistant on surveys, 1895-1896.

BASELINE, creek (I-3)
Athabasca River; this creek follows the 14th Base Line.

BASHAW, town (J-6)
After Eugene Bashaw, pioneer lumberman, who purchased the land where the town now stands from a Métis.

BASILICA, mountain (9,400 feet) (J-2)
From a fancied resemblance to a basilica.

BASSANO, town (M-6)
After the Marquis de Bassano, Canadian Pacific Railway shareholder; Lady Bassano, née Marie-Anne-Claire Lymes, was a native of Quebec. A dam was built near here as part of the C.P.R. irrigation scheme and led to the slogan "The best in the West by a dam site." (1884)

BASTION, peak (9,812 feet) (J-2)
Descriptive. From a fancied resemblance to a bastion. (1916)

BATH, creek and glacier (L-4)
This creek along which the C.P.R. approaches the Kicking Horse Pass from the east, was named when, on July 20, 1881, Major Rogers (whose name is commemorated in Rogers Pass in B.C.) of the C.P.R. engineering staff, took an involuntary bath in it when thrown from his horse. It appears as Noore's Creek on the Palliser map of 1863.

BATTLE, lake (J-5); river (J5-J8) and locality (J-6)
Flows southeast and northeast from the Fifth Meridian into Saskatchewan where it joins the North Saskatchewan River at Battleford. It

first appears on the Arrowsmith Map of 1802. The name is a translation of the Cree *no-tin-to-si-pi* or in Blackfoot *ke-chi-sab-wap-ta*. The Blackfoot and Crees fought near this river.

BAUERMAN, mount (7,800 feet)   (O-5)
After H. Bauerman (1835-1909), geologist, British Boundary Commission, Pacific to the Rockies. Hilary Bauerman, metallurgist, geologist, mineralogist was born in London in 1835 and studied in England and Germany. In the course of his career he travelled widely and worked in many parts of the world: Sweden, Lapland, Canada, Arabia, Mexico, Brazil, Asia Minor and the U.S.A. Later he became a professor of geology at Firth College, Sheffield and then at the Ordnance College at Woolwich.

BAWLF, village   (J-6)
Named in honour of Nicholas Bawlf sometime president of the Winnipeg Grain Exchange. The townsite was laid out in August, 1905.

BAZALGETTE, mount (8,000 feet)   (J-2)
After Squadron Leader Ian W. Bazalgette, V.C., D.F.C., Calgary, killed in World War II and who was the only Alberta winner of the V.C. in that conflict. (1949)

BEACH CORNER, locality   (I-5)
At the junction of the Jasper Highway and road to Edmonton Beach summer resort; literally "the corner where one turns off to the beach."

BEACON, peak (9,795 feet) and lake   (J-2)
Descriptive of its isolated position. (1922)

BEAR, hills   (J-6)
The name is derived from the Cree *mus-kwa-chi-si*; in Blackfoot *kyo-etomo*; in Stoney *o-zin-za-hen*. Dr James Hector notes: "The Blackfoot track continues to the S.S.E., but we now left it and turned off to the S.S.W. making for the south end of a low wooded hill called the *Musquachis* or Bear's Hill."

BEAR, lake   (G-2)
So named by unknown Metis because a bear had been killed there by one of his people. (1950)

BEARBERRY, locality and creek   (L-5)
Translation of Cree *a-chuk-i-si-pi*; in Stoney, *a-be-wap-tan* (Tyrrell); after the bearberries growing on the banks of the creek. (1909)

BEARSPAW, locality   (L-5)
After Chief Masgaahsid or Bear's Paw, who signed the Treaty at Blackfoot Crossing, September 22, 1877. (1879)

BEATTY, mount (9,841 feet)   (M-4)
Named after Admiral David Beatty, first Earl (1871-1936), Commander at the Battle of Jutland, 1916.

BEAUMONT, hamlet   (J-6)
So named because it is situated on a hill with a good view. It is said that the name was suggested by one John Royer about 1895.

BEAUVALLON, hamlet (I-7)
French for "beautiful vale"; the situation commands a beautiful view
of the North Saskatchewan River valley. (1909)

BEAUPRÉ, mount (9,115 feet) (J-2)
After a guide of the Sandford Fleming party, 1872. (1923)

BEAUVERT, lake (J-2)
French for "beautiful green", alluding to the colour of the lake.

BEAVER, hills (I-6)
On David Thompson's map, 1814; in Blackfoot, *kaghghik-staki-etomo*
(Nelson); in Cree *amisk-wa-chi* and in Stoney, *chaba-hei*, (Tyrrell).

BEAVER, lake and river (H-7)-(H-8)
The Turnor map, 1790, shows Beaver River. The Harmon map, 1820,
shows Beaver Lake and River.

BEAVERHILL, lake and creek (I-6)
These two features, immediately east of Edmonton take their name
from the Cree *amisk-wachi-sakhahigan* (Tyrrell). Beaverhill Lake appears as Beaver Lake on the Thompson map of 1814 which also
shows the Beaver Hills.

BEAVERLODGE, river and town (G-1)
The town is named after the river, which flows within one and a half
miles of it. The name Beaverlodge is from the translation of a Beaver
Indian word with the word "lodge" meaning a temporary dwelling.

In 1908, prior to the surveying of the township, the first settlers
arrived and took up squatters' rights in the valley. The first post office
was opened in 1910 and named Bellow since the name Beaverlodge
was already given to the office at Lake Saskatoon. When the E.D.
and B.C. Railway arrived in 1928, a new townsite was created about
one mile northwest of the original hamlet and about 100 buildings
were moved.

BEDDINGTON, locality (L-5)
After Beddington, Surrey, England. The name Beddington first appears
as *Beddingtone* in Domesday Book (1086)—the *tun* (habitation) of
Beadda, (Ekwall).

BEEHIVE, mountain (9,492 feet) (N-5)
Descriptive of outline; on B.C.-Alberta boundary.

BEEHIVE, THE, mountain (7,440 feet) (L-4)
Descriptive of outline. A familiar landmark near Lake Louise.

BEHAN, locality and lake (G-7)
Named after the cook on a survey party, 1912.

BEISEKER, village (L-6)
After one Thomas Beiseker who was at the head of the first group of
settlers who came to the area from the United States. His name was
given to the village; he later returned to the United States where he died.

BÉLANGER, mount (10,200 feet)   (J-3)
After André Bélanger, member of 1814 party to cross the Athabasca
Pass from Astoria; drowned in the Athabasca River below Brûlé Lake.
(1921)

BELL, mount (9,500 feet)   (L-4)
Named for Miss Nora Bell, member of the Alpine Club of Canada and
one member of a small party which made what was apparently the
first ascent. (1959)

BELLCOTT, locality   (N-8)
After Belle Cotterell, wife of the assistant general superintendent, British
Columbia district, Canadian Pacific Railway. Anstead, prior to 1914.

BELLOY, locality   (F-2)
After Madame Belloy, a Belgian operatic singer who sang during the
1914-1918 war for the Belgian Relief Fund. (1916)

BELLY, river   (O-6)-(N-6)
Various theories have been advanced for the origin of this name with
little agreement resulting. The Blackfoot called it *mokowanis* meaning
"belly" possibly named for the Atsina Indians whose tribal sign of a
rubbing gesture over the abdomen gave them the name of Belly People
or Big Bellies. A second theory states that the Atsina were a detached
segment of the Arapaho (on a reserve in Montana) and were regarded
as beggars or spongers; hence the tribal sign. Both theories refer to
them as "Belly People" (and this is thought by some to be incorrect),
"Big Bellies" or more familiarly "Gros Ventres." A third and totally independent theory states that the Indian term *mokowanis* comes from the
big bend or belly in the river as it makes a loop near Lethbridge.

BELVEDERE, locality   (I-5)
Formerly known as Pembina Crossing and Macdonald Crossing, after an
early settler, Gordon Macdonald; it was given its present name by
Robert Telfer, a former postmaster, since the post office when located
two miles south commanded a fine view. A belvedere is a raised turret
from which to view scenery. (1905)

BELYEA, lake   (A-7)
After A. P. C. Belyea, D.L.S., former Director of Surveys, Alberta,
1938-1947.

BENALTO, hamlet   (K-5)
An acronym meaning high hill. (1914)

BENJAMIN, creek   (L-5)
After Jonas Benjamin, Stoney Indian chief. (1917)

BENNETT, locality   (M-5)
After R. B. Bennett (1870-1947). Born in New Brunswick he came
to Calgary to practise law. He was a Member of the North-West Territories Legislature and from 1909-1911, a Member of the Legislative
Assembly of Alberta. In 1911 he was elected to Parliament and from
1930-1935 was Prime Minister of Canada. He retired to England in
1939 and in 1941 was created Viscount Bennett of Mickleham, Calgary and Hopewell. (1911)

BENNINGTON, peak (10,726 feet)   (J-2)
A peak of Mount Fraser (q.v.); after Bennington, Vermont, Simon Fraser's birthplace. (1922)

BENTLEY, village   (K-5)
One Major Macpherson, an American Civil War veteran, started a post office and store at the site of Bentley. Nearby was a sawmill where there was a popular sawyer named George Bentley. When it came to choosing a name the settlers wanted Macpherson but the men at the sawmill chose Bentley; as there were more sawmill hands than settlers the name Bentley won out. (1900)

BENTON STATION, locality   (L-8)
After the Benton Trail from Fort Benton, Montana, to Fort Macleod, Alberta.

BERGEN, locality and creek   (L-5)
Probably after Bergen, Norway. (1907)

BERGNE, mount (10,420 feet)   (K-3)
Named by A. O. Wheeler, D.L.S., founder of the Alpine Club of Canada, after Frank Bergne, Alpine Club, England who was killed while climbing with Wheeler in Switzerland in 1907. (1920)

BERLAND, river   (I-2)-(I-3)
After one Baptiste Berland mentioned by Father De Smet in 1846. It appears as Baptist River on the Thompson map of 1814. The name was changed to Berland in 1917 to avoid confusion with Baptiste River which flows into the North Saskatchewan.

BERRYMOOR, locality   (J-5)
Wabamun Lake; descriptive. (1910)

BERTHA, creek, lake and peak (8,000 feet)   (O-5)
Named after one Bertha Ekelund, an early resident of the area. She gained notoriety by attempting to pass counterfeit money and went to jail as a result. This and other exploits seem to have endeared her to the oldtimers of the area.

BERWYN, village   (F-3)
Said to be named after Berwyn, Denbighshire, Wales by one of the very early residents of the district. The settlement was named in 1922 when it became the "end of steel for a few years on the Edmonton, Dunvegan and British Columbia Railway." The village was incorporated in 1936. Prior to 1922 the settlement was located three miles east and was called "Bear Lake."

BESS, mount (10,500 feet) and pass (5,330 feet)   (I-1)
Named in 1911, after Miss Bessie Gunn, afterwards wife of M. C. McKeen, former M.L.A. for Lac St. Anne.

BETTS, creek   (E-1)
After Private Andrew M. Betts, of the Peace River district, killed in World War II. (1960)

16

BETULA BEACH, summer village (I-5)
Betula is the Latin for birch. When the summer village was erected various names were suggested but the name Betula Beach won out because of the birch trees in the area. (1960)

BEYNON, locality (L-6)
After H. Beynon Biggs, first postmaster. (1914)

BEZANSON, hamlet (G-2)
After A. M. Bezanson. original owner of townsite land here. (1915)

BICHE, LAC LA, lake (G-6)-(H-6)-(H-7)
Literal translation "lake of the red doe"; so called by early explorers from about 1790. Lac la Biche was on an important trading route; explorers came in from Fort George over a height of land down the Beaver River to Lac la Biche en route to the Athabasca River and north.

BICKERDIKE, locality (I-3)
Named after Robert Bickerdike (1843-1919). Bickerdike was a member of the Legislative Assembly of Quebec in 1897 and in 1900 was elected to the House of Commons in Ottawa and re-elected in 1904, 1908 and 1911, finally retiring in 1917. He was a Member of Parliament for the St. Lawrence constituency of Montreal.

BIDENT, mount (10,109 feet) (L-4)
So called from a fancied resemblance to a double tooth. (1904)

BIG, lake (I-5)
From the Cree, *mistihay sakigan* or large lake (Steele).

BIG CHIEF, lake (G-7)
After Solomon Cardinal, also known as Sam Cardinal and apparently referred to as "Big Chief." Born at Goodfish Lake on March 18, 1915, he joined the Canadian Army in 1944 and was killed in the Italian campaign that same year.

BIG KNIFE, creek and provincial park (K-7)
It is said that two Indians fought here and killed one another. One was known as "Big Man" and the other as "Knife." From this the Indians gave this place the name "Big Knife."

BIG VALLEY, village (K-6)
Descriptive; a wide open valley. (1907)

BIGHORN, range, river and Indian Reserve (K-3)
The name of the range is a translation of the Indian name. At one time this area was a noted habitat of the Rocky Mountain sheep or bighorn. The name appears on the Palliser map of 1863.

BIGORAY, river (I-4)
After Pilot Officer W. W. Bigoray, D.F.M., Redwater, killed in World War II. (1949)

BINDLOSS, hamlet (M-8)
Named after Harold Bindloss (1866-1945). A native of England, Bindloss spent some time in the British Colonies and in Western Canada.

He was a writer of "westerns" and no doubt gained material for his fiction when in Canada. He returned to England in 1896 where he resided for the remainder of his life.

BINGLEY, locality (K-5)
After Bingley, Yorkshire, England, birthplace of the first postmaster. (1910)

BINGLEY, peak (8,000 feet) (J-2)
Named by Dr. William Cheadle, noted traveller, whose birthplace was Bingley, Yorkshire. (1863)

BIRCH, hills, lake and creek (G-2)
Translation of Cree name, *waskwai*. Also see supplement.

BIRCHAM, locality (L-6)
Presumably after Bircham, King's Lynn, England.

BIRDSHOLM, locality (O-7)
After A. W. Bird, one time postmaster. (1914)

BISHOP, mount (9,300 feet) (M-5)
In honour of Air Marshall W. A. Bishop (1894-1956), V.C., D.S.O., M.C. In 1917 he brought down three enemy machines in one flight; in all he brought down 72 machines during World War I. (1918)

BISMARCK, locality (J-5)
After Otto von Bismarck (1815-1898), German statesman and Chancellor—known as the "Iron Chancellor"; it was originally a German settlement.

BISTCHO, lake and Indian Reserve (A-2)
Indian name meaning "big knife."

BITTERN, lake (J-6)
A translation of the Cree *mo-ka-ka-sioo*; after the large number of bitterns that frequented the lake shore.

BITTERN LAKE, village (J-6)
The village takes its name from the lake on which it is situated. When, in 1910, the C.P.R. branch line from Wetaskiwin was opened a station was located on the shore of Bittern Lake and given that name. Two miles away was the town of Rosenroll and it had long been the hope of its residents that the railway would come there. This was not to be as farmers in the district were taking their produce to Bittern Lake. Acting on the old adage, "If you can't beat them, join them," the citizens of Rosenroll decided to move their buildings to Bittern Lake and amalgamate with the village that had grown up there. On July 1, 1910, the confederation of the two towns was celebrated with the post office officially taking the name Bittern Lake.

BLACK DIAMOND, town (M-5)
Named from the coal mine operated by Addison McPherson which was the first industry of the district. The town "boomed" because of the discovery in 1914 of gas and oil in the Turner Valley field. (1907)

BLACK PRINCE, mount (9,500 feet) (M-4)
After a light cruiser destroyed in the Battle of Jutland, May, 1916.

BLACKFACE, mountain (9,407 feet) and creek (J-3)
Probably descriptive. (1922)

BLACKFALDS, village (K-5)
Originally named Waghorn by the Post Office Department in 1891.
At this time the Calgary and Edmonton Railway was built and the
railway company labelled its siding here "11th siding," later changing
the name to Blackfalds after a hamlet in Scotland. Waghorn Post
Office was changed to Blackfalds in 1902.

BLACKFOOT, Indian Reserve (M-6)
The name Blackfoot is a translation of this tribe's own name for itself,
siksikauwa and refers to their moccasins either because they were
painted black or blackened by the ashes of prairie fires.

BLACKHORN, peak (9,800 feet) (J-2)
Descriptive. (1916)

BLACKIE. village (M-6)
After John Stuart Blackie (1782-1874), Scottish publisher, founder
of the firm of Blackie and Sons. (1911)

BLACKMUD, creek (I-6)
Translation of Cree name, *kas-ki-te-oo asiski,* (Tyrrell).

BLACKROCK, mountain (9,580 feet) (J-2)
A sharp black peak. (1922)

BLACKSPRING, ridge (N-6)
In Blackfoot, *sicehkiscoh,* signifying black spring water.

BLACKSTONE, river (J-3)
Brazeau River; descriptive.

BLAIRMORE, town (N-5)
"Tenth Siding" was the first name given to what is now the town of
Blairmore when the C.P.R. laid its track through the Crowsnest Pass.
The camp later became known as "The springs." The townsite was
officially named "Blairmore" on November 15. 1898, after the Hon.
H. G. Blair, (1844-1907), Minister of Railways. Tradition reports that the
site had been named "Blair" but it was felt that this was too short a
name for a town so it was suggested that "more" be added to the name.
The suggestion was accepted and "more" was added giving the town
the name Blairmore. (A. Tiberg, Municipal Secretary, letter, August,
1970).

BLANE. mount (9,650 feet) (M-5)
Opal Range; after Sir C..R. Blane, Commander of the battleship H.M.S.
Queen Mary in World War I. The *Queen Mary* was destroyed by
German gunfire at the Battle of Jutland, May, 1916. (1922)

BLEFGEN, lake (H-6)
After T. F. Blefgen, Director of Forestry in Alberta, 1931-1948. (1953)

BLINDMAN, river   (K-5)
Flows into the Red Deer River. Shown as Wolf River on Thompson
map, 1814; Blind River on Palliser map, 1863. The name is a translation
of the Cree *pas-ka-poo*. It was named by the Crees because a war party
hunting in that area became snow blind. In Stoney it is *is-tap-ta* or
cham-bath-na-dab-wapta or "dead standing timber" river, (Tyrrell).

BLOOD, Indian Reserve   (N-6)
This, the largest Indian Reserve in Canada, is named after the Blood
Indians. The derivation of the name "Blood" is in doubt although
several likely explanations have been offered. Prince Maximilian of
Wied in his *Travels in the Interior of North America* (London, 1844)
stated that, before the Siksika divided into separate bands, the Siksika
or Blackfeet, the Kainah or Bloods and the Peigans were encamped in
the neighbourhood of several tents of Kutenais. The Blackfeet and
Kainah wished to kill the Kutenais but the Peigans opposed the idea.
However, some of the Kainah killed the Kutenais, took their scalps,
stained their faces and hands with the blood and then returned. Disputes
arose as a result of this cruel action; the tribes separated and the
murderers received the name of the Bloods.

BLUE, range   (M-4)
From blue appearance when seen from a distance through the haze.

BLUEROCK, mountain (9,100 feet) and creek   (M-5)
Descriptive.

BLUESKY, hamlet   (F-2)
Descriptive of the cloudless skies characteristic of the region. (1913)

BLUET, lake   (I-8)
French for "blueberry" as blueberries grow on the shore.

BLUFF, mountain (7,039 feet)   (N-5)
Descriptive.

BLUFFTON, hamlet   (F-2)
Named after Bluff Centre a post office located prior to construction
of the railway. (1922)

BOGART, mount (10,300 feet)   (L-5)
Named in 1904 after Dr. D. Bogart Dowling (1858-1925), Canadian
geologist. He was a pioneer in the field of coal, petroleum and natural
gas development.

BOLTON, mount (8,878 feet)   (M-5)
After Lambert Ernest Stanley Bolton (1880-1916), D.L.S., of the
Surveyor General's staff, Ottawa. He was killed in action in 1916.

BON ACCORD, village   (I-6)
"Bon Accord" is the motto of the City of Aberdeen, Scotland. It is
said to have been used as the password at the taking of the Castle in
Aberdeen from the English by the Aberdonians. Later Robert Bruce
authorized the use of the words as the motto. At the termination of
a civic function, it is usual to give the toast "Bon Accord"—"Happy
to meet, sorry to part, happy to meet again."

One evening in 1896, a meeting was convened at the home of Alexander (Sandy) Florence. Under the terms of the North-West Territories School Legislation, the purpose of the meeting was to set up a school district. At the suggestion of Sandy Florence (who hailed from Aberdeen), "Bon Accord" was accepted as the name of the new school district. Later it became the name of the post office and was retained as the name of the hamlet and ultimately the village. (1964)

BONHOMME, ROCHE, mountain (8,185 feet)   (J-2)
It resembles a man's face; it is mentioned in Grant's *Ocean to Ocean*, 1873.

BONNET, peak (10,290 feet) and glacier   (L-4)
Descriptive of the summit. (1890)

BONNYVILLE, town and municipal district   (H-7)
After Reverend Father Bonny who established the first Roman Catholic Church in the district in 1910 near Moose Lake two miles west of the present town. Father Bonny had been a missionary in Africa prior to coming to Canada. In the same year that Father Bonny established his church, a post office was opened and named Bonnyville in honour of Father Bonny.

BONNYVILLE, BEACH, summer village   (H-7)
On the east shore of Moose Lake; after the town of Bonnyville. (1960)

BOOM, mountain (9,047 feet), lake and creek   (L-4)
In 1908 when Boom Lake was named, the driftwood in it resembled a lumberman's boom.

BOONE, creek and lake   (G-1)
After Boone Taylor, well-known oldtimer who lived at Swan Lake, B.C. prior to World War I. He hunted, trapped and acted as guide to many of the later settlers looking for homesteads. He was the first person to have a lease on Fish Creek (local name, Alberta side). It is known as Boone Creek and the lake from which it flows as Boone Lake.

BOSCHE, ROCHE À, mountain (6,966 feet)   (J-2)
A French name which may be a corruption of the word "bosse" meaning a hump. It is mentioned in Grant's *Ocean to Ocean*, 1873, and Grant notes for the date of September 2, 1872: "Opposite camp to the north, the hump of the Roche à Bosche stood out prominently . . ."

BOSWELL, mount (8,000 feet)   (O-5)
After Dr. W. G. Boswell, veterinary surgeon, British Boundary Commission, Lake of the Woods to the Rockies, (1872-1876).

BOTHA, village and river   (K-6)
After General Louis Botha (1862-1919), a famous Boer general. (1909-village; 1916-river).

BOTTREL, locality   (L-5)
After Edward Botterel, early settler. The name was misspelt when first officially recorded.

BOULE, ROCHE, mountain (7,230 feet)   (J-2)
Located west of Brûlé Lake on the Athabasca River, it takes its name
from the French *boule* meaning "ball." It appears as Bullrush Mountain on the Palliser map of 1863.

BOUNDARY, creek and **BOUNDARY CREEK,** locality   (O-5)
The creek flows into the U.S.A across the forty-ninth parallel.

BOURGEAU, mount (9,575 feet), lake and range   (L-4)
Named for Eugene Bourgeau (1813-1877); born in the south of France,
he was attached to the Palliser Expedition as botanist. Cosson in the
Palliser Report says: "Bourgeau, it is true, was not a learned man, but
by his aptitude for natural history, he made good the deficiencies in
his early education. His frank good nature gained him friends every-
where he travelled." He was recommended by Sir W. Hooker of Kew
Gardens, England.

BOW, river (L-3)-(N-7), glacier (L-3), range (L-3), lake (L-3), falls (L-4),
peak (9,194 feet) (L-4)
The Bow River which rises at the Bow Glacier and flows into Bow
Lake and on through the Rockies to Calgary to become part of the
South Saskatchewan River system, takes its name from the Cree *ma-
na-cha-ban* meaning "bow", according to Tyrrell. This is a reference to
the availability along its course of wood suitable for making bows, a
fact of which the Indians took full advantage. It appears on the
Arrowsmith map of 1801 as Askow or Bad River and on the Arrowsmith map of 1822 as Bow or Askow River. Bow Hills appear on the
Arrowsmith map of 1822.

   Bow Lake and Hector Lake (q.v.) were known as *minismeimme*
in Stoney and *oskowwioosipi sagahegun* in Cree, both names meaning
Coldwater Lakes.

   In 1832 the Hudson's Bay Company constructed a trading post on
the Bow River west of where Calgary now stands. It was known as
Peigan Post, Bow River Fort, or more familiarly as Old Bow Fort. Its
object was to lure the Blackfeet and Peigan Indians away from the
American traders on the Missouri River but the Blood Indians who
were supposed to trade at Fort Edmonton were jealous and would not
let their allies come to trade. Owing to the constant threat of attack
resulting from this situation, Old Bow Fort was abandoned early in 1834.

BOW ISLAND, town   (N-7)
Bow Island was named after the Bow River and according to the old
timers a mistake was made in the naming of the town. The Bow and
Belly Rivers join north of the village of Grassy Lake and the town
of Bow Island was originally planned where the village of Grassy
Lake now stands.

   An amusing local tradition states that two ladies in imminent
danger of permanent spinsterhood put on a determined effort to win
two bachelors. The first said she was "out to win a Fred" (Winnifred)
while the second retorted "Before you do a beau I'll land" (Bow
Island).

BOW VALLEY, provincial park   (L-4)
From the Bow River valley in which it is situated. See also Bow, river.

BOWDEN, village (K-5)

There are two explanations of how Bowden received its name. The first is that it was named after Bowden near Manchester, England. The second is that a surveyor named Williamson who was working on the Calgary and Edmonton Railway was asked when they reached the siding what to name it and jokingly replied "Call it by my wife's maiden name Bowden." This was agreed upon.

BOWELL, hamlet (N-8)

After Sir Mackenzie Bowell (1823-1917), Canadian Minister of Customs, 1878-92; Prime Minister of Canada, 1894-96. He and Sir John Abbot were the only Prime Ministers who sat in the Senate while holding office.

BOWEN, lake (C-7)

For Colonel R. E. Bowen, commanding 202nd Battalion, Edmonton, during the First World War.

BOWHAY, lake (B-5)

After Flight Lieutenant S. L. Bowhay, King's Commendation, Three Hills, Alberta, killed in World War II.

BOWLEN, mount (10,000 feet) (L-4)

Peak No. 3 of the Ten Peaks, (q.v.). It can be seen from Moraine Lake in the Valley of the Ten Peaks; after the Honourable Dr. J. J. Bowlen (1876-1959), Lieutenant Governor of Alberta, from 1950 until his death on December 16, 1959.

BOWMANTON, locality (N-8)

After Mrs. Whitson, née Bowman, wife of a local farmer. (1913)

BOYD, creek (J-5)

In honour of Flying Officer William Boyd Anderson of Craigmyle, killed in World War II. (1950)

BOYER, river and Indian Reserve (C-4)

It appears as Bouille River on Arrowsmith map, 1854, and may be after Charles Boyer, the North West Company trader referred to by Sir Alexander Mackenzie in a letter dated Athabasca, 22 May, 1789, as "a very fit person for the Peace river."

BOYLE, village (H-6)

For John Robert Boyle (1871-1936), Minister of Education, Alberta, 1913; later Honourable Justice Boyle of the Supreme Court of Alberta. (1914)

BOYNE LAKE, locality (H-7)

Named in 1905 after the Battle of the Boyne, 1689.

BRACHIAPOD, mountain (8,300 feet) and lake (L-4)

The west slopes are said to be literally covered with brachiapods and fossil corals. (1911)

BRADSHAW, locality (O-6)

Named in 1912 after William Bradshaw, rancher.

BRAGG CREEK, hamlet, provincial park (M-5)

Named in 1911 after George Bragg, earliest settler.

BRAITHWAITE, mount (7,000 feet)   (I-1)
After Dr. Edward Ainslie Braithwaite (1862-1949). A native of England he came to Canada and joined the North-West Mounted Police in 1884, performing medical duties for the Force. In 1885 during the Riel Rebellion he was medical attendant to Colonel A. G. Irvine's column, caring for the wounded from Duck Lake and Batoche.

In 1892 he left the Mounted Police to establish a medical practice in Edmonton and four years later was named that city's coroner and medical health officer. He helped to form the first western Canadian medical association and was president for the Alberta area. In the course of his long career he was well known for his services to Indians, traders and early residents of the area.

BRANT, hamlet   (M-6)
Named in 1905 by its founder, E. E. Thompson of High River; brant geese were very plentiful in 1905 on the lakes in the vicinity.

BRAZEAU, mount (11,386 feet) (K-3), range (K-3), river (J-3), lake (K-3)
After Joseph E. Brazeau, an employee of the Hudson's Bay Company. Brazeau came of a prominent Creole family in St. Louis, Missouri and entered the fur trade in 1830, working on the Yellowstone and Missouri Rivers. Later he joined the Hudson's Bay Company, serving as postmaster and clerk from 1852 to 1864 at Edmonton, Rocky Mountain House and Jasper House. Brazeau was a linguist and according to Palliser "spoke Stoney, Sioux, Salteau, Cree, Blackfoot and Crow—six languages, five of which are totally distinct from one another. Being of an old Spanish family and educated in the United States, he also spoke English, French and Spanish fluently." Brazeau was a great help to the Palliser Expedition and Palliser comments: "Of Mr. Brazeau, the gentleman in charge of the Rocky Mountain House, I have to speak in terms of the highest praise."

BREAD, creek   (K-4)
So called because during a forest fire in 1919 bread for all the camps was made at a camp by this creek.

BRECCIA, creek   (J-2)
From a large amount of rock breccia near its mouth.

BRERETON, lake   (H-5)
In honour of Pte. (A/C) Alexander Brereton, Victoria Cross winner in World War I. (1953)

BRETON, village   (J-5)
After Douglas Corney Breton, (1883-   , Simonstown, S.A.), a United Farmers of Alberta Member of the Legislative Assembly for Leduc, 1926-1930. (1926)

BRETT, mount (9,750 feet)   (L-4)
After Honourable R. G. Brett, M.D., Lieutenant Governor of Alberta, (1915-1925); pioneer resident of Banff. (1903)

BREWSTER, mount (9,380 feet), glacier and creek   (L-4)
For John Brewster who arrived in Banff, December, 1887. His family was well known in connection with the Brewster Transportation Company.

BRIDGLAND, mount (9,600 feet) and creek (J-2)
North of the Yellowhead Pass; after M.P. Bridgland, D.L.S., who
made extensive surveys in the Rocky Mountains. (1918)

BRIÈREVILLE, locality (H-7)
Established in 1917 and named after J. C. O. Brière, first postmaster.

BRIGHTVIEW, locality (J-6)
The name of the first postmaster's farm; probably descriptive. (1907)

BROCK, lake (I-5)
Northwest of Wabamun Lake; named in 1950 in honour of Corporal
George W. Brock, M.I.D., Edmonton, killed in World War II.

BROCK, mount (9,445 feet) (M-5)
Opal Range; after Rear Admiral Brock, engaged in the Battle of
Jutland, 1916. (1922)

BROCKET, hamlet (N-6)
After Brocket Hall, seat of Lord Mount Stephen (1829-1921), Hat-
field, Herts, England. He was connected with the building of the
C.P.R. (1897) See also Banff.

BROOKS, town (M-7)
After N. E. Brooks, divisional engineer, Canadian Pacific Railway at
Calgary; died at Sherbrooke, Quebec, May 12, 1926. The name was
selected from a list submitted by E. Crocker to the postal authorities
and coincided with the selection of the same name by the C.P.R.

BROSSEAU, hamlet and lake (I-7)
After Edmond Brosseau, merchant and farmer, who was born at
Laprairie, Quebec in 1842 and for many years resident in Alberta.

BROWN, mount (9,156 feet) (K-2)
Athabasca Pass; named by David Douglas, 1827, "in honour of R.
Brown, Esq., the illustrious botanist"; Robert Brown (1775-1858) was
a famous British botanist.

BROWNFIELD, locality (K-7)
Established in 1907 and named after C. D. Brownfield, first postmaster.

BROWNVALE, hamlet (F-3)
For J. H. Brown, early settler.

BRUCE, hamlet (J-7)
For A. Bruce Smith, former manager, Grand Trunk Pacific Telegraph
Company; formerly Hurry Post Office; changed to Bruce, 1909.

BRUDERHEIM, village (I-6)
Literally "home of the brethren or brothers". A group of members of
the Moravian Church had migrated from Poland to Volhynia, Russia.
In 1893-94 this group sent one Andreas Lilge to Canada to find a suitable site for a settlement. As soon as he had located it, more settlers
came, among them Mr. Lilge's two brothers, William and Ludwig. It
was in honour of these three brothers, Andreas, Ludwig and William
Lilge that the settlers decided to name their new home "Bruderheim"
—home of the brothers. Name originally spelt "Bruederheim."

BRÛLÉ, lake, creek, hill, point rapids, hamlet   (J-2)
From the French *brûlé* meaning "burnt" presumably after stands of burned timber noticed along its shores by the early explorers.

BRUSSELS, peak (10,370 feet)   (K-3)
After Captain Fryatt's ship (see Fryett, mount); Brussels Peak and Mount Fryatt are on the south and north sides of Fryatt Creek respectively.

BRYANT, mount (8,600 feet)   (J-2)
East of Miette Range; named in 1960 after Frank Bryant, former warden of Jasper Park, chief warden at Waterton Lakes Park, superintendent of Kootenay National Park.

BRYCE, mount (11,507 feet)   (K-3)
After Viscount James Bryce, one time president of the Alpine Club, London, England; British Ambassador at Washington, D.C., 1907-1912. (1898)

BUCHANAN, lake   (C-5)
Named in 1949 for Flight Lieutenant D. S. J. Buchanan, D.F.C., Edmonton, killed in World War II.

BUCHANAN, ridge   (O-5)
After Senator William Asbury Buchanan (1876-1954), founder, editor and publisher of the *Lethbridge Herald*. He was also the first Provincial (Legislative) Librarian and served in the first Alberta government as Minister of Municipal Affairs.

BUCKTON, creek   (C-7)-(D-7)
Named in 1914 after A. Scott Buckton, D.L.S.

BUFFALO, lake   (K-6)
Palliser notes that it received its name "from the resemblance (long ago but not now) of its outline to a buffalo hide stretched out for the purpose of being dressed, the small stream ('la queue') representing the tail of the animal." From the number of buffalo bones found there, it seems to have been a favourite buffalo hunting ground. It was known in Cree as *mustus*; in Stoney *ta-toong-gama* (Tyrrell).

BUFORD, hamlet   (J-5)
The settlers originally came from Buford, North Dakota, hence the name. (1903)

BULLER, mount (9,000 feet)   (M-4)
After Lieutenant Colonel H. C. Buller, Princess Patricia's Canadian Light Infantry; killed in the First World War. (1922)

BULLHORN, coulee   (O-6)
In Blackfoot, *pomepisan* or Grease Pound creek; a buffalo pound was built here and the meat was boiled for grease.

BULLPOUND, creek   (M-7)
In Blackfoot, *stomaxah piskan* or buffalo bull pound; a number of bull buffalo were killed here in a pound.

BULLSHEAD, hill and creek (N-8)
In Blackfoot, *in-e-oto-ka,* or "buffalo head", so named because of its shape (Dawson).

BULWARK, locality (K-7)
Formerly Lindsville. Named after the coronation of King George V, 1911. (1916)

BULYEA, mount (10,900 feet) (L-3)
After the Honourable George Hedley Vickers Bulyea (1859-1926), first Lieutenant Governor of Alberta, 1905-1915. (1920)

BURDETT, village (N-7)
After Angela, Baroness Burdett-Coutts (1814-1906) who was a shareholder in the North-West Coal and Navigation Company Ltd. The Canadian Pacific Railway wanted coal from the mines at Lethbridge and at first (1885-1886) it was shipped by boat to Medicine Hat but this proved too slow and too costly and subject to the vagaries of the water level of the river. A narrow gauge railway (known irreverently as the "Turkey Track") was built from Lethbridge to Medicine Hat; later it was extended to the Montana border. Baroness Burdett-Coutts' name is also commemorated in the village of Coutts (q.v.).

BURKE, mount (8,340 feet) (N-5)
Named in 1919 after one D. C. Burke, rancher and forest ranger.

BURLEIGH, creek (I-2)
For J. H. Burleigh, former ranger, who almost lost his pack outfit in muskeg on the bank. (1947)

BURMIS, locality (N-5)
After two residents, Burns and Kemmis. (1901)

BURNEY, mount (9,625 feet) (M-4)
After Admiral Sir Cecil Burney who led the First Battle Squadron in the Battle of Jutland, 1916. (1922)

BURNS, mount (5,039 feet) and lake (M-5)
After Pat Burns (1856-1937), Calgary, owner of land near the lake. Known as the "Cattle King", Burns built up a large meat packing business. In 1931 he was called to the Senate and sat until 1936 when he resigned.

BURRISON, lake (B-6)
After Leading Sergeant Richard Burrison, M.M., Chauvin, killed in World War II. (1949)

BURSTALL, mount (9,000 feet), creek and lakes (M-4)
After Lieutenant General Sir H. E. Burstall. (1918)

BUSH, pass (7,860 feet) (K-3)
At the head of the Bush River, B.C. which was so called from dense forest (bush) on the banks of the river.

BUTTRESS, mountain (8,809 feet) and lake (J-2)
Probably descriptive. (1916)

BYERS, lake   (I-5)
Situated on land originally owned by people named Byers. (1950)

BYNG, mount (9,760 feet) and pass   (M-4)
After General Julian, First Viscount Byng, of Vimy; in command of the
Canadian Army Corps, May, 1916-June, 1917; Governor General of
Canada, 1921-1926. (1918)

BYRON, hill and creek   (O-5)
Crowsnest River; after small mining townsite owned by the Byron Creek
Colleries.

— C —

CACHE, lake   (H-7)
A translation of the Cree name, *astachikuwin*. The Indians at one time
had a cache here for buffalo meat and hauled it to their winter camp
as needed.

CADOMIN, hamlet, mountain (7,877 feet) and creek   (J-3)
Contraction of Canadian Dominion Mine; named by F. L. Hammond,
president, Cadomin Coal Company. (1913)

CADOTTE, lake and river   (F-4)
After Jean Baptiste Cadotte (1723-ca. 1803) who became a fur trading
partner of Alexander Henry the Elder. In 1796 he turned the business
over to his two sons, Jean Baptiste II (1761-1818), who was a partner
from 1801-1803 in the North West Company; and Michel, (1764-1836),
who also served with the North West Company. The river is referred to
as Cadotte's River in the journal of Archibald McDonald under date of
August 25, 1828.

CALAHOO, hamlet   (I-5)
After William Calahoo, a Metis of Iroquoian origin. (1915)

CALDER, lake   (F-5)
After Paul B. Calder of Edmonton, former bush pilot who was killed
in a flying accident in 1933. (1954)

CALDWELL, locality   (O-6)
Named in 1900 after D. H. Caldwell, first postmaster. (1900)

CALGARY, city   (L-5)
The second city in Alberta takes its name from the ancestral estate
of Colonel J. F. Macleod (1836-1894) on the Isle of Mull in the Hebrides in Scotland. It is a Gaelic word and is translated as "clear,
running water". On August 18, 1875. "F" Troop of 50 men of the North-
West Mounted Police under Inspector E. A. Brisebois set out from Fort
Macleod to establish a post at the junction of the Bow and Elbow Rivers.
The troop arrived at the site in a few days and commenced to erect a post
which was ready by Christmas of that year.

Inspector Brisebois wished to name the post after himself but
Colonel Macleod, then Assistant Commissioner of the Force, decided on
the name "Calgary" and Calgary it became.

CALLING, lake and river and CALLING LAKE, hamlet (G-6)
From a translation of an Indian name. The lake makes a loud noise
when freezing up each year owing to its depth.

CALMAR, town (J-5)
After Kalmar, Sweden; the first postmaster, C. J. Blomquist, came from
Kalmar in 1895. (1900)

CALUMET, lake and river (D-7)
Named after the Pierre du Calumet posts of the North West Company
and the Hudson's Bay Company. The pipestone (calumet) cliffs were
some three miles away.

CAMBRAI, mountain (10,380 feet) (K-3)
After Cambrai, France which Canadian troops entered in October, 1918.
(1920)

CAMERON, lake and falls (O-5)
Named after Major-General D. R. Cameron, British Commissioner on the
International Boundary Commission, Lake of the Woods to the Rockies,
1872-1876.

CAMPSIE, locality (I-5)
Named in 1909 after Campsie, Scotland, William Wallace, the first
postmaster, being a Scotsman.

CAMROSE, city (J-6)
After Camrose, Pembrokeshire, Wales; name selected from the British
postal guide in 1905.

CAMSELL, lake (A-7)
After Charles Camsell (1876-1958), prominent geologist. Charles Camsell was born at Fort Liard, N.W.T., the son of a chief factor of the
Hudson's Bay Company. He was educated in Manitoba and later at
Queen's, Harvard and the Massachusetts Institute of Technology. In
1900 he was an assistant on a geological survey trip to Great Bear Lake
and the Coppermine area. He was geologist in the Geological Survey
from 1904-1920, deputy minister of mines 1920-1935 and deputy minis-
ter of mines and natural resources and Commissioner of the Northwest
Territories from 1935-1946. He was prominent on the Dominion Fuel
Board, the National Research Council and received numerous awards.
In 1935 he was created C.M.G.

CANICHE, peak (8,873 feet) (J-2)
From a fancied resemblance of the summit to a poodle's head. *Caniche*
is French for "poodle."

CANMORE, town (L-4)
Said to have been named after Malcolm III (d.1093), a Scottish king.
He was known as Canmore or the "large headed" and was a son of
Duncan I. He became king in 1054 after defeating the usurper Macbeth.

CAPPON, locality (L-8)
After Professor James Cappon (1854-1939), Queen's University; name
suggested by J. W. Jake, a graduate of Queen's. (1912).

CARBON, village (L-6)
There are coal mines in the vicinity; named in 1904.

CARBONDALE, hamlet (I-6)
After its coal deposits.

CARBONDALE, hill (5,921 feet) and river (N-5)
From a coal mine on the river. (1918)

CARCAJOU, hamlet (D-3), pass and creek (J-2)
French for wolverine. (Hamlet, 1923)

CARDIFF, hamlet (I-5)
After Cardiff, Wales; the name was suggested by its coal mines. (1907)

CARDINAL, river and mount (8,000 feet) (J-3)
Named in 1918 after Jacques Cardinal, fur trader, whose grave is on the bank of the river. The mountain was named in 1922.

CARDSTON, town and municipal district (O-6)
After Charles Ora Card (1839-1906), son-in-law of Brigham Young and a pioneer of Cache Valley, Utah. In 1886 Mr. Card left Logan, Utah with Bishop Isaac Sundaland and Elder James W. Hendricks to find a new home for members of the Church of Jesus Christ of Latter Day Saints (Mormons). The following year the main company of Mormons arrived, consisting of ten families who took up squatters' possession on Lees Creek, the present site of Cardston.

CARIBOU, mountains (B-4)-(B-5)
Probably suggested by large numbers of caribou in these mountains.

CARLOS, locality (K-5)
The applicant for the post office was J. Sleeper, son of Carlos Sleeper, of Minnesota. (1914)

CARMANGAY, village (N-6)
After C. W. Carman and his wife (née Gay), former residents. (1907)

CARNWOOD, locality (J-5)
An error for Cornwood, name of a parish, Devonshire, England.

CAROLINE, village (K-5)
The first Caroline post office was opened in 1908 by Mr. and Mrs. Harvey Langley. In choosing the name they used that of their only child, Caroline. When the village was organized in 1952 the name was used since the post office was already so named.

CARSTAIRS, town (L-5)
After the town of Carstairs, Lanarkshire, Scotland. The first settlers were ranchers and of Scottish descent.

CARTHEW, mount (8,600 feet) (O-5)
After William Morden Carthew, D.L.S., Lieutenant, 49th Battalion. C. E. F., killed at Ypres, June 1, 1916. (1916)

CARVEL, locality (I-5)
After *Richard Carvel*, a novel by Winston Churchill (1874-1965). (1911)

CASCADE, mountain (9,836 feet) and river (L-4)
This well-known feature overlooking the town of Banff, takes its name from a translation of the Indian name "mountain where the water falls" which was abbreviated by Hector in 1858. *Pamasas wapta* is the Stoney and *kakishikwenightsipi* is the Cree name of the river, referring to a murder in which an Indian is said to have cut off the head of a companion (see Cuthead Creek).

CASSILS, locality (M-7)
After Charles Cassils of Cassils, Cochrane and Company of Montreal. He was an associate of the Cochrane Ranch Company and on the books of the company he is listed as a "gentleman."

CASTOR, town and creek (K-7)
According to the secretary-treasurer of the town (1970) the origin of the town name is not certain and although no documentary evidence supports it, it is generally believed that the townsite was named for Castor Creek which divides the town in two. Castor is a Latin word for beaver which are still to be found in the waters of the creek.

CAUTLEY, mount (9,418 feet)· (M-4)
After R. W. Cautley (1873-1953), D.L.S., A.L.S., B.C.L.S., member of the Interprovincial Boundary Commission (1913-1924) which surveyed the Alberta-British Columbia boundary.

CAW, creek (H-2)
In honour of Captain Bruce Edward Ashton Caw, M.C. and bar, of Vegreville.

CAYLEY, village (M-5)
Named for Hugh S. Cayley member of the Council of the North-West Territories for Calgary. Cayley was a native of Toronto and was publisher of the *Calgary Herald*. He was first elected to the Council of the North-West Territories in July, 1886, and remained a member until its dissolution. He was then elected to the Assembly of the North-West Territories, June 30, 1888.

CEREAL, village (L-8)
So named on account of its adaptability for the raising of cereal crops. From times of earliest settlement it gained a reputation for large yields of all grains. (1911)

CHABA, river, peak (10,540 feet), icefield and glacier (J-2)
A. P. Coleman who explored this area in 1892 notes when following this stream that: "As there were endless beaver dams and trees cut by beaver along its course we named it Chaba River from the Stony word for beaver." Chaba Peak is said to have also been named by Coleman after a Stoney Indian, Job Beaver, who had also explored the area.

CHAMPION, village (M-6)
Originally called Cleverville after one Martin G. Clever an early settler in the district. After the railway arrived the name was changed to Champion and the buildings moved to the present site. There are said to be two origins of the name: (1) after H. T. Champion of Alloway and Champion, bankers of Winnipeg and (2) the name of a railway engineer at the time the name was changed.

31

CHANCELLOR, locality   (L-6)
   The reference in the name is to the then German Chancellor (Bülow)
   prior to the First World War. Chancellor was a German settlement.
   (1913)

CHARD, hamlet   (F-7)
   After one A. Chard, former freight and traffic supervisor for the Alberta Government, prior to 1928.

CHARLES STEWART, mount (9,315 feet)   (L-4)
   After Honourable Charles A. Stewart (1868-1946). A native of Ontario.
   Stewart came to Alberta where he settled at Killam in the early years
   of the twentieth century. He was elected to the Legislative Assembly of
   Alberta as a Liberal in 1909 and was re-elected in 1913, 1917 and 1921.
   From 1912 to 1913 he was Minister of Municipal Affairs and from 1913
   to 1917 Minister of Public Works for the Sifton administration. From
   1917 to 1921 he was Premier of Alberta, the last Liberal premier prior
   to the defeat of the Liberals by the United Farmers of Alberta. Stewart
   became a Member of the House of Commons and sat for many years
   as a member from Alberta. He served as Minister of the Interior, Minister of Mines and Superintendent General of Indian Affairs from 1921
   to 1930. In 1936 he was appointed Chairman of the International Joint
   Commission.

CHARLTON, mount (10,500 feet)   (J-3)
   Named by Mrs. M. Schäffer after H. R. Charlton, then general advertis-
   ing agent, Grand Trunk Pacific Railway. (1911)

CHATEH, hamlet   (C-2)
   Formerly known as Assumption it was named Chateh, November 18,
   1970 in honour of a chief who signed the original treaty for the native
   people in 1900. The native people requested the change.

CHAUVIN, village   (J-8)
   After George Von Chauvin, director, Grand Trunk Railway, London,
   England. (1908)

CHEADLE, locality   (L-6)
   After William Butler Cheadle (1835-1910) noted traveller and co-author
   with Lord Milton of *Northwest Passage by Land*. Milton and Cheadle
   crossed Canada (via the Yellowhead Pass) to the Caribou country in
   1862 and the book is based on Cheadle's diary. (1884)

CHEPHREN, mountain (10,700 feet) and lake   (K-3)
   After Chephren or Khafre, fourth pharaoh of the Fourth Dynasty of
   Egypt and builder of the second of the great pyramids. He was the
   son of Khufu or Cheops the builder of the Great Pyramid and reigned
   c.2540-2514 B.C. although some authorities (Herodotus among them)
   claim he reigned as long as fifty years. Mount Chephren was originally
   known as Pyramid Mountain but the name was changed in 1918 to
   avoid confusion with Pyramid Mountain near Jasper.

CHERHILL, hamlet   (I-5)
   After A. P. Stecher, first postmaster, with "hill" added. (1911)

CHESTER, mount (10,000 feet) (M-4)
After H.M.S. *Chester* engaged in the Battle of Jutland, 1916. (1922)

CHETAMON, mountain (8,400 feet) (J-2)
Stoney Indian word for "squirrel"; two rocks on the arête resemble squirrels. (1916)

CHIGWELL, hamlet (K-6)
After Chigwell, Essex, England. The name first appeared in its present form in England in 1190.

CHILD, lake (C-2)
An Indian child died tragically here.

CHILD LAKE, Indian Reserve (C-2)
See Child, lake. (1912)

CHIN, hill, locality and coulee (N-7)
From Blackfoot *mistoamo*, meaning "beard"; from the shape of the hill when seen from a distance.

CHINCHAGA, river (D-2)
A Beaver Indian name meaning "beautiful" or "wonderful" river.

CHINOOK, village (L-8)
After the warm dry winds from the Rockies. See supplement. (1910)

CHIP, lake and CHIP LAKE, locality (I-4)
A shortened form of Buffalo Chip Lake, the name by which it was originally known. The modern name Chip Lake first appears on a map in 1865. The lake was also known as "Bull Dung" lake and "Dirt" lake.

CHIPEWYAN, lakes and river (E-6)
For origin see Fort Chipewyan.

CHIPEWYAN LAKE, trading post, (E-6)
For origin see Fort Chipewyan. (1944)

CHIPMAN, creek (N-5)
After J. E. Chipman of the Halifax Ranch Company.

CHIPMAN, village (I-6)
After Clarence Campbell Chipman (1856-1924), Private Secretary to Sir Charles Tupper when Minister of Railways and Canals, (1882-1891); then appointed Chief Commissioner, Hudson's Bay Company, (1891-1911), London Eng. (1905)

CHISHOLM MILLS, hamlet (H-5)
After Thomas Chisholm a tie contractor for the E.D. and B.C. Railway. Chisholm was a Klondike pioneer, having run the Aurora Saloon and Dance Hall at Dawson City in the days of the gold rush. He was a huge man, standing over six feet, weighing over 240 pounds and it is said that he wore a watch chain of gold nuggets across his chest and that this "looked almost as large as a logging chain" (according to J. W. Judge, railway pioneer). He died penniless in 1936.

CHOKIO, locality (N-6)
Said to be a corruption of chok-ieo, the Indian pronunciation of the English "choke-cherries", which the Indians used to sell to the workmen constructing the railway. (1904)

CHOWN, mount (10,890 feet), glacier and creek   (I-1)
    After Reverend S. D. Chown, D.D. (1853-1933), formerly General
    Superintendent, Methodist Church. (1912)

CHRISTIE, mount (10,180 feet)   (J-3)
    Named by Hector in 1859 after William Joseph Christie (1824-ca.1886),
    Chief Factor for the Hudson's Bay Company at Edmonton from 1858-
    1871. He was in charge there when the Palliser Expedition wintered at
    the Fort.

CHRISTINA, lake and river   (E-7), (F-7)-(G-7)
    After Christina Gordon, sister of the former postmaster at Fort Mc-
    Murray. Changed from Pembina to avoid duplication. (1911)

CINQUEFOIL, mountain (7,412 ft.) and creek   (J-2)
    The cinquefoil or five-finger grows in the vicinity. (1916)

CIRQUE, peak (9,768 feet) and lake   (L-3)
    Descriptive, the stream from its south front falls into a great cirque or
    amphitheatre.

CLAIRE, lake   (C-6)
    On maps since 1874; corruption of Clear; "Clear Water" lake in Sir
    Alexander Mackenzie's journal, October 10, 1792.

CLAIRVAUX, mountain, creek and glacier   (J-2)
    Intended to express its situation at the head of a "clear valley."

CLANDONALD, hamlet   (I-8)
    Formerly named Wellsdale, it received its present name when a group
    of Scottish settlers proposed a change. A meeting was held and the
    name Clandonald chosen. Presumably the Scots were in the majority.

CLARESHOLM, town   (N-6)
    There are two explanations of the origin of this name. Neither is certain;
    each is credible. The first is that it was after the home of a super-
    intendent of the railway named Niblock; his wife's Christian name was
    Clare. The second is that a motherly lady whose name was Clare ran a
    boarding house at this point when the branch line of the C.P.R. from
    Calgary for Fort Macleod was being built. Many workers lived there
    and spoke of "going to Clare's home." So the present name came into
    being.

CLARINDA, locality   (O-7)
    After Mrs. T. Clarinda Clark, mother of Miss F. Clark, postmistress.
    (1911)

CLARK, range   (O-5)
    After Captain William Clark (1770-1838) of the Lewis and Clark expedi-
    tion, 1806. It was this expedition that first reached the mouth of the
    Columbia River after an overland journey across the United States.
    Clark became Governor of the Northwest Territory (U.S.A.) in 1813
    and was Superintendent of Indian Affairs until 1820 when Missouri
    became a state. In 1822 he was again Commissioner of Indian Affairs.
    (1917)

CLAYSMORE, locality (I-7)
Possibly after Claysmore, Middlesex, England. (1905)

CLEAR, hills (E-2)
A descriptive name.

CLEAR HILLS, Indian Reserve (E-2)
See Clear, hills.

CLEARWATER, river, mountain (10,420 feet) and lake (K-4)
North Saskatchewan River; Clearwater River on Thompson map, 1814; descriptive of the river.

CLEARWATER, river (E-7)
Athabasca River; Washacumow or Clear Water River on Turnor map, 1790; in Stoney, *mnith-ow wap-ta*, (Tyrrell).

CLINE, mount (11,027 feet) and river (K-3)
Known as "Waputeek or White Goat" river on Palliser map, 1859; after Michael Cline (Klyne, Clyne, Klein, Kline), born 1781; employee of the North West Company and the Hudson's Bay Company. He was in charge at Jasper House, 1824-25 and 1829-34. He retired to Red River, 1837 and was living in 1843. Cline River was formerly called Cataract River. Hector says that his Indian guide reported a trail up the White Goat River from Kootenay Plain to Jasper House, travelled by a trader named Cline, who used it when collecting provisions for the winter; the peak was named by J. N. Collie.

CLIVE, village (K-6)
After Robert, 1st Lord Clive, (1725-1774), British soldier and statesman, one of the creators of British power in India. Formerly known as Valley City and probably before that as Urquhart. (1909)

CLOVER BAR, hamlet (I-6)
After Thomas H. Clover who was born in 1809. A natural wanderer, he was one of the California "forty-niners." In 1858 he was on the Fraser and by the "sixties" he was washing gold on the North Saskatchewan near Edmonton. He was last heard of in 1897 when he was at Leroy, North Dakota.

CLYDE, village (I-6)
After George D. Clyde, the first postmaster and early settler. In the early 1900's Mr. Clyde homesteaded here and as time passed he carried a small stock of the bare essentials and his home became a stopping place for early settlers coming into the area. On August 1, 1906, a post office designated Clyde was established at his residence with Mr. Clyde as postmaster; thus prior to the coming of the railway there was a district known as Clyde. The railway laid out a townsite immediately south of Mr. Clyde's property with the name of the already existing post office being used. Any buildings that had sprung up around the original post office were ultimately moved to the new site. (Letter, Sec.-Treas., 1970)

COALDALE, town (N-6)
According to the files of the C.P.R. (quoted in the Alberta Jubilee booklet of Coaldale) Elliott T. Galt, son of Sir Alexander T. Galt erected a residence at the river bottom south of the High Level (Leth-

bridge) bridge and to distinguish it from the growing town of Coal Banks (now Lethbridge) named it Coal Dale. The C.P.R. when wishing to name the sidings established on its road to the east (to Medicine Hat) commemorated the name of Mr. Galt's house and so Coaldale came into being.

COCHRANE, town and lake   (L-5)
After Senator M. H. Cochrane (1823-1903). In 1878 the Cochrane Ranch was established and 1881 the ranch was incorporated into the Cochrane Ranch Company. It was owned by Senator Cochrane and was the first big ranching company in the west. The local manager was Colonel James Walker, a veteran from the North-West Mounted Police.

COLD, lake   (H-8)
"Coldwater" lake on Turnor map, 1790. It appears that the lake was so named on account of the very cold water at all seasons of the year. The local Crees—before the coming of the white man—called the lake Cold Lake in Cree.

COLD LAKE, town and Indian Reserve   (H-8)
After the lake nearby.

COLEMAN, mount (10,262 feet)   (K-3)
After A. P. Coleman (1852-1939), geologist at the University of Toronto. Coleman made a number of explorations in the Rockies between the North Saskatchewan and Athabasca rivers studying the geology of the area and generally exploring. He also explored the Mount Robson region in B.C.

COLEMAN, town   (N-5)
Named in 1904 by A. C. Flummerfelt, president of the International Coal and Coke Company after his youngest daughter. The town came into being as a result of the development of large coal deposits and construction of the C.P.R. from Lethbridge to Kootenay Lake via the Crowsnest Pass.

COLIN, mount (8,815 feet) and range   (J-2)
After Colin Fraser (ca. 1805-1867) a servant of the Hudson's Bay Company. Fraser was born in Scotland and came to Canada in 1827 as Sir George Simpson's private piper. When Simpson travelled on his tours of inspection it was his custom to have Fraser piping when they arrived at a trading post; this is said to have greatly impressed the Indians. Fraser became a trader and from 1835 to 1849 was in charge of Jasper House. He later served at other posts and died at Lac St. Anne in 1867.

COLINTON, hamlet   (H-6)
Named by J. M. Milne who had an interest in the townsite, after his former home, Colinton, Edinburgh, Scotland. Kinnoull P.O. until 1913. Another version is that it was for Colin Fraser, early fur trader.

COLLIE, creek   (I-2))
Flows southeast into the Wildhay River and was named after J. N. Collie, F.R.S., London, England—alpinist, who with Dr. Mumm, is reported to have visited this area in 1910 and later years. (1946).

COLQUHOUN, creek (G-2)
After Flight Lieutenant Ian L. Colquhoun, M.I.D., Edmonton, killed in World War II. (1951)

COLUMBIA, mount (12,294 feet), glacier and icefield (K.-3)
After the Columbia River which was named in 1792 by Captain Robert Gray of Boston, after his vessel. (1899)
The location of the mouth of the Columbia River had eluded mariners for some time. Captain Vancouver missed it in 1792 on his voyage up the west coast although he suspected its location. The reason it was not easily found was—and is—the presence of a dangerous bar at its mouth. In 1792, Captain Robert Gray noticing the movement of the water, decided to explore and at high tide, with all sails set he successfully crossed the dangerous bar and entered the mouth of the river which he named for his ship the *Columbia*. His discovery helped strengthen the American claim to the territory.

COMMITTEE PUNCH BOWL, lake (K-2)
This small mountain tarn is the centre one of three located at the summit of Athabasca Pass. Athabasca Pass was at the highest point on the famous express route of the fur trade overland from the east via the Saskatchewan and Athabasca Rivers to the Big Bend of the Columbia and the Pacific coast. It was not uncommon for parties passing that way to regale themselves on reaching this point—particularly if a high official of the fur trade was present. The circular shape of the lake gave it its name; the waters divide here—one stream to the Pacific, the other to the Arctic.

CONJURING, creek (I-6)
North Saskatchewan River. Name suggested by that of Wizard Lake from which it flows; the Cree name is *paw-ga-mow*, literally "vomiting" creek or *miteoo* (Tyrrell). Hector, 1858, has *Ecapotte's creek*.

CONN, lake (H-7)
After Leading Steward J. R. Conn, M.I.D., Hillcrest, killed in World War II. (1951)

CONNELLY, creek (N-5)
After Connelly brothers, residents in the vicinity.

CONNEMARA, station (M-5)
After Connemara, Ireland.

CONNOR CREEK, locality (I-4)
After James Connor, early settler. (1919)

CONRAD, locality (N-7)
After Charles Conrad, partner in I. G. Baker and Company, early trading company of Fort Benton, Montana. (1914)

CONSOLATION, valley, pass and lakes (L-4)
East of Moraine Lake and named by Wilcox, as he was "very much pleased with the place" which contrasted favourably with the desolation of the neighbouring Valley of Ten Peaks. (1899)

CONSORT, village (K-8)
Known as Sanderville Post Office prior to 1911. It received its present
name at the time of the coronation of King George V. The adjacent
places of Loyalist, Veteran, Throne and Coronation (q.v.) all received
their present names at this time.

CONWAY, mount, (10,170 feet), glacier, range and creek (L-3)
Named by Collie after Sir Martin Conway, famous mountain climber;
he climbed in the Himalayas, Andes, Alps, etc. President of the Alpine
Club of Great Britain, 1902-1904. (1902)

COOKING, lake (I-6)
Translation of Cree *opi-mi-now-wa-sioo*; a favourite Indian camping
ground.

COOKING LAKE, hamlet. (I-6)
See Cooking, lake.

COPITHORNE, ridge (M-5)
The name was presumably derived from the family name of Copithorne
who were old settlers in the locality.

COPPER, mountain (9,130 feet) (L-4)
Named by Dr. G. M. Dawson after copper prospects located near its
summit by Healy and O. and J. S. Dennis.

CORNWALL, mountain (9,700 feet) (M-5)
After the Cruiser *Cornwall,* engaged in the Battle of Jutland, 1916. (1922)

CORONACH, mountain (8,078 feet) and creek (J-2)
So named because of the howling of coyotes; Coronach is Gaelic for
funeral dirge. (1916)

CORONADO, locality (I-6)
After Coronado, California from Coronado Butte, Arizona, honouring
Francisco Vasquez de Coronado, sixteenth century Spanish explorer.
Means "crowned". Name suggested by one A. J. Fraser. (1921)

CORONATION, mountain (10,420 feet) (K-3)
Named by Collie in 1901 on the Coronation Day of King Edward VII
and Queen Alexandra. Collie notes: "We did not forget that today,
August the 9th was Coronation Day and it was a pity, perhaps that we
could not have celebrated it on the top of Mount Forbes. Tea and a
little weak whiskey and water were the most generous fluids we possess
wherein to drink their Majesties' health; but as a memento of the
occasion we named a fine peak to the south, with a drapery of the
whitest snow and a singularly beautiful glacier clinging to its northern
face—Coronation Peak."

CORONATION, town (K-7)
Named by the Canadian Pacific Railway in 1911 at the time of the
coronation of King George V.

CORONET, mountain, (10,340 feet), glacier and creek (J-3)
Maligne Lake. From the shape of the mountain. (1923)

CORRAL, creek (L-4)
Bow River. After a horse corral near the mouth used during construction days on the Canadian Pacific Railway.

CORY, mount (9,154 feet) (L-4)
North of the Bow River. After William Wallace Cory, Deputy Minister of the Interior (1905-1930). It is the mountain with the "hole-in-the-wall" in it which can be seen from the highway. (1923)

COSTIGAN, mount (9,775 feet) (L-4)
After Hon. John Costigan (1835-1916). A native of New Brunswick he was first elected to the Legislative Assembly of that province in 1861. In 1867 he was elected to the House of Commons and served as Minister of Inland Revenue from 1882-1892, Secretary of State from 1892-1894, and Minister of Marine and Fisheries from 1894-1896. He was called to the Senate in 1907. (1904)

CÔTÉ, mount (7,844 feet) and creek (I-2)
After Senator Jean Léon Côté (1867-1924), Edmonton; 1893-1904, D.L.S., Western Canada and Yukon. First elected to the Legislative Assembly, Alberta, 1909. He was Provincial Secretary, 1918-1921, and was called to the Senate, 1923. (1925)

COUGAR, mountain and creek (M-5)
Elbow River. After the cougar or mountain lion.

COUSINS, locality (N-8)
After William Cousins, one time prominent businessman of Medicine Hat.

COUTTS, river (H-5)
Saulteux River; after G. M. Coutts, member of a survey party. He died about 1911.

COUTTS, village (O-7)
After Angela Georgina, Baroness Burdett-Coutts (1814-1906), English philanthropist and a stockholder in the Alberta Railway and Irrigation Company. A member of the prominent English banking family of Coutts, she was born in London and was the youngest daughter of Sir Francis Burdett. She inherited a vast fortune from the actress Harriet Mellon, the second wife of her grandfather, Thomas Coutts, the banker. At this time she took the name and arms of Coutts in addition to her own. In 1871 she was created a peeress in her own right. In 1881 she married William Ashmead Bartlett who took her name. Not only was she a shrewd investor but her charities were extensive and she personally administered many of them herself. She was buried in Westminster Abbey. See also Burdett, village.

COWLEY, village (N-5)
Named by a rancher, F. W. Godsal; while watching his cattle wandering across the prairie, he was reminded of Gray's "lowing herd winds slowly o'er the lea."

CRADOCK, locality (N-6)
After Rear Admiral Sir Christopher Cradock who perished in the naval battle of Coronel, November 1, 1914. (1915)

CRAIGMYLE, village   (L-7)
After an estate in Scotland. (1913)

CREMONA, village   (L-5)
According to Mrs. C. J. Haggerty (letter, August, 1970), Secretary-Treasurer of the Village, it was in 1906 that a Mr. and Mrs. Smith-Jackson arrived from England and opened a store about one mile west of the present village site. They applied to the Post Office Department to have the store named "Honley" after their home town in England. It was felt, however, that this would be confused with Hanley, Saskatchewan and the suggestion from the Post Office was to name the place Cremona. Mrs. Smith-Jackson approved the name which has since remained. Presumably it was after the city in Italy. (1906)

CRESSDAY, station   (O-8)
After W. Creswell and Tony Day, ranchers. (1922)

CROOKED, creek   (O-5)
Translation of Cree name, *wawakatinau*; descriptive.

CROSSFIELD, village   (L-5)
Named after the chief surveyor of the Canadian Pacific Railway, it was incorporated as a village on September 14, 1907.

CROW INDIAN, lake   (O-7)
After the Crows, a Siouan tribe forming part of the Hidatsa group.

CROWFOOT, glacier and mountain, (9,500 feet)   (L-3)
From its resemblance to a crow's foot. (Mountain, 1959)

CROWFOOT, locality and creek   (M-6)
After Crowfoot, head chief of the Blackfoot tribe at the signing of Treaty No. 7 in 1877. Later he refused to join Sitting Bull in his fight against the white man. "Tell the Great Mother", he told the Mounted Police, "we have been loyal and that we know she will not let her children starve." He was born ca. 1836 and died in 1890.

CROWLODGE, creek   (N-6)
Translation of Blackfoot *ataw-is-toik-akwapi* or *mastowistooek-okapi*, "the lodges with crows painted" (Nelson); the Blackfoot name is *ahkisikaseme* or Medicine Root creek because the Indians dig roots here for use as medicine (Steele).

CROWSNEST, mountain (9,138 feet) lake, river, pass (4,453 feet), locality   (N-5)
From a translation of the Cree Indian name, *kah-ka-ioo-wut-tshis-tun*, it does not commemorate the slaughter of the Crow Indians by the Blackfoot (who named it *ma-sto-ceas*) when they got them into a corner or "nest" but merely refers to the nesting of the crows near the base of the peak—literally "the nest of the crow or raven." The first mention of the name is by Captain Blakiston of the Palliser Expedition who notes under date of December 15, 1858: "I have not mentioned the existence of two other passes across this portion of the mountains called the Crow-nest and Flathead Passes, the former in the British, the latter in American Territory. The Crow-nest pass of which I have marked the general direction on the plan follows up the Crow-nest

River, a tributary of the Belly River into the mountains and gains the west side near 'The Steeples'. By report of the natives it is a very bad road and seldom used. I observed the old trail coming in from the plains on the left bank of the Crow-nest River." Blakiston does not explain why the Indians considered that this was such a bad road; perhaps it was choked with fallen timber. It is an easier road than the North Kootenay Pass and is now traversed by the southern (Kettle Valley) line of the C.P.R. and Highway No. 3.

CRUMMY, lake   (D-3)
After Flying Officer George K. Crummy, Grande Prairie, killed in World War II. (1964)

CUMMINGS, locality   (J-7)
After Cummings Brothers, general merchants, John T. Cummings being first postmaster. (1908)

CURRIE, mount (9,268 feet) and creek   (M-4)
In honour of General Sir Arthur Currie (1875-1933). A native of Ontario, Currie went to British Columbia in 1894 where he taught in Victoria and was also in insurance and real estate. From 1897 to 1914 he served in the B.C. Brigade, Canadian Garrison Artillery and by 1909 had risen to command the regiment as Lieutenant-Colonel. In 1914 he was in command of the 50th Regiment Gordon Highlanders and in August of the same year became Commander of the 2nd Brigade which he took overseas. In recognition of his service at the Second Battle of Ypres and at St. Julien he was promoted Colonel, Brigadier-General and Major-General and Commander of the First Canadian Division. After Vimy Ridge in 1917 he was created K.C.M.G., Lieutenant-General and Commander of the Canadian Corps which position he retained until the end of the war. In 1919 he became the first General in the Canadian Army. From 1920 to 1933 he was Principal and Vice-Chancellor of McGill University, Montreal. (1918)

CUTHEAD, creek   (L-4)
Cascade River. Translation of Stoney Indian name; according to legend, a Cree Indian who had eloped with a Stoney woman was overtaken here and beheaded.

CYPRESS, hills   (N-8)
Shown on Palliser map, 1865. According to Palliser the early Canadian hunters and traders called all evergreens "le Cypres." It was a natural development for them to call the tree covered hills in what is now Southern Alberta the "Montagne de Cypres." The name was later anglicized to the Cypress Hills. The Cree called them *mi-na-ti-kak* meaning beautiful upland; the Blackfoot *aiekunekwe* or Grizzly Bear Hills and in Stoney *pa-ha-toonga* (Tyrrell).

CYPRESS HILLS, provincial park
See Cypress, hills

CZAR, village   (K-8)
A Russian settlement. (1909)

— D —

DABBS, lake (H-7)
East of Lac la Biche; after Pilot Officer H. E. Dabbs, D. F. C., Daysland, killed in World War II. (1951)

DALEMEAD, locality (M-6)
After Dr. Ellwood Mead, an irrigation specialist, and "dale" from its situation in a valley. (1914)

DALHOUSIE, mount (8,000 feet) (J-3)
Named by Southesk, 1859, after 11th Earl of Dalhousie (1801-1874), "at whose house my journey to America was first suggested." He was Secretary for War during the Crimean War and nephew of the 9th Earl who was Governor General of Canada.

DALMUIR, locality (I-6)
After Dalmuir, near Glasgow, Scotland. (1913)

DALROY locality (L-5)
Named about 1907 by the Canadian Pacific Railway Company after G. M. McElroy, early settler, with the Scottish prefix *dal* meaning "dale" or "valley."

DALY, mount (10,342 feet) (L-4)
After C. F. Daly, president, American Geographical Society, 1864-1899. (1898)

DAPHNE, island (E-7)
Athabasca River; after Daphne, daughter of J. N. Wallace, D.L.S. (1925)

DAPP, hamlet, creek and lake (H-5)
After David A. Pennicuick, former accountant of the E. D. and B. C. Railway. It was Eunice Post Office until 1917. His initials D.A.P. plus an extra "p" form the name.

DARRAH, mount (9,038 feet) (O-5)
After Captain Charles John Darrah, R.E., astronomer, British Boundary Commission, Rockies to the Pacific, 1858-1862. (1917)

DARWELL, hamlet (I-5)
Darwall was the name chosen by settlers but the "a" changed to "e" for someone's preference. (*West of the Fifth*)

DAVID, mountain (8,986 feet), creek and lake (K-3)
After David Thompson (1770-1857), who travelled through the Howse Pass, 1806-7.

DAVIDSON, lake (B-6)
After Warrant Officer II (CSM) William Davidson, M.M., Edmonton, killed in World War II. (1949)

DAYSLAND, village (J-7)
After one E. M. Day, local land owner. (1905)

42

DEADHORSE, coulee (M-6)

Forty horses of the R.N.W.M.P. died here on the march to the West, 1874 (Steele).

DEADMAN, hill (L-5)

Between Ghost and Bow Rivers; in Cree, *chipei watchi*; Hector says: "There was once a great battle fought here and there is a grave built in the wood on the top of the hill, in which the slain were buried." It is probably the hill west of the Ghost in the angle it makes with the Bow.

DEADMAN, lake (I-5)

In Indian *hahpeukaketactch* or "man-who-got-stabbed"; a Cree was stabbed here in a drunken row (Steele). It was also known in early days as Berland Lake, after a fur trader.

DEBOLT, hamlet, creek (G-2)

After H. E. Debolt, postmaster. (1923)

DECOIGNE, locality (J-2)

After François Decoigne, yellow-haired trapper, after whom the Yellow-head Pass (q.v.) is named. (1926)

DECRENE, locality (G-5)

After a contractor who constructed a portion of the E.D. and B.C. Railway. (1914)

DEL BONITA, locality and Port of Entry (O-6)

Spanish words meaning "of the pretty." (1914)

DELIA, village (L-6)

"A petition by local homesteaders was sent to the Post Office Department asking that a post office be provided and named Delia. A man by the name of A. L. Davies homesteaded in the area and operated a stopping house named 'Delia's Stopping House' as his wife's name was Delia. In 1913 the C.N.R. purchased land for a townsite which was called 'Highland' as it was the highest point on the railroad between Saskatoon and Calgary. With the town being called Highland and the Post Office Delia, there was considerable confusion and a great deal of correspondence between local people, the Government and the Railway, so the name was changed to Delia." (Olive K. Martin, Secretary-Treasurer, Village of Delia, August 18, 1970 letter).

DELPHINIUM, creek (J-2)

After the wild delphiniums near its headwaters. (1960)

DELTAFORM, mountain (11,225 feet) (L-4)

From its resemblance to the Greek letter delta ($\triangle$). It is number eight of the Ten Peaks, (q.v.).

DEMAY, lake and station (J-6)

The lake was named in 1893 after a settler. It was formerly Flat Lake which is a translation of Cree *ka-ta-ta-kwa-cha-o-ka-mak* (Tyrrell); *tatakwachaw* means flat (Lacombe).

DEMMITT, locality (G-1)

After Chelsea Thomas Demmitt who settled in the area in 1919 following service with the American Expeditionary Force in France.

DENHART, locality (M-7)

After a farmer who settled in the district. (1914)

DENNIS, locality (M-8)

After one Colonel J. S. Dennis, Department of Colonization and Development of the Canadian Pacific Railway. (1910-12)

DENT, mount (10,729 feet) (K-3)

After one C. T. Dent, sometime president, Alpine Club, England. (1899)

DEOME, creek (H-2)

For one Deome Findley who had a trapline on this creek. (1947)

DERWENT, village (I-7)

C.P.R. men named it after Derwent Waters, England. This name appears as long ago as ca. 730 when Bede wrote of *Deruuentionist fluuii* (Derwent River); ca. 890 it appears as *Doerwentan,* stream. The name appears in several counties for different features in England. A British river name *Derventio* found, as a name of a place on the Yorkshire Derwent (*Derventione*) derived from British *derva* 'oak', Welsh *derw,* etc. The name means "river where oaks were common'. Derwentwater comes from the name and appears as Derwentwater in 1210 in records of Furness Abbey and as *Derewentwater* on 1234 Close Rolls, (Ekwall).

DESJARLAIS, locality (I-7)

After one David Desjarlais, first postmaster.

DE SMET, ROCHE, mountain (8,330 feet) also range (J-2)

After Pierre Jean De Smet (1801-1873) Belgian missionary who worked for many years among the Indians of the Western and North Western States. De Smet emigrated to America in 1827 where he entered the Jesuit novitiate and was ultimately ordained. He was sent to the Oregon country in 1840 and the following year, established a mission to the Flathead Indians. In 1845 he crossed the mountains by Whiteman Pass and visited Fort Edmonton; the next year he returned by Athabasca Pass. He endured many hardships while with the Indians. He recounts in a letter how the mountain was named for him: "They (the Iroquois Indians) begged leave to honour me before my departure with a little ceremony to prove their attachment and that their children might always remember him who had first put them in the way of life. Each one discharged his musket in the direction of the highest mountain, a large rock jutting out in the form of a sugar loaf and with three loud hurrahs gave it my name."

DE VEBER, mount (8,494 feet) (I-1)

After Hon. Leverett George de Veber (1849-1925) who was born at St. John, N.B. and received his medical training at St. Bartholomew's Hospital, London, and at the University of Pennsylvania. He practised medicine at Lethbridge. In 1898 he was elected to the North-West

Territories Assembly and in 1905 to the first Legislature of Alberta; he served as Minister without Portfolio from 1905-1906. In 1906 he was called to the Senate. He died in Ottawa in 1925.

DEVILLE, locality (I-6)
After Dr. Edouard Gaston Deville, LL.D., I.S.O., D.L.S., D.T.S., (1849-1924). Surveyor-General of Canada, (1885-1924). He is the father of Canadian Photogrammetry. (1909)

DEVILS HEAD, mountain (9,174 feet) (L-4)
Translation of the Cree name *we-ti-kwas-ti-kwan*; in Stoney, *si-ham-pa* (Tyrrell). Sir George Simpson says it bears "a rude resemblance to an upturned face."

DEVILS THUMB, THE—mountain (8,066 feet) (L-4)
Between Lakes Louise and Agnes; descriptive.

DEVON, mountain (9,855 feet) (L-3)
Pipestone Pass. The Devonian geological formation is well developed here. (1923)

DEVON, town (J-5)
Named for the Devonian formation in which the Leduc Oil Field lies.

DEWBERRY, village (I-8)
After the berry. (1907)

DE WIND, mount (8,000 feet) (J-2)
Berland Range; after Lieutenant Edmund De Wind, V.C. (posthumously) Calgary, killed in World War I. (1949)

DE WINTON, hamlet (M-5)
After Major General Sir Francis De Winton, G.C.M.G., C.B. (1835-1901), military secretary to the Marquis of Lorne, then Governor General. He organized the De Winton Ranch Company, also known as Brecon ranch.

DIADEM, peak (11,060 feet) (K-3)
Sunwapta River. It was climbed by J. Norman Collie, 1898, and so named by him because it was crowned by a "diadem" of snow about 100 feet high.

DIAMOND CITY, hamlet (N-6)
The coal mine at this point was named Black Diamond Mine but when a post office was about to be opened, it was found the name had already been used and the alternative Diamond City was selected.

DIAMOND DICK, creek (G-2)
Named after homesteader Dick Harrington who gained reputation for his ability to tie a diamond hitch on pack horses. (1962)

DICKINS, lake (A-2)
After C. H. (Punch) Dickins (1899-   ), D.F.C., of Victoria, B.C., formerly of Edmonton and Toronto, famous northern bush pilot who was the first Canadian to cross the Arctic Circle by air. Later he was one of the founders of Canadian Pacific Airlines. (1953)

DICKSON, hamlet and creek **(K-5)**
After Dickson creek, which after Benedickson, a very early settler from Norway. (1906).

DICKSON, lake **(G-1)**
Northwest of Albright Lake after Flying Officer C. A. Dickson, A.F.C., Edmonton, killed in World War II. (1952)

DIDSBURY, town **(L-5)**
Didsbury derives its name from Didsbury in Manchester, England. The first settlers were descendents of Dutch Mennonites who left their homes in Pennsylvania, U.S.A. and migrated as United Empire Loyalists to Waterloo County, Ontario. In 1893 Sir J. A. Macdonald, Prime Minister of Canada, requested Jacob Shantz to select a site in Western Canada for the Mennonite group. Didsbury was chosen and Mr. Shantz constructed an immigration hall, a barn and well in preparation for settlers. In payment for his work he received a quarter section of land from the government. In 1894 Mr. Shantz returned to Waterloo County and selected 34 hardy young people to become the first settlers. Didsbury was incorporated as a village in 1905 and as a town on September 27, 1906 (From: *Echos of an Era*, Kinette Club of Didsbury, Didsbury, 1969). Didsbury is a name of ancient origin being derived from *Dedisbiry* (Assize Rolls, 1246) and *Diddesbiry* (Assize Rolls, 1276) "*Dyddi's burg*", (Ekwall).

DILLION, river **(G-8)**
A family name of J. N. Wallace, D.L.S., who surveyed the Fourth Meridian in 1909-10.

DIMSDALE, locality **(G-2)**
After Henry George Dimsdale, engineer on the construction of the E.D. and B.C. Railway.

DINA, locality **(J-8)**
After Dina Sand, the only girl living in the district when the post office was opened, (intended to be pronounced "Deena" as in Norwegian). (1908)

DINANT, locality **(J-6)**
Named by François Adam, a pioneer settler, after his home town in Belgium; formerly Pretty Hill Post Office. (1911)

DINOSAUR, provincial park **(M-7)**
In the area where the dinosaurs once roamed.

DINOSAUR, ridge (5,550 feet) and creek **(H-1)**
From the fancied resemblance of the ridge to this prehistoric animal. (1923)

DOGPOUND, locality and creek **(L-5)**
In Cree, *mizekampehpoocaha* or "wolf caught in buffalo pound" (Steele). Tyrrell gives the Cree name as *ko-ma-tas-ta-moin* or "stolen horse (or dog) creek", and the Stoney name as *so-mun-ib-wapta*. It is "Edge Creek" on the Palliser map, 1865. Another suggestion is that

the name comes from the pounding of the dogs' paws on the frozen creek as the braves returned to winter camp from hunting. The area was a favourite Cree winter camp. (1900)

DOLOMITE, pass, peak (9,828 feet) and creek (L-3)
The peaks in the vicinity resemble the Swiss "Dolomites." (1897)

DOME, glacier (K-3)
From Snowdome mountain—descriptive.

DONALDA, village (J-6)
Changed from Eidswold P.O. in 1911. After Donalda Crossway of Coburg, Ont., a niece of Sir Donald Mann (1853-1934), vice-president, Canadian Northern. (1911)

DONATVILLE, locality (H-6)
After one Donat Gingras, early settler. (1914)

DONNELLY, village (F-3)
After an official of the E.D. and B.C. Railway. (1915)

DORENLEE, locality (J-6)
After W. O. Dore, a former postmaster.

DORMER, river and mountain (9,080 feet) (L-4)
From ridges terminating like dormer windows above the valley.

DOROTHY, locality (L-7)
After Dorothy Wilson, the first and only baby in the district when the post office was opened. (1908)

DOUAI, mountain (10,830 feet) (K-3)
On the Alberta-B.C. Boundary; after the celebrated fortified town in northeastern France; in commemoration of its occupation on October 18, 1918, by the Canadians in conjunction with other Allied troops. (1920)

DOUGLAS, mount (11,017 feet), lake and creek (L-4)
After David Douglas (1798-1834), botanist who crossed the Rockies in 1827. Douglas was born in Scotland and at an early age entered the Scone Palace Gardens as an apprentice gardener, later attending lectures in botany at the University of Glasgow. He was appointed a botanical collector for the Horticultural Society of London and in 1823 went to the United States and Upper Canada. The following year he set out via Cape Horn for the Pacific Northwest where he spent two years exploring and discovering new varieties of trees and plants as well as collecting seeds and specimens. The Douglas fir was named for him. In 1827 he crossed the mountains via Athabasca Pass with the Hudson Bay express and continued with them as far as Norway House and then spent some time collecting botanical specimens in the Red River district before embarking at York Factory for England. In 1830 he returned to the Pacific Northwest, spent some time in California and then travelled north to Fort St. James by way of the Okanagan Valley, Fort Kamloops, Fort Alexandria and the Fraser, Nechako and Stuart Rivers. He returned to the Columbia and sailed

for Honolulu and while in Hawaii he fell into a bullock pit and was gored to death by a trapped animal. He kept a meticulous journal entitled *Journal during Travels in North America, 1823-1827* which was not published in full until 1914.

DOVERCOURT, locality (K-5)
H. Lee, the first postmaster, came from Dovercourt, Harwich, England. (1912)

DOWLING, lake and station (K-7)
Named by J. B. Tyrrell, 1886, after Donaldson Bogart Dowling (1858-1925), geologist, Geological Survey of Canada (1884).

DRAGON, peak (9,500 feet) (K-3)
From the shape of a rock near the summit. (1921)

DRAPER, locality (E-7)
After Thomas Draper, president, McMurray Asphaltum and Oil Company. (1925)

DRAYTON VALLEY, town (J-5)
After a village in Hampshire, England, from which the wife of W. J. Drake, postmaster, came. It was changed from Power House, 1920.

DRIEDMEAT HILL, lake and creek (J-6)
Translation of Cree *ka-ke-wuk* (Tyrrell). It is said that, at one time, the Indians covered the entire hill with buffalo meat, drying it in the sun. The lake is Kihumoo lake on Pinkerton's map, 1814, and on Harmon map, 1820.

DRIFTPILE, locality, river and Indian Reserve (G-4)
Translation of Cree name of river, at the mouth of which driftwood piles up.

DROMORE, mountain (8,600 feet) (J-2)
After Dromore, County Down, Ireland, which is Celtic for "great ridge." (1916)

DRUMHELLER, city (L-6)
After Samuel Drumheller, a pioneer in the Alberta coalfields. He came to Alberta from Walla Walla, Washington and opened his coal mine in 1918 shortly after the first one was opened by Jesse Gouge. He died February 28, 1925 in Los Angeles. (1911)

DRUMMOND, mount (10,250 feet) and glacier (L-4)
At the headwaters of the Red Deer River. Named by Dr. G. M. Dawson, 1884, after Thomas Drummond, assistant naturalist in Franklin's second Arctic Expedition, 1825-1827. On October 2, 1825, he left Fort Assiniboine to proceed up the Athabasca River to the Rocky Mountains which he reached October 14. He wintered on the Berland River.

DRYWOOD, creek (O-5)
Oldman River; descriptive. A translation of the Indian name of the creek; in Blackfoot, *ohsaksitoti,* or "backfat" river, from the fat on the back of a buffalo.

DUCHESS, village   **(M-7)**
After the Duchess of Sutherland, wife of the Fourth Duke; he acquired an extensive farm at Brooks. (1911)

DUFFIELD, station   **(I-5)**
After George Duffield Hall, Boston, Massachusetts. (1911)

DUHAMEL, locality   **(J-6)**
After the Most Reverend Joseph Thomas Duhamel (1841-1909), Roman Catholic Archbishop of Ottawa. Originally it was a trading post in 1870's known to the Indians as *notikiwin seppe*—Battle River. Later known as Battle River Crossing, it was one place where the river could be forded without difficulty. In 1880 when the five LaBoucan brothers were there it was known as LaBoucan settlement. In 1892 when the post office was established the settlement was given the name of Duhamel in honour of Archbishop Duhamel who presented a bell to the mission there under Father Bellevaire. François Adam was the first postmaster.

DUNGARVAN, mountain (8,500 feet) and creek   **(O-5)**
After Dungarvan, County Waterford, Ireland. (1915)

DUNMORE, station   **(N-8)**
After the 7th Lord Dunmore, who visited the West in 1883 and was a large shareholder in the Canadian Agricultural Coal and Colonization Company. As Lord Dunmore was going west on one occasion he killed a moose. When returning he used the jawbone to repair his Red River cart and thus the city of Moose Jaw got its name. (1883)

DUNSHALT, locality   **(L-6)**
Named by A. McLean, who came from Dunshalt, Fifeshire, Scotland about 1907.

DUNSTABLE, locality   **(I-5)**
Named by the Post Office Department probably after Dunstable, Bedfordshire, England. *Dune stapla* (Ekwall). (1908)

DUNVEGAN, locality   **(F-2)**
Originally a trading post named after the ancestral castle of the McLeods in Scotland. Archibald Norman McLeod of the North West Company, according to Harmon, October 10, 1808, "used to winter here while in Athabasca." The first ascertained reference to the name is in Simon Fraser's journal, 1805.

DURLINGVILLE, locality   **(H-8)**
After F. Durand and Islin, early settlers in the area. (1908)

DURWARD, locality   **(N-6)**
After *Quentin Durward*, novel by Sir Walter Scott (1771-1832). (1913)

DUSTY, lake   **(J-6)**
In Cree, *ko-pwa-o-wa-gas-takh* (Tyrrell).

DUTCH, creek   **(N-5)**
West fork of Oldman River. After a prospector, a Dutchman who "was reported to have found some very valuable minerals on this stream", was murdered by his partner.

DUTHIL, locality   (L-4)
    After Duthil, Invernesshire, Scotland. (1883)

DUVERNAY, hamlet   (I-7)
    After Ludger Duvernay (1799-1852), founder of the Société St. Jean-Baptiste in 1834; changed from South Bend, 1908.

— E —

EAGLE, lake and hill   (M-6)
    In Blackfoot, *petoomoxecing*, many eagles having been killed in the locality. Tyrrell gives the Cree name of the hill as *ki-hi-a-watis* and the Stoney name as *mha-moos-ni-bin*. It is said that the eagles disappeared from the hills in 1898 after a forest fire.

EAGLESHAM, village   (F-3)
    May be after Eaglesham, Renfrewshire, Scotland. (1916)

EARLIE, locality and lake   (J-8)
    Error for Airlie, after the song *The Bonnie House of Airlie*. It was decided to submit the name Airlie for a promised post office but the person who sent the name to the Post Office Department spelt it Earlie. (1910)

EAST ARROWWOOD, creek   (M-6)
    In Blackfoot, *nehts-ziks-kway*, meaning arrowwood place (Nelson).

EASTBURG, locality   (I-5)
    After A. E. East, postmaster.

EASTGATE, locality   (I-6)
    After Eastgate, Rochester, England, the former home of C. J. Woodward, postmaster. (1909)

EASYFORD, locality   (J-4)
    There was an "easy ford" of the Pembina River in the vicinity.

EBON, peak (9,600 feet)   (K-3)
    This peak shows black amid a line of snowclad mountains. (1918)

ECKVILLE, town   (K-5)
    After A. E. T. Eckford, early settler. It seems that a contest was held for naming the townsite and a Miss Hattie Mitzner (later Mrs. Hattie Stephens) came up with the name Eckville and this was the name chosen. (Mrs. M. K. Schofer, Secretary-Treasurer, Town of Eckville, letter, August, 1970)

EDBERG, village   (J-6)
    After Johan A. Edstrom, postmaster. Johan Edstrom (1850-1910) soon after arriving opened a store and post office (1900); at that time the nearest post office was at Duhamel. He decided to call the post office Edberg from *Edstrom* and "berg" meaning hill in Swedish. (*Memoirs of the Edberg Pioneers*, S. Edstrom and F. Lundstrom, 1955). (1902)

EDEN, lake (I-5)
Named by the man who owned the quarter section and who had a fur farm called Lake Eden Fur farm.

EDGERTON, village (J-8)
After H. H. Edgerton, Grand Trunk Pacific Railway, engineer. (1908)

EDITH, mount (8,380 feet) (L-4)
After a Mrs. J. F. Orde (née Edith Cox), Ottawa who visited Banff with Lady Macdonald in 1886.

EDITH CAVELL, mount (11,033 feet) (J-2)
Named in 1916 after Edith Cavell (1865-1915), English nurse shot by the Germans in 1915. In the days of the fur trade it was known as "La Montagne de la Grande Traverse" for it was the landmark for the route via the Whirlpool River and Athabasca Pass to the Columbia and thence to the Pacific Coast.

Edith Cavell was matron of a Belgian Red Cross hospital in Brussels to which many wounded allied prisoners of war were sent. She was also a member of a group engaged in aiding some two hundred allied soldiers trapped behind German lines to rejoin their armies. Under German martial law this activity was regarded as treason and punishable by death. When Edith Cavell was captured and tried she made no attempt to deny her activities. Her defence was simply that as a nurse it was her duty to save lives. The lives of these men she declared would be forfeit if they were caught so she helped them to escape and this, in her judgment, was saving lives. She was accordingly condemned to death and executed by a firing squad on October 12, 1915.

The first suggestion that a mountain be named after Edith Cavell is attributed to Sir Richard McBride, then Premier of British Columbia, who proposed the loftiest peak in Canadian territory, Mount Robson, be named in her honour; others in the Rockies and those near Quebec City were also suggested. With this strong support Prime Minister Sir Robert Borden asked the Geographic Board of Canada to deal with the proposal. The mountain was selected and in March, 1916, was officially named Edith Cavell. (*Canadian Nurse* 68: 23-26, February, 1972)

EDMONTON, city (I-6)
The capital of Alberta takes its name from Fort Edmonton, or, as it was first known, Edmonton House, built in 1795 by William Tomison at the mouth of the Sturgeon River some twenty miles downstream from the present site of the city. Tomison built it for the Hudson's Bay Company a short distance from Fort Augustus of the North West Company at the time when rivalry between the companies was at its keenest. Edmonton House came into operation on October 13, 1795. It in turn was named for Edmonton, Middlesex, England, now a suburb of Greater London. Tomison is said to have named Edmonton House as a compliment to his clerk, John Peter Pruden, a native of Edmonton, England. The name Edmonton first appears in a letter dated November 12, 1795 from Tomison to James Spence at Buckingham House. Fort Augustus and Edmonton House were abandoned in 1802 and re-located near the present city. In 1810 these, in turn were abandoned and new

forts built down river with outposts further up the river. This proved to be an unwise decision and in 1813 the two new forts were again located within the present city area, on the site of the City power plant on Rossdale Flats. When the Hudson's Bay Company and the North West Company were amalgamated the name Fort Augustus was dropped and the name Fort Edmonton adopted. The traders had wished to name the new post Fort Sanspareil but Fort Edmonton was chosen and accordingly perpetuated. In 1825 there was severe flooding and finally in 1830 Fort Edmonton was moved to higher ground, near the site of the Alberta Legislative Building where it remained until it was demolished in 1915. With the close of the fur trade era a settlement grew up around the fort and became the nucleus of the city. Edmonton became a city in 1904 and the provincial capital in 1905.

According to Ekwall's *Oxford Dictionary of English Place Names*, the name "Edmonton" goes back to Anglo-Saxon times. In Domesday Book (1086) it appears as *Adelmetone* and as *Edelmetone* in the Pipe Rolls of 1130 and again in the Book of Fees of 1256 as *Edelmestun*. It was originally Eadelm's *tun* (habitation). The name is immortalized in William Cowper's humorous poem *John Gilpin* (1782): Mistress Gilpin informs her husband:

> "Tomorrow is our wedding day,
> And we will then repair
> Unto the Bell at Edmonton
> All in a chaise and pair . . ."

Gilpin is on his wild ride . . .

> "Thus all through merry Islington
> These gambols he did play,
> Until he came unto the Wash,
> Of Edmonton so gay.

> At Edmonton his loving wife
> From the balcony espied
> Her tender husband, wondering much
> To see how he did ride."

EDSON, town and river   (I-3)
After Edson J. Chamberlain (1852-1924), vice-president, general manager, Grand Trunk Pacific, later president of it and G.T.R. (1911)

EDWAND, locality and creek   (H-6)
After Edward Anderson, first postmaster; it is a combination of *Edwa*rd and *Ande*rson. (1904)

EDWIN, creek   (E-7)
After Edwin Gay, Lloydminster, member of a survey party.

EGG LAKE, locality   (H-7)
Near Missawawi (Big Egg), Lake, which was probably named after eggs of wild fowl. (1897)

EGREMONT, hamlet   (I-6)
After Egremont, England, the former home of R. C. Armstrong, first postmaster. The name originates from Aigremont in Normandy, France. (1908)

EIFFEL, peak (10,091 feet) and lake   (L-4)
Named in 1908 after a natural tower rising for about 1,000 feet to the top of the mountain, which suggested the Eiffel Tower, Paris, France.

EISENHOWER, mount (9,390 feet)   (L-4)
Changed from Castle Mountain in 1946; after General Dwight D. Eisenhower (1890-1969). Supreme Commander of Allied Forces, Europe, World War II. He was President of the United States of America from 1953-1961. Hector (1858), liked it to a gigantic castle.

ELBOW, river   (M-5)
The river flows eastward from the Rockies to the 'elbow' about five miles south of Calgary, where it turns abruptly northward. *Hokaikshi* of David Thompson, 1814; *hokaikshi* or Moose River on Arrowsmith's map, 1859; *o-toos-kwa-na* in Cree; *nm-no-tho-ap-ta* in Stoney (Tyrrell); up to 1880, often called Swift creek.

ELBRIDGE, locality   (H-6)
After Elbridge Deval, prospective first postmaster, who died suddenly. (1916)

ELCAN, locality   (O-7)
Last part of "tabernacle" reversed. The name of the town Taber is the first part of the word. These places were originally Mormon settlements.

ELDON, locality   (L-4)
Named in 1883 probably after John Scott, third Earl of Eldon.

ELEPHAS, mountain (9,810 feet)   (K-2)
Elephas is Latin for elephant; named from fancied resemblance of rocks near mountain top to elephant heads. (1922)

ELK, island   (I-6)
Astotin Lake; so named as many elk were found in the locality, now part of the National Park.

ELK, range   (M-4)
The mountains are at the head of the Elk River, British Columbia, which are so called from the number of elk formerly found near here.

ELK ISLAND, locality and national park   (I-6)
Named for the many elk found on the islands in the area.

ELK POINT, town   (I-7)
Elk Point derived its name from Elk Point, South Dakota, U.S.A. which was the home of Mr. Highby, the first postmaster who opened a post office in 1907. The surrounding district was first surveyed in 1885 and the first townsite survey was registered on February 12, 1927. Elk Point became a village on May 31, 1938 and a town on January 1, 1962.

ELKWATER, hamlet and lake   (N-8)
Translation of Blackfoot *ponokiokwe*.

ELLENWOOD, lake (G-2)
After Corporal R. W. Ellenwood, M. M., Edmonton, killed in World
War II. (1952)

ELLERSLIE, locality (I-6)
After Ellerslie, one of the manors of Sir William Wallace (ca. 1270-
1305), the Scottish insurgent against Edward I of England.

ELLIOTT, peak (9,425 feet) (K-3)
After Elliott Barnes, son of a rancher who lived at the foot of the
peak; he climbed the mountain in 1906 when eight years old. (1907)

ELLIOTT, river (D-4)
After Lieutenant Elliott Greene, Third Battalion, C.E.F., assistant on
a survey party. (1913)

ELLS, river (D-6)-(E-6)
After S. C. Ells, Department of Mines, who made a traverse of this
river and an examination of the bituminous sand deposits of the
McMurray district. (1923)

ELLSCOTT, hamlet (H-6)
After L. Scott, A. and G.W.R., purchasing agent; formerly Glenshaw
Post Office. It was changed to Ellscott, 1916.

ELMWORTH, locality (G-2)
Said to have been named after a place in Massachusetts. (1920)

ELNORA, village (K-6)
In 1908 the settlers had asked for the settlement to be named Stewart-
ville but the Post Office Department turned this down as there were
already a number of communities known by this name which had been
proposed after a student minister. The people then met at the house of
A. Hogg and it was decided that the community should be called
Elnora by combining the first two names of Mrs. *El*inor Hogg (Mrs.
A. Hogg) and Mrs. *Nora* Edwards (Mrs. W. Edwards). A. Hogg arrived
in 1906 and William Edwards in 1908. (*Hayes Municipality*, 1967).

ELPOCA, mountain (M-5)
The mountain is at the head of the Elbow River and of Pocaterra
Creek, (q.v.). It was named after George Pocaterra (1882-1972). (1920)

ELTHAM, locality (M-6)
Probably after Eltham, London, England; Elta's ham (homestead),

ELYSIUM, mountain (8,025 feet) and pass (J-2)
Overlooks fine meadows; an allusion to Elysian Fields. (1916)

EMBARRAS, rivers (C-7), I-3) and locality (I-3) Athabasca River and
McLeod River. Both rivers so called from quantities of driftwood that
obstruct them making it necessary to portage everything.

EMBARRAS PORTAGE, locality (C-7)
See Embarras, river

EMIGRANTS, mountain (8,376 feet) (J-2)
After the gold-seekers mentioned by Milton and Cheadle, who travelled
by the Yellowhead Pass to the Cariboo in 1862. (1916)

EMIR, mountain (8,584 feet)   (J-2)
A descriptive name alluding to its prominence. (1916)

EMPRESS, village   (L-8)
After Queen Victoria proclaimed Empress of India, 1872. (1913)

END, mountain   (L-4)
South fork of Ghost River; this peak is at the "end" of the range. (1884)

ENDLESS CHAIN, ridge   (J-3)
Descriptive.

ENGADINE, mount (9,750 feet)   (M-4)
After a German cruiser engaged in the Battle of Jutland, 1916. (1922)

ENILDA, hamlet   (G-4)
First name (reversed) of the wife of J. Tompkins, postmaster. (1913)

ENSIGN, locality   (M-6)
After the old Canadian Red Ensign. (1909)

ENTRANCE, hamlet and provincial park   (I-3)
Near the former entrance to Jasper National Park. (1915)

ENTWISTLE, village   (I-5)
"The village is named after Mr. James D. Entwistle who was an early settler of the Magnolia District which is about six miles east. He was an engineer on the Grand Trunk Railway and originally from Ontario but lived most of his adult life in Winnipeg and Edmonton. He moved west about 1904-05. His son, Bill, had the first store in the village and ran a freight haul from Stony Plain west by horse and wagon." (Mrs. A. Burke, Secretary-Treasurer, Village of Entwistle, letter, September, 1970). (1908)

EON, mount (10,860 feet)   (M-4)
Probably descriptive of the ages that elapsed during the slow elevation of the mountain. (1917)

ERASMUS, mount (10,700 feet)   (K-3)
Named after Peter Erasmus (1834-1931) noted guide and trader. The son of a Danish father and French (Metis) mother, he was born at Red River and educated for the Anglican ministry which he never entered. Instead he went to Edmonton as interpreter for the Reverend Thomas Woolsey the newly arrived Wesleyan missionary. When he arrived at Fort Edmonton he went with Mr. Woolsey to the Wesleyan mission at Pigeon Lake and most of his time was spent with the Indians on the plains.

In 1858 he joined the Pallier Expedition as guide and interpreter and remained with it throughout its explorations. He is referred to many times in the Palliser report.

When the Palliser party finished its work Erasmus remained in Edmonton until 1862 when he settled on the northeast shore of Whitefish Lake where the Reverend Henry B. Steinhauer had established a Methodist mission. Here he built himself a house and store and for part of the time acted as a fur buyer for the Hudson's Bay Company and for the rest as an independent merchant. He made regular trips to

Winnipeg by Red River cart. When the Riel Rebellion broke out in 1885 Erasmus hastened to Edmonton for recruits and ammunition for loyal Indians under Chief Pakan but when he returned he found his home burned to the ground and his store looted.

Erasmus was associated with the McDougalls in their missionary work at Victoria settlement (now Pakan) acting as guide, interpreter and translator for many years. He was interpreter for the Dominion Government when the different treaties were made with the Indians. In recognition of this the Government awarded him a pension for life.

EREBUS, mountain (10,324 feet) (J-2)
A "dark" rock precipice faces northeast. (1916)

EREMITE, mountain (9,500 feet), glacier and creek (J-2)
Descriptive; a solitary peak. An eremite is a hermit. (1916)

ERIN LODGE, locality (F-2)
Erin is the poetic name of Ireland; "lodge" was added to distinguish it from other "Erins." (1917)

ERITH, locality and river (I-3)
East branch of Embarras River; probably after Erith, Kent, England.

ERMATINGER, mount (10,080 feet) (J-2)
After Edward Ermatinger, of the Hudson's Bay Company (1796-1876). Ermatinger entered the service of the Company in 1818 and served at York Factory and Upper Red River between 1818 and 1825. From 1825-1826 he was posted to the Columbia Department. He retired from the fur trade in 1830 and went to live in Upper Canada. After his retirement he wrote several books. (1921)

ERMINESKIN, Indian Reserve (J-6)
Cree Indian Reserve; name of the chief of the band of Indians who occupy this Reserve. (1885)

ERNEST, creek (N-5)
Oldman River; after Ernest Ernst who discovered coal just below the "gap" where the Bow River issues from the mountains.

ERRIS, mount (9,320 feet) (N-5)
After Erris, a headland on the west coast of Ireland. (1915)

ERSKINE, hamlet and lake (K-6)
After Thomas Erskine, British jurist, (1750-1823). (1905)

ESCARPMENT, river (K-3)
Siffleur River; probably descriptive.

ESPLANADE, mount (7,521 feet) (J-2)
Descriptive; it is a flat-topped ridge. (1916)

ESTHER, locality (L-8)
Named after Mrs. Anna Esther Landreth, daughter of the first postmaster, Y. B. Olsen; she was the first girl settler in the district. (1914)

ETHELWYN, locality (I-8)
After the wife of the first postmaster, H. M. Jones. (1910)

ETZIKOM, hamlet and coulee (N-8)
Blackfoot for valley "coulee"; also known in Blackfoot as *misloonsisco* or "crow springs" coulee, as Crow Indian war parties used to water here. It was Endon Post Office until 1916.

EUCERVUS, ridge (M-4)
Head of the Cascade and Panther Rivers; after the deer seen on the ridge. Latin *cervus* meaning deer. (1923)

EVANS, mount (10,460 feet) (J-2)
Name suggested by G. E. Howard, 1914, after Captain E. R. G. R. Evans, R.N., (1881-1957), second in command of the British Antarctic Expedition and commander after the death of Captain Scott in 1912. In the First World War Evans was commander of H.M.S. *Broke*. In one incident the *Broke* engaged six German destroyers and sank two. In the course of the action some Germans managed to jump aboard the *Broke* but were repelled by Evans and his men. For this action Evans became known as "Evans of the *Broke*". Later he attained the rank of Admiral and was raised to the Peerage as Lord Mountevans.

EVANSBURG, village (I-4)
After Harry Marshall Erskine Evans (1876-   ), of Edmonton. (1914)

EVAN-THOMAS, mount (9,500 feet) and creek (M-4)
Opal range; after Rear Admiral H. Evan-Thomas (1862-1928) who fought at Jutland, 1916. (1922)

EXCEL, locality (L-8)
So named because the early settlers thought it had an excellent situation. (1911)

EXCELSIOR, mount (9,100 feet) and creek (J-3)
A high peak; descriptive. (1916)

EXSHAW, hamlet, mountain (5,800 feet) and creek (L-4)
This was named after a son-in-law of Sir Sandford Fleming who was a director of the cement company operating here. (Mountain, 1965)

— F —

FABYAN, hamlet (J-7)
After Fabyan, New Hampshire. (1909)

FAIRFAX, lake (J-3)
Originally named Lohoar Lake after someone of this name who was drowned in 1916 in attempting to save two boys. He was in a boat with them when it capsized. He told the boys to hang on to the boat while he swam to shore but drowned on the way. The boys were rescued. Name changed to Fairfax Lake but origin of "Fairfax" unknown.

FAIRHOLME, range (9,315 feet) (L-4)
North of Bow River; on Palliser map, 1859. The range was named by Palliser after his sister, Grace, who married June 15, 1853, William Fairholme, of Greenknowe, Berwickshire, Scotland.

FAIRVIEW, mountain (9,001 feet), creek and pass (L-4)
South of Lake Louise; describes the fine view.

FAIRVIEW, town and municipal district (F-2)
Land near the townsite of Fairview was first surveyed by provincial surveyors in 1908 and the first homesteaders came in the winters of 1910-11-12. Four miles south of the present townsite was a water hole or natural reservoir in the ravine along the trail to Dunvegan where incoming settlers watered their stock. It was near this hole that in 1910 a thriving hamlet sprang into being when pioneers arrived with bull teams and the hamlet was named "Waterhole." Among the early settlers was one H. L. Propst who named his homestead "Fairview" and when the municipal district was organized on December 9, 1914, it was named Fairview Municipal District No. 858 with executive offices at Waterhole, then the centre of the district. The E. D. and B.C. Railway was extended thirteen miles from Berwyn to Whitelaw in 1924 and fifteen miles west to Fairview in 1928 where it reached mile 365.8, the present site of Fairview which was surveyed in the same year by C. B. Atkins, A.L.S. The question arose for a name for the townsite and E. J. Martin suggested "Fairview" to the railway and so it was named. The hamlet of Waterhole being off the railroad was moved to Fairview. Fairview achieved village status on March 28, 1929 and became a town on April 25, 1949. (*History of Fairview*).

FAIRYDELL, locality (I-5)
Probably descriptive. (1910)

FAITH, locality (O-8)
After Faith, daughter of James Sergeant, first postmaster. (1911)

FALHER, town (F-3)
The village of Falher was named after the Reverend C. Falher, O.M.I., who arrived at Grouard, 1889. He was noted for his ability to speak the Cree language. Father Falher spoke of the district as the "Happy Hunting Ground" of the Indians because of the large number of fox found in the district where cayuses wintered in the open on great quantities of peavine. The hamlet was organized as a village in 1923, disorganized in 1926, again organized in 1929, and as a town in 1955. (1913)

FALLENTIMBER, creek (L-5)
Red Deer River; descriptive; it is a translation of the Cree name *kow-ikh-ti-kow*; in Stoney, *o-ta-ha-wap-ta*.

FALUN, hamlet and creek (J-5)
After a mining town in Sweden from which early settlers came. Falun in Sweden is noted for its copper mines. (1904)

FARBUS, mountain (10,550 feet) (K-3)
After Farbus village, on the eastern slope of Vimy Ridge, France, in commemoration of the Canadians who fought there. (1920)

FARQUHAR, mount (9,400 feet) (N-5)
After Lieutenant-Colonel F. D. Farquhar, D.S.O., commanding the Princess Patricia's Canadian Light Infantry and who was killed in World War I. (1917)

FARRELL, lake   (F-5)
After Conway Farrell, D.F.C., former bush pilot associated with Canadian Pacific Airlines. (1954)

FARRELL, lake and creek   (K-6) (K-7)
After the earliest settler. (1907)

FATIGUE, mountain (9,667 feet), creek and pass   (L-4)
Descriptive of climber's sensations when climbing it. (1888)

FAUST, hamlet   (G-4)
After E. T. Faust, locomotive engineer. (1914)

FAWCETT, hamlet, lake and river   (H-5)
The hamlet was known as French Creek until 1914, when it was renamed Fawcett after S. D. Fawcett (b. 1882), D.L.S., engineer during construction of Edmonton, Dunvegan and British Columbia Railway. The name was selected by the railway.

FAWN LAKE, locality   (I-5)
After a small lake of same name which probably commemorates some occurrence in connection with a young deer. (1911)

FAY, mount (10,612 feet)   (L-4)
Bow range; after Professor Charles E. Fay, Appalachian Mountain Club, Boston, Massachusetts. (1904)

FEDERAL, locality   (K-7)
Named after the Federal Government.

FEDORAH, locality   (I-6)
After Sardou's drama *Fédora* in which Sarah Bernhardt played the role of the Princess Fedora. Fedora is the correct spelling. (1908)

FELIX, creek   (I-3)
Oldman creek; after Felix Plante a trapper in the district. (1946)

FERGUSON FLATS, locality   (I-7)
After W. R. Ferguson, first postmaster. (1912)

FERINTOSH, village   (J-6)
Name proposed by a local resident, Dr. J. R. McLeod, Member of the First Legislature of Alberta, 1905; after Ferintosh, Ross, Scotland. Name of whisky mentioned in a Burns' poem.

FERN CREEK, locality   (J-5)
From a nearby creek on which ferns grew at one time. (1913)

FERRYBANK, locality   (J-6)
Known first as Fairy Bank but changed to Ferrybank December 1, 1905. Fairy Bank was so named from the peculiar shape of the ravine or canyon.

FESTUBERT, mountain (8,274 feet)   (O-5)
After the village, east of La Bassée, France, where Canadian troops fought, 1915. (1917)

FIDDLE, range, river, pass and peak (J-2)
Athabasca River; the missionary De Smet, in a letter, 1846 refers to the river as "Violin." Fiddle range appears on the Palliser map, 1865. H. J. Moberly says that it is the "translation of *ke-too-che-gun*, a Cree word signifying a musical instrument. When the wind strikes the mountain from a certain direction, it sounds like a 'G' fiddle string."

FIDLER, point (B-7)
On the north shore of Athabasca Lake after Peter Fidler (1769-1822), Hudson's Bay Company, who built Nottingham House near Chipewyan, 1802; he made extensive explorations in what is now western Canada. (1922)

FINCASTLE, locality (N-7)
Viscount Fincastle was a title of the Earl of Dunmore. (See Dunmore). (1915)

FINDLEY, creek (I-2)
Muskeg River; after Deome Findley who had a trap line on this creek. (1947)

FIREBAG, river (D-7)
Athabasca River; fire making materials were carried in a firebag in early times before the advent of matches. J. W. Sullivan, secretary, Palliser Expedition refers to "the bag used by the Indians and half-breeds for carrying their flints and steels, touchwood, smoking weed, etc., better known as 'sac à commis'."

FISH, creek (M-5)
Translation of Blackfoot name, *siokame* or black fish.

FISHER, range and peak (10,050 feet) (M-5)
East of Kananaskis River; the range was named by Palliser, probably after a family, one of whose members accompanied him on a hunting excursion near New Orleans in 1847.

FITZALLEN, locality (I-7)
After a Mr. Fitzallen, one time secretary of the town of Vegreville. (1931)

FITZGERALD, hamlet (A-7)
Slave River; the name was changed from Smith Landing in 1915, honouring Inspector Francis Joseph Fitzgerald (1867-1911), Royal North-West Mounted Police, who, with Constables Kenny and Taylor and ex-Constable Cater, perished on the Peel River in February, 1911, while on McPherson-Dawson patrol.

FITZGERALD, locality (N-8)
After Edward Fitzgerald, sometime purchasing agent of the Canadian Pacific Railway.

FLAGSTAFF, hill and county. (K-7)
Palliser gives the Cree Indian name of the hill as *hiskiwaornis kahkohtake,* or Flag-hanging hill; he describes it as a place of assembly of the Sarcees. The county takes its name from the hill.

FLATBUSH, hamlet and creek (H-5)
From the nature of the country. (1916)

FLATHEAD, range (O-5)
South of Crowsnest Lake; after the Flathead Indians of western Montana.

FLEET, hamlet (K-7)
Hub Post Office until 1912; probably named by the Canadian Pacific Railway after their fleet of ships or for the British fleet.

FLETCHER, lake and channel (B-7)
After J. A. Fletcher, D.L.S. who in 1916 surveyed the area and the 30th Base Line. (1962)

FLOATINGSTONE, lake (H-7)
A lone stone stands up 12-15 feet out of the lake. The name is a translation of the Cree name *assinkagama*.

FLORANN, locality (O-7)
Named for *Flor*ence Whitney and *Ann* Grady who owned and operated a small country store at this point about 1909. (1913)

FLYINGSHOT, lake, settlement (G-2)
From the fact that ducks were shot during flight over the lake which lies between two feeding grounds.

FOCH, mount (10,430 feet) and creek (L-4)
After Marshal Ferdinand Foch (1851-1929), Generalissimo of the Allied Forces, 1918. (1918)

FOISY, locality (I-7)
After Aladin Foisy, first postmaster. (1919)

FOLDING, mountain (9,330 feet) (J-2)
Southeast of Brûlé Lake; from the "folded" rock strata that compose it.

FOLDING MOUNTAIN, creek (J-2)
See Folding, Mountain. (1960)

FOOTHILLS, locality (J-3)
Formerly Mudge; it is in the foothills. (1913)

FOOTNER, lake (B-3)
Near the head of Meander River; after Hulbert Footner, author of *New Rivers of the North* (1913). He travelled in the area in 1911 going down the Peace River to Fort Vermilion and overland to Hay River; then to Peace River again, over to Lesser Slave Lake, down to Athabasca Landing and finally to Edmonton. (1922)

FORBES, mount (11,852 feet) and creek (K-3)
Named by Hector after Professor James David Forbes (1809-1868), Scottish scientist; sometime Principal of the United College of St. Andrews, Scotland.

FORDING, pass (7,544 feet) (N-5)
This pass goes from the head of the Fording River, B.C. to the Highwood River. Fording River was named by Dr. G. M. Dawson in 1884 as his party forded it several times.

FOREMAN, locality (K-6)
After E. R. Foreman, first postmaster.

FORESTBURG, village (J-7)
Carl Farvolden, Secretary-Treasurer of Forestburg writes in a letter dated August, 1970: "One or two old timers say it was named after a Forestburg in South Dakota from which one old timer came in the late 1800's or early 1900's. There is, apparently, a Forestburg in Ontario as well and there were a few people from Ontario in the early days. However, it is difficult to say definitely. Apparently when the C.N.R. came here in 1915 the post office was Duxbury and was situated about two and a half miles south of the present village. I suppose no one could feel right about calling the new village "Duxbury" so something else was dreamed up either by one of the old timers or by some official of the C.N.R." Originally descriptive.

FORGET, mount (6,959 feet) (I-1)
After the Honourable Amédée Forget (1847-1923), Banff; Senator, 1911-23; Lieutenant Governor of the North-West Territories, (1898-1905). (1925)

FORGETMENOT, pass (5,899 feet) (I-1)
From the abundance of this flower. (1963)

FORK, lake (H-7)
This lake is shaped like the prongs of a fork. (1916)

FORMBY, lake (F-8)
After a suburb of Liverpool, England; 'Forni's By' (farm), Ekwall.

FORSHEE, locality (K-5)
There is a place of this name in Virgina, U.S.A. (1919)

FORSTER, reservoir (M-7)
After the original homesteader by the name of Forster and on whose former property this reservoir is located. (1968)

FORT, hills and creek (O-7)
Athabasca River; the Hudson's Bay Company and the North West Company had trading posts in the vicinity.

FORT, island (I-7)
North Saskatchewan River; Fort George was moved to this island, 1801; it was called "Isle of Scotland" by David Thompson.

FORT ASSINIBOINE, village (H-5)
Athabasca River; the building of a Hudson's Bay Company post here in 1823 is referred to by John Work in his journal, September 24, 1823: "About noon arrived at a new house which Mr. McDonald, the gentleman who is superintending the building, calls Fort Assiniboyne. It is

situated on the north bank. This is the house that was to have been built at McLeod branch." It was the northern point on the portage from Fort Edmonton to the Athabasca River en route to Fort Vancouver via Athabasca Pass and Boat Encampment and was in operation the year round at least in 1827. In 1859 Dr. Hector stated the place consisted of a few ruinous huts on the left bank of the river but it was not then in use the year round.

FORT CHIPEWYAN, hamlet (C-7)
Fort Chipewyan was named for the Chipewyan Indians; the name means "pointed skins." Fort Chipewyan, one of the most famous of the fur trade posts was first built by Roderick Mackenzie of the North West Company in 1789 on a rocky point projecting into Lake Athabasca. In 1799 the post was relocated on its present site on the north side of the lake.

After the union of the Hudson's Bay Company and the North West Company the former company operated the post to the present. It was one of the best known posts and was referred to as "Little Athens" because of its amenities of civilization in the wilderness.

FORT KENT, hamlet (H-8)
Name suggested by a former resident of Fort Kent, Maine, U.S.A. (1922)

FORT MACLEOD, town (N-6)
Fort Macleod was the first Mounted Police post in Alberta and takes its name from Colonel James F. Macleod (1836-1894) (see also Calgary) who led the Force on its march across the plains in 1874. The original post was built on an island in the Oldman River late in 1874 where it remained until moved southwest a short distance from the present town. It was immediately successful in stamping out the illegal whisky trade that had flourished previously.

Fort Macleod was known to the Blackfeet as *stamix-otokanokowy* or bullshead's home as Colonel Macleod was known to the Indians as "Bull's Head" because he had a buffalo head over the door of his residence. The crest of his family is a bull's head.

FORT McMURRAY, town (E-7)
A former trading post at the junction of the Athabasca River and Clearwater River. David Thompson descended the Athabasca River in 1799 and arrived at the Fort of the Forks "where a bold river comes in." In 1870, Fort McMurray was established by Factor H. J. Moberly on the site of the Forks Fort and named after Chief Factor William McMurray, who was in charge of Ile à la Crosse about that time.

FORT SASKATCHEWAN, town (I-6)
On the North Saskatchewan River. The first N.W.M.P. post north of Calgary was built in 1875 under Inspector W. D. Jarvis. The citizens of Edmonton complained that the post was not built nearer Edmonton but surveys for a railroad through the Yellowhead Pass crossed the river at that point and the site was considered suitable for transport purposes. The railroad was not built through the Yellowhead Pass but the post remained. In Cree *aimaganis* or soldiers' house (Tyrrell).

FORT VERMILION, hamlet   (C-4)
There have been several trading posts in this area and not all have
been named "Fort Vermilion." In 1788, Boyer of the North West
Company built the "Old Establishment" at the mouth of the Boyer
River but in 1792 the "New Establishment" was built some 40 miles
upstream from the present hamlet. It was also known as "Fort du
Tremble", "Old Aspin Fort" and "Finlay's Post." In 1799 it was
abandoned. In that year "Upper Fort Vermilion" or "Lafleur's Post"
was built some 17 miles downstream from the mouth of Keg River.
"Fort Vermilion" some 24 miles below Keg River was built in 1800
and operated until 1828.

The Hudson's Bay Company built its first fort "Mansfield Post"
near the present hamlet in 1802 and abandoned it three years later.
In the pattern of the time when the two rival fur trading companies
were in keen competition the North West Company built "Fort Liard"
about 1804 and closed it in 1805-06. It was in 1828 that the Hudson's
Bay Company built "Fort Vermilion" on the site of the present hamlet.
This post remained in use until modern times and there is still a trading
post at the present hamlet. The name probably comes from red ochre
deposits in the vicinity.

FORTH, locality   (K-5)
South of Red Deer; after the Scottish river. (1920

FORTRESS, mountain (9,908 feet), lake and pass (4,388 feet)   (K-2)
Descriptive; the mountain resembles a fortress. (1892)

FORTUNE, mount (9,250 feet)   (M-4)
Spray River; after a destroyer sunk at the Battle of Jutland. (1922)

FORTY MILE, coulee and county   (N-7)
Southwest of Medicine Hat; the coulee is about forty miles long. (1912)

FOSSIL, mountain (9,665 feet)   (L-4)
Head of the Red Deer River; from the numerous fossils in the limestone
on its slopes. (1908)

FRANCHÈRE, peak (9,225 feet) (J-2) and locality   (H-7)
Astoria River; after Gabriel Franchère, author of *Relation d'un voyage
à la Côte du Nord-Ouest de l'Amerique Septentrionale*, Montreal. 1820.
It is the first published description of a journey through the Rockies
by way of the Columbia River and Athabasca Pass and River. (1917)

FRANCIS, lake   (G-7)
Northeast of Lac la Biche; after an Indian, Philip Francis. (1951)

FRANK, village   (N-5)
After H. L. Frank who opened the first coal mine there. It was the
scene of a tremendous rock slide in 1903 when on April 29, some
ninety million tons of rock crashed down from Turtle Mountain
destroying part of the town and taking 70 lives. (1901)

FRASER, mount (10,726 feet) and glacier   (J-2)
Comprising Bennington, McDonell and Simon peaks; it was named after
Simon Fraser (1776-1862), explorer of the Fraser River, 1808.

FREEDOM, locality   (I-5)
Dusseldorf was the name until 1919.

FREEMAN, Indian Reserve   (G-4)
It was a reserve for a family of Indians named Freeman. (1905)

FREEMAN, river   (H-4)
Time-expired servants of the fur-trading companies were called
"freemen."

FRENCH, lake   (C-6)
After a trapper known as "Frenchy" who lived in a cabin by the lake.
After his death the name "French" was given as a memorial to his
family. (1963)

FRENCH, mount (10,510 feet)   (M-4)
After Field Marshal J. D. P. French (1852-1925), Viscount of Ypres
and of High Lake, Commander-in-Chief, British Army, 1914-15. (1918)

FRESHFIELD, mount (10,945 feet), creek, glacier and icefield   (L-3)
Named by Stutfield and Collie after Sir Douglas Freshfield, F.R.G.S.,
of the Alpine Club, England. (1897)

FRESNOY, mountain (10,730 feet)   (K-3)
After Fresnoy, in the Department of Aisne, France, ten miles northeast
of St. Quentin. Named in commemoration of its capture by the Canadians, April 13, 1917. (1920)

FRIEDENSTAL, locality   (F-2)
After Friedensthal, Romania; the 'h' was dropped. (1913)

FROG, lake, creek and locality   (I-8)
The lake is on the Palliser map, 1863; translation of Cree name, *ah-yik-
sa-kha-higan*, (Tyrrell). Frog Lake was the scene in 1885 of the
massacre of nine people by a band of Big Bear's Indians at the outbreak of the Riel Rebellion.

FRYATT, mount (11,026 feet) and creek   (J-2)
After Captain Fryatt, shot by the Germans on July 27, 1916, on a
charge of having attempted to ram a submarine. (1921) See also
Brussels, peak

FURMAN, locality   (N-5)
After John Furman, early settler. (1911)

— G —

GABLE, mountain (9,625 feet)   (L-4)
Descriptive; a long ridge with gable-like slopes facing west. (1919)

GABRIEL, lake   (K-5)
It appears as Gabriel's Hill lake on Palliser map, 1863 and as Gabriel
Lake on Arrowsmith map, 1859. From the hill, Hector, in January,
1858, had his first view of the Rocky Mountains. It is probably after
Baptiste Gabriel, whom Palliser describes as "a first rate trader and
a smart little hunter."

GADSBY, lake (K-6)
After James Gadsby, trapper, trader and settler in the area. (1894)

GADSBY, village (K-6)
After M. F. Gadsby, Ottawa. (1909)

GAETZ, creek and lakes (K-5)
After the Reverend Leonard Gaetz (1841-1907) pioneer homesteader and Methodist Minister of Red Deer. See also Red Deer, city.

GAHERN, locality (O-6)
After H. G. Ahern, postmaster.

GAINFORD, hamlet (I-5)
After Gainford, Durham, England; Seba Post Office until 1910. The name is from the Old English *gegn*, direct (as of a road) and ford. It appeared first as *Geagenforda* (1050) and *gaineford* (1196), (Ekwall).

GALAHAD, village (K-7)
Probably after the famous knight of the Round Table. (1907)

GALARNEAU, creek (L-7)
See Galarneauville, locality

GALARNEAUVILLE, locality (L-7)
After G. P. Galarneau, first postmaster, (1914)

GALATEA, mount (10,300 feet) and creek (M-4)
After a cruiser engaged in the Battle of Jutland, 1916. (1922)

GALLOWAY, locality (I-3)
After D. E. Galloway, assistant to the president of the Grand Trunk Pacific Railway; later assistant vice-president, Canadian National Railway, Montreal. (1911)

GALT, island (N-8)
After the Galt family of Lethbridge. See also Coaldale.

GALWEY, mount (7,800 feet) and creek (O-5)
After Lieutenant Galwey, R.E., assistant astronomer, British Boundary Commission, Lake of the Woods to the Rockies. (1917)

GAP, locality and lake (L-4)
From the "gap" in the Rockies where the Bow River issues from the mountains.

GAP, THE, pass (N-5)
A conspicuous gap where the Oldman River forces its way through the Livingstone Range.

GARDEN PLAIN, locality (K-7)
Probably descriptive. (1910)

GARDENVIEW, locality (I-5)
Probably descriptive.

GARFIELD, locality (L-5)
After James Garfield, President of the United States, March 4-July 2, 1881.

GARGOYLE, mountain (8,834 feet)   (J-2)
A stream flows from its base as from a gargoyle or spout. (1916)

GARRINGTON, locality   (K-5)
After Garrington, son of H. C. Monday, postmaster. (1908)

GARSON, lake   (I-8)
After C. N. Garson, manager of the Hudson's Bay Company post at
Onion Lake, Saskatchewan; changed from Whitefish, 1911.

GARTH, mount (9,970 feet)   (K-3)
After John McDonald of Garth (1774-1860), early fur trader. He
entered the service of the North West Company in 1791. In 1799 he
built Rocky Mountain House on the North Saskatchewan River and
the following year became a partner in the Company. In 1807 he established Fort Gibraltar at the junction of the Red and Assiniboine
Rivers. By 1813 he was posted to the Columbia where he took over
Fort Astoria. He retired in 1815.

GARTLY, locality   (L-6)
Gartly is a parish in Aberdeenshire, Scotland. (1914)

GASS, mount (9,400 feet)   (N-5)
After L. H. Gass, D.L.S., survey assistant (1913-1915) to J. A. Calder;
killed in action 1917.

GATINE, locality   (L-6)
After Mrs. Gatine, a housekeeper for railway construction crews.

GAUNCE, mount, (7,501 feet)   (I-3)
After Squadron Leader Lionel M. Gaunce, D.F.C., Lethbridge and
Sylvan Lake. Killed in World War II. (1949)

GAUTHIER, creek   (I-3)
After a trapper. (1947)

GEIKIE, locality and lake   (J-2)
After Sir Archibald Geikie (1835-1924), eminent Scottish geologist,
one time Director-General of the British Geological Survey. (locality,
1912; lake, 1958)

GEM, locality   (M-7)
Probably a descriptive name. (1914)

GENDARME, mountain (9,586 feet)   (J-2)
French for "policeman", because the mountain is supposed to stand
on guard. (1911)

GENESEE, locality   (J-5)
Genesee was named by one Bert White who had come from Genesee,
Idaho and his suggestion was adopted by a meeting of settlers of the
area. His house may still be seen to-day. Genesee, Idaho takes its
name from a town of the same name in New York State. The name
is said to come from an Iroquoian word meaning "valley beautiful."
(*Frontier Days in Leduc and District*, 1956). (1916)

GENEVA, lake   (I-7)
Named when Lake Geneva Post Office was opened in 1910; the post
office probably was named after Lake of Geneva, Switzerland.

GEORGE, creek (K-6)

After George Buxenstein, president of the German Development Company.

GERHARTS, lake (I-5)

After the people who owned the land on which the lake is situated. (1950)

GERRY, lake (F-2)

After Pilot Officer R. T. Gerry, Roll of Honour, Battle of Britain, Lethbridge. Killed in World War II. (1949)

GHOST, river (L-4)-(L-5)

It appears as Dead Man River on Palliser map, 1860; in Cree, *chi-pe-isi-pi* and in Stoney, *winc-hin-ai-wap-ta* (Tyrrell); in Blackfoot, *op-skoonakaz*, "river with rapids" (Nelson). A ghost was seen going up and down this river, picking up the skulls of the dead, who had been killed by the Crees, (Erasmus). There are many Indian graves on the river (Steele). The combatants slain in a battle were buried in the woods on the top of Deadman Hill (q.v.).

GHOSTPINE, lake and creek (K-6) (L-6)

About 1830 or earlier on the shores of Pine Lake the Blackfoot Indians raided a sleeping camp of Crees and murdered every man, woman and child in the band. Only one Cree warrior survived having been away from the camp on a hunting expedition at the time. When he returned and found all his family and friends murdered and mutilated, the Cree painted his face black in mourning then set out on the trail of the Blackfeet. The lone Cree managed to kill and scalp many of the rival tribesmen, stealthily raiding their camps at night or else ambushing any brave who became separated from the main group. For years afterwards, Crees avoided Pine Lake. They thought the region was haunted by ghosts of the murdered people and it contained a weird looking pine tree; therefore the place was called Ghost Pine Lake. The Ghostpine Creek flows from here and forms a junction with the Red Deer River, shortly after joining Three Hills Creek. (*M.D. of Kneehill, 1904-1967* by L. Grace Gore, 1968)

GHOSTPINE CREEK, locality (K-6)

See Ghostpine, lake and creek

GIBBON, pass (7,400 feet) (L-4)

Named for J. M. Gibbon, secretary and founder of the Trail Riders, an organization making a ride in the Rockies each season. (1958)

GIBBONS. village (I-6)

After the farmer who owned the station ground.

GIBRALTAR, mountain (9,000 feet) (M-5)

From the fancied resemblance to the famous rock.

GILT EDGE, locality (J-8)

Edward Monaghan, early homesteader, looked over the district, and pronounced it "gilt edge." (1908)

GIROUARD, mount (9,875 feet) (L-4)
After Colonel Sir E. Percy Girouard, K.C.M.G., D.S.O.; born in Montreal 1867; graduated, Royal Military College, Kingston, 1884; Director of Railways, Sudan Expedition, 1896-98 and Boer War, 1899-1902; High Commissioner and Commander-in-Chief of Northern Nigeria, 1907-08; Governor and Commander-in-Chief of East Africa Protectorate, 1909-12; Director General of Munitions Supply, 1915. (1904)

GIROUXVILLE, village (F-3)
May be for Rev. H. Giroux, O.M.I. (1869-1956) or the pioneer Giroux family. (1915)

GLACIER, lake and river (K-3)
North Saskatchewan River; named by Hector; it receives the discharge of a large glacier.

GLADSTONE, mount (7,777 feet) and creek (O-5)
After W. S. Gladstone, an "old timer", and former employee of the Hudson's Bay Company. In a sawpit near the creek he whip-sawed lumber and made the windows and doors for Fort Macleod. He was also one of the builders of Fort Whoop-Up.

GLADYS, locality (M-5)
In the early days mail for the Gladys district, northeast of High River, was usually brought out by some settler who had driven to town for supplies. One couple who frequently performed this service was Charles and Gladys Harkness. "As people said 'Let's go to Gladys' for the mail' that seemed the logical suggestion for a name for the proposed post office. So it came about that the Postal Department gave the name 'Gladys' to a new post office at the home of Charles Harkness, S.W. 14, 20-29-W4 on January 1, 1890." (*Gladys and Dinton through the years*, 1965).

GLASGOW, mountain (9,680 feet) and creek (M-5)
After a cruiser engaged in the Battle of Jutland, 1916. (1922)

GLEICHEN, town (M-6)
Originally 12th Siding; on C.P.R. from Medicine Hat, Named after the German Count Albert Edward Wilfred Gleichen, born 1863. He was a financial backer of the C.P.R. and travelled over the railway with the directors in 1883. Village of Gleichen was erected by Order in Council dated January 24, 1899 and the name published in *North-West Territories Gazette*, February 15, 1899. Gleichen became a town in 1910. The Count was the son of Admiral Prince Victor of Hohenlohe-Langenburg, an officer in the Royal Navy, who retired for health reasons in 1866. The Count's son Major General Lord Edward Gleichen, K.C.V.O., C.B., C.M.G., D.S.O. retired from the British Army in 1919 after 38 years of service. In his autobiography, *A Guardsman's Memories* he states that he visited Canada in 1906. He says in a letter to the Gleichen Town Secretary dated December, 1925, "I have never visited Gleichen myself, as I came on my trip to B.C. in 1906 from U.S. but I remember the clerk's astonishment at Calgary when I signed a telegram in my own name. He thought I had borrowed it from the town. I noticed it was pronounced Gleeshen in those parts; it should of course be pronounced Glaikhen (kh as in Scots 'loch')" [actually gutteral German]. On June 15, 1939, Baron Von Stuterheim, a German

newspaper correspondent injected a bit of romance into this frequently mispronounced place-name. On that fine morning the Baron got off the train at Gleichen, not to view the town but to see some Indians. The name of Gleichen made him curious and his first remark on meeting Indian Agént Gooderham was "Ah, Mr. Gutterheim (giving the German pronunciation Glaikhen) do you know how it got that name?" When told, Stuterheim interjected "No, no, not good enough. I'll tell you the rest of the story."

"In the 11th century the first Count Gleichen, a crusader whose castle was in my native province of Schleswig-Holstein, near a place called Gottingham got into the Turkish Court at Constantinople. He was there for some time and as his family did not accompany him the favorite daughter of the Sultan became his constant companion. The Sultan was pleased and everyone was happy till the day the Count was ordered to return to his homeland. The Sultan voiced his regrets, but stated there was now a strong bond between the two countries since his daughter would be Gleichen's wife. The Count was in a dilemma; a wife and family awaited his return to Germany! He pondered over the situation and finally wrote to his wife and told her everything and added that if she wanted to see him again it must be with another woman, the Sultan's daughter. She understood and accepted this condition. On returning he built a second castle and the two castles are still to be seen." (F. D. Creighten, Secretary-Treasurer, Town of Gleichen letter, 1970)

GLEN LESLIE, locality   (G-2)
After T. Leslie, first postmaster. (1914)

GLENBOW, locality   (L-5)
A glen on the Bow River. (1907)

GLENDON, village   (H-7)
From the maiden name of mother of J. P. Spencer, former postmaster. (1912)

GLENDOWAN, mountain (8,771 feet)   (O-5)
After Glendowan range, County Donegal, Ireland (1915)

GLENEVIS, hamlet   (I-5)
Suggested by John A. McLeod, early settler, whose wife came from Glennevis, Cape Breton Island, N.S.; one "n" is omitted. (1913)

GLENFORD, locality   (I-5)
"Glen" and last syllable of name of Thomas Rutherford, first postmaster. (1909)

GLENHEWITT, locality   (J-5)
After J. J. Hewitt, first postmaster. (1913)

GLENWOOD, hamlet   (O-6)
After Glen, son of E. J. Wood, owner of the surrounding land. (1911)

GOAT, range (9,260 feet)   (M-4)
Translation of Indian name—wap-u-tik; named by Palliser.

GODDARD, hamlet (O-7)
After Ernest Goddard, a former postmaster. (1911)

GOLDEN DAYS, summer village (J-5)
Reminder of the golden days of summer. (1965)

GOLDEN EAGLE, peak (10,000 feet) (K-3)
A reference to the number of golden eagles seen in the vicinity of the peak. (1920)

GOLDENROD, creek (I-2)
Probably descriptive; from the great growth of goldenrod in the vicinity.

GOLDSMITH, creek (G-4)
After Sandy Goldsmith, member of a survey party.

GOOD HOPE, locality (I-6)
Descriptive of the "good hopes" of the settlers; liable to be confused with Good Hope Fort, Mackenzie River. (1907)

GOODFARE, locality (G-1)
Formerly known as Kempton; probably descriptive. (1919)

GOODWIN, locality (G-2)
After two early ranchers. (1923)

GOOSEQUILL, lake (K-6)
Translation of Cree name, *manikwanan.*

GOPHER HEAD, locality (K-6)
From the shape of a hill near the first post office. (1908)

GORDON, lake and river (E-8)
After William Gordon, former postmaster, Fort McMurray.

GORGE, creek (I-3)
Flows through a gorge to reach a river. (1946)

GORMAN, mount (7,800 feet) (K-2)
After A. O. Gorman, D.L.S. who was employed on subdivision re-surveys and base line surveys. He served as chief of the legal surveys division and assistant surveyor general in the Mines and Technical Surveys, Alberta-B.C. Boundary Surveys. (1925)

GOUGH, lake (K-6)
Named by J. B. Tyrrell after a teamster with a geological survey party, 1884.

GOULD DOME, mountain (9,490 feet) (N-5)
Named by Lieutenant Blakiston of the Palliser Expedition in 1858 after British naturalist John Gould (1804-1881). Blakiston notes: "after the distinguished British naturalist, I named it 'Gould's Dome'."

GOURIN, locality (H-6)
After the capital of the French canton from which Joseph Ulliac, postmaster and first settler, came in 1914, with his family of seventeen persons. (1923)

GRAHAM, creek (F-8)
After Graham Davies of Lloydminster, member of a survey party.

GRAINGER, locality (L-6)
After F. W. Grainger, an early settler, from England. (1912)

GRAMINIA, locality (J-5)
From Latin *gramen*, grass. (1908)

GRANDE CACHE, town (I-2)
A "cache" is a place where trappers stored extra supplies on the trail. (1963)

GRANDE PRAIRIE, city and county (G-2)
French name meaning "big prairie", the largest prairie area in the district. To the North West Company traders the open area was known as Buffalo Plains. To Father Grouard (later Bishop Grouard) the gently undulating wilderness was "la grande prairie." From 1906 on it began to attract attention as a potential farming area. Surveyors, geologists, etc. had scouted the region and written on it as the "fertile belt." By 1908 promotion was active and in 1910 the "City of Grande Prairie" was the slogan of the promotor who had a complete map of the new "city" in his Edmonton office for all to see. The city was named for "la grande prairie." From 1908 on settlers poured into the region and in 1916 the railway came. Grande Prairie became a city on January 1, 1958.

GRANDIN, locality (H-6)
After Monsignor Vital-Julien Grandin (1829-1902); born at St. Pierre-sur-Orthe, Laval, France. He entered the Oblates, December 28, 1851, came to St. Boniface, 1854 and died at St. Albert, Alberta, 1902. He was the first Bishop of St. Albert. (1911)

GRANDVIEW, summer village (J-5)
The name was chosen because of the height of land above Pigeon Lake and the view afforded by the high lakefront land. The name was a natural name because of the nature of the property. The name Summer Village of Grandview was chosen since this area is commonly known as the Grandview area. Incorporated January 1, 1967. (Ronald C. Delamater, Secretary-Treasurer, letter, August, 1970).

GRANLEA, locality (N-7)
Combination of grain and lea, suggesting the rich agricultural products of the district. (1913)

GRANTA, station (M-6)
Granta is the old Saxon name of the River Cam which flows through Cambridge, England. It was suggested by Van Schaik and Fairburn, two Cambridge University graduates, who purchased tracts of land in the vicinity. (1913)

GRANTHAM, locality (M-6)
After town and borough of Grantham, Lincolnshire, England. (1913)

GRANUM, town (N-6)
Formerly known as Leavings, the station and post office were changed to Granum, October 1, 1907. It was first called Leavings, because it

was the point where the Macleod-Calgary trail left Willow Creek. Granum is Latin for "grain" and was suggested by Malcolm McKenzie, M.L.A., (d.1913).

GRASSY, mountain (6,700 feet)   (N-5)
Crowsnest River; descriptive.

GRASSY, ridge   (J-2)
Descriptive. (1916)

GRASSY ISLAND, lake   (K-8)
Descriptive.

GRASSY LAKE, village   (N-7)
In 1874 as Jerry Potts led the first contingent of the North-West Mounted Police across the area, a Mountie who had pestered him with countless questions asked if water could be obtained in a slough which was covered with reeds. Potts replied, "The only things you can get out of a slough in August is grass. This is the driest part of the Northwest. There are bullfrogs ten years old that don't know how to swim." The name is a translation of the Blackfoot word *moyi-kimi* (Nelson). The lake is now dry.

GRATZ, locality   (I-7)
Birthplace, in Germany, of J. Vogel, first postmaster. (1913)

GRAY, lake   (H-5)
After Lieutenant R. H. Gray, V.C., D.S.O., M.I.D., Calgary, killed in World War II.

GREASE, creek   (L-5)
So called from the bushes of notched-leaved birch, which for some mysterious reason, is named "greasewood." The Cree name is *to-muna;* Stoney name is *sna-tin-da-wap-ta.*

GREAT WEST, ridge   (L-5)
Name suggested because Great West Timber Company worked this ridge some years ago. Remains of two of their camps are at the base of the ridge. (1941)

GREEN COURT, hamlet   (I-4)
Named by Mr. Hamilton Baly, first postmaster, who taught at The King's School, Canterbury, Kent, England and who named it Green Court after the playground. (Changed to two words in 1950). The following is from an interview with J. B. Bickersteth in Canterbury, England by Stanley Williams (*Edmonton Journal,* June 8, 1970): "But his fondest recollection is coming upon a clearing in the bush near Whitecourt. He stopped his horse and asked where he was. 'Green Court' came the reply. It turned out the knot of stump farmers who were breaking the land here were 'old boys' of King's School, Canterbury. They had named their settlement after the court outside their cathedral school." (1908)

GREEN GLADE, locality   (K-8)
Name descriptive.

GREENLAWN, locality (I-8)
The original post office was built on a grassy slope. (1908)

GREENOCK, mountain (6,881 feet) (J-2)
After Greenock, Scotland. The name means "sunny hill" and the mountain was climbed on a sunny day. (1916)

GREENSHIELDS, locality (J-8)
After E. B. Greenshields, Montreal, director, Grand Trunk Pacific Railway; Holmstead Post Office until 1909.

GREGG, mount (8,300 feet), lake and river (J-3)
After J. J. Gregg, settler and prospector.

GREGOIRE, lake and river (F-7)
After an early settler.

GREGOIRE LAKE, provincial park and Indian Reserve (F-7)
See Gregoire, lake.

GREISBACH, mount (8,800 feet) (J-2) and locality (I-6)
In honour of W. A. Griesbach (1878-1945). He was born in Qu'Appelle, Sask., but raised in Edmonton and served in the South African War. He was called to the Bar in 1901 and in 1905 and 1906 he was an alderman for Edmonton. In 1907 he became Mayor. In 1914 he enlisted and went overseas as Major and the following year was promoted Lieutenant-General to command the 49th Battalion. In 1917 he was promoted Brigadier-General to command the 1st Canadian Infantry Brigade. He received the D.S.O., C.M.G. and C.B. He was elected to the House of Commons in 1917 and in 1921 was called to the Senate. He was promoted Major-General and in 1940 was Inspector General for Western Canada. He retired on March 31, 1943 for health reasons and died two years later. (1954)

GREW, lake (E-6)
After J. Grew, Indian Affairs Branch, Department of Mines and Resources who reported the name of Deep Lake which was later changed to "Grew Lake." (1953)

GRIFFIN, creek (F-3)
After Thomas Griffin, first white settler on the creek; died 1919. (1912)

GRIMSHAW, town (F-3)
After Dr. M. E. Grimshaw, Peace River Medical Officer for Central Canada Railway. The land around Grimshaw was surveyed for homesteads in 1910 and homesteaders began to arrive around 1911-12. The land on which the town now stands was the homestead of Albert Edward Craddock who arrived from British Columbia in 1912. The railway arrived in 1921 and the townsite was first surveyed by Alfred Driscoll in September of that same year. Subsequent surveys were made in 1927-28. The town was named to honour the late M. E. Grimshaw, M.D., a doctor who had given unstinted service for many years to the early settlers throughout the Peace River district. Dr. Grimshaw was born at Kingston, Ontario. He practised medicine at Innisfail in 1912 and at Medicine Hat in 1913, then moved to the Peace River District to establish a practice in 1914. He was Mayor

of Peace River in 1922 and subsequently started a medical practice at Fairview in 1929 where he died in November the same year. (Henry Bulholzer, Secretary-Treasurer, Town of Grimshaw, letter, August, 1970.) (1922)

GRISETTE, mountain (8,200 feet) (J-2)
A peak of "grey" limestone. (1916)

GRIZZLY BEAR, creek (J-8)
In Cree, *mist-a-ya* (Tyrrell).

GROSMONT, locality (H-6)
French for "big mountain"; after a hill to the north. (1912)

GROTON, locality (O-7)
After Groton, South Dakota, former home of A. J. Peterson, first postmaster. (1913)

GROTTO, mountain (8,880 feet) (L-4)
Named 1858 by E. Bourgeau, botanist, Palliser Expedition; it contains a large cave with a high-arched roof, narrow at the mouth.

GROUARD, hamlet (G-4)
Formerly Lesser Slave Lake Post Office; changed to Grouard, 1909; after Monsignor Emile - Jean - Marie Grouard (1840-1931), Vicar Apostolic of Athabasca diocese; author of *Les Eldorados du Nord-ouest; Excursion au Mackenzie et au Klondike*, Lyons, 1901, and *Soixante ans de mon apostolat*, 1922.

GROUARD MISSION, hamlet (G-4)
After Bishop Grouard. See Grouard, hamlet.

GULL, lake (K-5)
In Cree, *kiaskus;* "Gull" on Arrowsmith map, 1859; "Long" on David Thompson map, 1814; in Stoney, *pi-cha-tto-amna* (Tyrrell).

GULL LAKE, summer village (K-5)
See Gull, lake.

GUNN, hamlet (I-5)
After Peter Gunn (1864-1927); born in Thurso, Scotland, he came to Canada, 1883. For twenty-seven years he was with Hudson's Bay Company as Factor at Lac Ste. Anne. He was a Member of the Alberta Legislative Assembly, 1909-1917.

GURNEYVILLE, locality (H-7)
After the maiden name (Gurney) of the wife of Alex Hall, first postmaster. (1910)

GWYNNE, hamlet (J-6)
Formerly known as Diana Post Office, the name was changed to Gwynne on March 1, 1906 after Julia Maude Gwynne, the second wife of Sir Collingwood Schreiber (1831-1918). He became the Federal Deputy Minister of Railways in 1892 and played a major part in the building of the National Transcontinental Railway (the Grand Trunk Pacific Railway).

HABAY, hamlet (C-2)
After a pioneer missionary in the district. (1954)

HABEL, creek (K-3)
After Dr. Jean Habel, Berlin, Germany. He explored the region in
1901 and died a year later. (1907)

HADDO, peak (10,073 feet) (L-4)
After George, Lord Haddo, eldest son of the Marquis of Aberdeen
and Temair. (See Aberdeen, mount).

HADDOCK, locality (I-4)
After Maude Haddock, one time postmistress. (1915)

HAGLUND, creek (H-2)
After a trapper whose trapline included this creek. (1946)

HAIDUK, peak (9,540 feet), creek and lake (L-4)
Probably after Haiduk district, Hungary or Hideghut (Haiduk), village,
Romania.

HAIG, glacier (M-4)
After Field Marshal Earl Haig (Sir Douglas Haig), (1861-1928), Commander-in-Chief of the British Forces in France during World War I.
(1922)

HAIG, mount (8,565 feet) (O-5)
After Captain R. W. Haig, R.A., astronomer, British Boundary Commission, Pacific to the Rockies, 1858-1862.

HAIGHT, locality (J-6)
Possibly after Captain Haight, for many years transport officer of
Hudson's Bay Company down the Athabasca River.

HAIR, lake (A-7)
Name derived from shape of lake. (1961)

HAIRY HILL, village (I-7)
Known as Soda Lake Post Office prior to 1907. It is so named as
buffalo shed their hair on the hill in the spring.

HALCOURT, locality (G-1)
H. Halcourt Walker submitted a number of names of early settlers
and Halcourt was selected. (1913)

HALCRO, Indian Reserve (G-3)
After Thomas Halcro, an Indian who obtained severalty under Treaty
No. 8. (1905)

HALFWAY LAKE, locality (H-6)
So named as it is equidistant from Athabasca Landing (now
Athabasca) and Edmonton. Translation of Cree Indian name, *abitau*,
(Tyrrell).

HALIFAX, lake (O-6)
After Halifax Ranch Company; a lease of 100,000 acres was granted in May, 1882, in the vicinity to J. E. Chipman and others of Halifax, Nova Scotia.

HALKIRK, village (K-7)
After Halkirk, Caithness, Scotland. "My father, now deceased, was one of the original first settlers in the district; he was a blacksmith; with a shop in the country close to his homestead. When the townsite was located and surveyed, he purchased a lot and moved in before the rails. He told me that all first purchasers were given an opportunity to choose a name. If you showed no interest, C.P.R. chose a name, if you had a strong local choice, then that was used. The man who asked them to choose had a list of suggested names and my father and two other residents picked this (Halkirk) from list because one of them liked the sound. It is supposedly a place name from Scotland. My people moved here in summer of 1909, house was completed Sept. 1, 1909, I was born Dec. 27, 1909, and first baby, so I am stuck with Halkirk for a middle name." (Mr. John H. Ainsworth, Secretary-Treasurer, letter, September, 1970).
     Halkirk, Scotland (near John O'Groat's) was the birthplace of Malcolm Groat who came to Edmonton in 1861 where he settled; Groat Estate, Groat Road and bridge were named for him. (1909)

HALLIDAY, locality (L-7)
After Howard Hadden Halliday (1878-   ) who was Member of the House of Commons for Bow River from 1917-1921. (1920)

HALSBURY, locality (M-7)
After the Earl of Halsbury (1823-1921), Lord Chancellor of England. (1914)

HAMELL, mount (6,986 feet) (I-2)
A geologist who worked in this area states that the Indians informed him that Hamell was a local hunter here some years ago. (1953)

HAMILTON, lake (G-6)
After E. H. Hamilton, geological assistant, Geological Survey. (1885)

HAMLET, locality (L-6)
After William Hamlet, railway employee, Fort William, who won the Croix de Guerre in World War 1. (1922)

HAMLIN, locality (I-7)
The name was suggested by one R. H. Perly whose mother came from Hamelin, England. The "e" was omitted by the Post Office Department. (1913)

HAMMER, hill (M-6)
In Blackfoot, *poxatsis* or "stone hammer"; a Cree Indian, while sleeping, was killed with a hammer wielded by an Indian woman.

HAND, hills, creek and lake (L-7)
So called owing to their likeness to an outstretched hand. Tyrrell notes: "They are called by the Crees *michichi ispatinan* or Hand Hills on account of their resemblance to the outstretched fingers of

the hand, the top of the table land not being flat but composed of five ridges which radiate from a centre lying to the southeast." In Stoney, Tyrrell mentions them as being called *o-chun-um-bin*. Another version is that the name means "little hand." A Blackfoot chief who was killed on one of these hills had one small hand, according to Peter Erasmus. Tyrrell's version seems the most likely. See also Michichi, hamlet and creek.

HANNA, town   (L-7)
After D. B. Hanna (1858-1938), president, Canadian Northern Railway, chairman. Ontario Liquor Commission; Cooperville P.O. until 1913. David Blythe Hanna was born in Scotland and came to Canada in 1882. He was associated with the Grand Trunk, New York West Shore and Buffalo Railway, Manitoba and Northwestern Railway and the Lake Manitoba Railway and Canal Company. In 1902, he was third vice-president of Canadian Northern and in charge of its operation upon incorporation. During his term of office Canadian Northern built its line from Saskatoon to Calgary and with the community becoming one of the most important divisional points along the line it was most appropriate that Hanna be named after the railway's illustrious executive. That is how Hanna received its name.

When the Canadian Government purchased Canadian Northern Railroad in 1918, Hanna resigned. Then he was appointed first president of the Board of Directors by the Canadian Government to control and direct the Canadian National. In 1922, he retired from railway service. He was, then, appointed first chairman of the Liquor Control Board of Ontario and when he had set up the administrative machinery, he retired in 1928. (*Pioneer Days of Hanna and District,* 1962)

HANSEN, lake   (H-8)
After Pilot Officer L. L. H. Hansen, M.I.D., Lethbridge, killed in World War II. (1951)

HANTS, locality   (M-6)
After Hampshire (Hants) county, England. (1900)

HARDIEVILLE, hamlet   (N-6)
After W. D. L. Hardie, then superintendent of the Galt coal mine which was opened here in 1909. Later, he was Mayor of Lethbridge. (1910)

HARDISTY, mount (8,900 feet) and creek   (J-2)
Named by Hector in 1859, after Richard Hardisty. See Hardisty, town.

HARDISTY, town   (J-7)
After Senator Richard Hardisty (1831-1889), Chief Factor, Hudson's Bay Company, as were his father and grandfather; for many years he was in charge of the Edmonton district. He was the last Chief Factor of Fort Edmonton. At Battle River, he established a trading post. (Secretary-Treasurer, Town of Hardisty, letter, September, 1970) (1906)

HARGWEN, locality   (I-3)
After a friend of the chief clerk of the Grand Trunk Pacific Railway. (1911)

HARKER, lake (A-7)
Named after a distinguished British geologist, Alfred Harker (1859-1939). He was prominent in the field of metamorphic and igneous petrology. (1958)

HARLECH, locality (J-4)
Probably, after the ancient capital of Merionethshire, Wales. (1914)

HARMATTAN, hamlet (L-5)
Named by the Post Office Department. The Harmattan is the name given to a hot, dry, parching wind that blows during December, January and February on the Atlantic coast of Africa, bringing a high, dense haze of red dust which darkens the sky. The natives of the area rub their bodies with oil or fat while this parching wind is blowing.

HARMON VALLEY, locality (F-3)
After Daniel Williams Harmon, North West Company; author of *A Journal of Voyages and Travels in the Interior of North America.* He was in charge at Dunvegan, 1808-1810.

HAROLD, creek (G-2)
After Leading Sergeant Raymond Alexander Harold, M.I.D., Calgary, killed in World War II. (1951)

HARPER, creek (C-5)
After C. J. Harper, D.L.S., member of survey party.

HARRIS, mount (10,825 feet) (L-3)
After one L. E. Harris, D.L.S., who was first to climb the mountain in 1919.

HARTLEY, creek (D-7)
After the late John Stephen Hartley, Stoker First Class of Ashmont, Alberta. (1963)

HARTSHORN, locality (K-7)
After D. H. Hartshorn, first postmaster. (1910)

HARVEY, lake (J-2)
After Horace Harvey (1863-1949), Chief Justice of Alberta from 1910-1949. Harvey was born and educated in Ontario. In 1890, he was called to the Ontario Bar and in 1893, to the Bar of the North-West Territories. He practised law in Calgary and in 1896 became Registrar of Land Titles for Southern Alberta (the old District of Alberta). In 1900, he was Deputy Attorney-General of the North-West Territories and in 1904, Puisne Judge of the Territorial Supreme Court. In 1907, he held the same position in the newly organized Supreme Court of Alberta, which he held until 1921, when the courts were reorganized, and he was made Chief Justice of the Trial Division. From 1924 until 1949 he was Chief Justice of the Appellate Division of the Alberta Supreme Court. In 1940, he was Chairman of the Mobilization Board for National War Services. (1954)

HARVEY, mount (8,000 feet)   (I-1)
After Lieutenant F. M. W. Harvey, V.C., M.C., of World War I.
He was later made Brigadier; he was from Fort Macleod, Alberta.
(1949)

HARVEY, pass   (L-4)
After the first person who crossed it in winter, one Ralph L. Harvey.
(1959)

HARWOOD, lake   (C-7)
After Colonel Harwood, commanding 51st Battalion, Edmonton. (1916)

HASTINGS, lake and creek   (I-6)
Both features were named by J. B. Tyrrell after one Tom Hastings, a
member of the 1884 Geological Survey party. The Cree name of the
lake is *a-ka-ka-kwa-tikh*, "the lake that does not freeze." The Cree name
for the creek is *kak-si-chi-wukh* or "swift current." Hastings Ridge
(q.v.) was also named by Tyrrell for the same man.

HASTINGS, ridge   (N-5)
Named by J. B. Tyrrell after Tom Hastings, member of 1884 Geological
Survey party. See also, Hastings, lake and creek.

HAT, mount (5,995 feet)   (H-1)
One peak resembles a hat.

HAULTAIN, mount (8,600 feet)   (J-2)
After Sir Frederick W. G. Haultain (1857-1942). A native of England,
Haultain was educated in Canada and came west to practise law at
Fort Macleod in 1884. From 1888 to 1905 he was the Member for
Fort Macleod in the Territorial Legislature and played a major part
in guiding the Territories toward provincial autonomy. When, in 1905
the provinces of Alberta and Saskatchewan were formed, he became
Leader of the Opposition in the latter province. In 1912, he was
appointed Chief Justice of Saskatchewan and in 1916, he was knighted.
From 1917 to 1939 he was Chancellor of the University of
Saskatchewan.

HAUNTED, lakes   (K-6)
As told by C. J. Mott, one time owner of the Haunted Lake ranch, the
legend is that on a bright moonlight night, an elk's head and antlers were
seen out on the ice near the middle of the lake. Two young braves from
an Indian camp on the south side were determined to get them but before
they reached the spot, the antlers were observed to move about
mysteriously. While the braves looked on in wonder, the ice broke and
the two disappeared. They are said by the Indians to haunt the lakes ever
since.

HAVEN, creek   (K-3)
After a rancher who had a grazing lease in this valley.

HAWKINS, locality   (J-7)
After the accountant, office of vice-president, Grand Trunk Pacific
Railway. (1909)

HAWKINS, mount, (8,800 feet)   (O-5)
After Lieutenant-Colonel J. S. Hawkins, R. E., Commissioner, British Boundary Commission, Pacific to the Rockies, 1858-1862. (1917)

HAY, lake   (F-2)
In Cree, *a-pi-chi-koo-chi-was*, meaning "little swamp" (Tyrrell). Presumably from the lush growth of grass.

HAY LAKES, village   (J-6)
Descriptive of large hay meadows in the vicinity.

HAYNES, creek and locality   (K-6)
Named in 1893 after Isaac Haynes who had resided on it since 1891. The locality also takes its name from Mr. Haynes.

HAYS, hamlet   (N-7)
Name selected by Prairie Farm Rehabilitation Administration officials to honour David Hays, manager of the former Canada Land and Irrigation Company, long active in promoting irrigation. (1952)

HAYTER, hamlet   (K-8)
After Hayter Reid, the superintendent of the Canadian Pacific Railway hotels and formerly Indian Commissioner at Regina. Later, he became Deputy Superintendent General of Indian Affairs. (1909)

HAZELDINE, locality   (I-8)
After Hazeldean, Sussex, England. From the Old English *denu* meaning a valley; the first part of the name probably alludes to the tree, (Ekwall).

HEAD, mount (9,122 feet) and creek   (M-5)
Named by Palliser after Sir Edmund Head, Governor of Canada, 1854-1861 and Governor of the Hudson's Bay Company, 1863-1868. The name is on the Palliser Expedition map, 1863.

HEALY, creek   (L-4)
Named by Dr. G. M. Dawson in 1884, after Captain John J. Healy, sometime manager of North American Trading and Transportation Company, Dawson, Yukon. Healy and his associates, J. S. and O. Dennis, located copper claims on a neighbouring mountain.

HEATH, creek   (N-5)
After William Heath, a settler, about 1885.

HEATH, locality   (J-8)
After the chief official of the Grand Trunk Pacific Railway, Water Supply Department (1908)

HECTOR, mount (11,135 feet), glacier, lake and creek   (L-3)
Mount Hector was named in 1884 by Dr. G. M. Dawson of the Geological Survey of Canada after Sir James Hector, M.D. (1834-1907). Hector was born in Edinburgh and received his medical education at the university there. From 1857-1860, he was surgeon and geologist and second in command to the Palliser Expedition. In 1861, he was

appointed geologist to the Provincial Government of Otago, New Zealand and from 1865-1905, was Director of the Geological Survey of New Zealand. In 1904, he revisited the scenes of his Canadian explorations.

HEINSBURG, hamlet (I-8)
After John Heins, first postmaster "Burg"—old word for fort (1913)

HEISLER, village (J-7)
After Martin Heisler, from whom the townsite was purchased. (1915)

HELMET, mountain (8,600 feet) and creek (J-3)
A local name reported in 1925. Probably descriptive.

HELMSDALE, locality (L-5)
After Helmsdale, Scotland.

HEMARUKA, locality (K-7)
A compound of Helen, Margaret, Ruth and Kathleen, daughters of A. E. Warren, general manager, Canadian National Railways, Toronto. Formerly Zetland after Zetland, Huron county, Ontario. (1927)

HENDAY, mount (8,800 feet) and locality (J-2)
After Anthony Henday, fur trader and the first European to set foot in what is now Alberta and to visit the Blackfeet Indians as well as to view the Rockies.

Virtually nothing is known of Henday's early life except that he grew up in the Isle of Wight in England. He was actively engaged in smuggling and was apprehended and outlawed. He entered the service of the Hudson's Bay Company in 1750, and was posted to York Factory on Hudson Bay. The purpose of his trip inland was to try to persuade the Indians to come to the Bay to trade but in the course of his journey he soon concluded that the Indians would not do this for it was too far and the French posts were convenient for them to receive a good price for their furs. Henday realized that the Company would have to build posts inland.

In the course of his travels Henday met the Blackfoot and in October 1754, after having crossed the plains, climbed a hill near where the town of Innisfail now stands and viewed the main range of the Rockies some 80 miles distant. He was the first white man to see them, the fabled "Shining Mountains." Henday wintered in the area with the Blackfeet and returned to the Bay the following spring. In 1759-1760, he made one more journey inland but this was not as extensive as his first. He returned to England in 1763, and was granted a pension by the Company. His subsequent life is unknown. (1954)

HENRY, mount (8.626 feet) (J-2)
After William Henry, early North West Company fur-trader. (1917)

HENRY HOUSE, locality (J-2)
After William Henry, North West Company, who built a trading post at the junction of the Miette and Athabasca Rivers, 1811. It is referred to in 1814 as having been abandoned. (1912)

HENRY MACLEOD, mount (10,789 feet)   (K-3)
After H. A. F. MacLeod, Canadian Pacific Railway engineer, who made a reconnaissance survey up the Maligne valley in 1875. (1923)

HENSON, lake   (A-7)
Named after an English geologist, a pioneer in the field of geophysical exploration who died early in a promising professional career.

HERCULES, locality   (I-6)
After E. Hercules Murphy, first postmaster. (1912)

HERMIT, creek   (H-1)
Not far from a cabin known as the hermit's cabin. (1947)

HERON, island   (C-6)
After F. J. Heron who made this his trapping headquarters for many years; he was from Fort Smith, N.W.T. (1963)

HESKETH, locality   (L-6)
After Colonel J. A. Hesketh, assistant division engineer of the Canadian Pacific Railway, Winnipeg. He graduated from the Royal Military College, Kingston in 1883. (1921)

HESPERO, locality   (K-5)
After Hesper the evening star. Pitcox Post Office until 1916.

HIDDEN, lake   (M-4)
Descriptive.

HIGH DIVIDE, ridge   (J-3)
Refers to the high divide crossed by the Bighorn trail between Hinton and McLeod River. (1945)

HIGH LEVEL, town   (C-3)
Descriptive. Incorporated as a town, 1965.

HIGH PRAIRIE, town   (G-3)
From the nature of the surrounding country. The Cree Indians named the High Prairie region *muskatayosips* meaning "Prairie River" after the main stream in the district. Settlement began at turn of the century but was sparse until 1912 when the railway came. When steel reached High Prairie many more came and a small community was established on the Prairie River. At first this community was called Prairie River but in 1910 the name was changed to High Prairie when the Post Office officials advised that there was another settlement of the original name. High Prairie was incorporated as a village on April 6, 1945 and as a town on January 10, 1950.

HIGH RIVER, town   (M-5)
The name of the town of High River is contracted from the Highwood River (q.v.) which flows through the town and originally in flood would flow either northeast along its present course or southwest along the Little Bow. The Indians therefore named it *itspitsi* which is Blackfoot for "High". The term was also used to describe the high cottonwood trees along its banks, hence the name "Highwood." The early traders used the easier pronunciation of "Spitzee" to describe the area surrounding the Highwood or High River.

Bell's map of 1872 refers to the river as the *Iskasquchow* while on David Thompson's map of his explorations of 1784-1812 the name "Spitchee" River appears. The map of the Warre and Vavasour expedition and Laurie's map of 1870 use the name Highwood River. (J. M. Tupkal, Secretary-Treasurer, Town of High River, letter, August, 1970)

HIGHROCK, range   (M-5)
From the precipitous, rocky character of it's summit as compared with the hills at its base.

HIGHTOWER, creek   (I-2)
After Pilot Officer C. E. Hightower, D.F.C., Beverly; killed in World War II. (1948)

HIGHVALE, locality   (I-5)
A. C. Brooks, the postmaster, came from Highgate, Ontario. (1909)

HIGHWOOD, range and river   (M-5)
The Highwood River (*ispasquehow*) appears on the Palliser map of 1865; as *spitchee* on the David Thompson map of 1814 and *spitchi* or *ispisquehow* on the Arrowsmith map of 1859. It was called the High Woods River by Blakiston. It is a translation of the Indian name *ispitsi* (Spitzee) and is so called because the river is on nearly the same level as the surrounding prairie instead of in a "bottom" or coulee. As a result, the belt of timber along the stream is much "higher" than usual and can be seen from a considerable distance. The Blackfoot name of the upper portion of the river is *sapow* or "wind" river. See also High River, town.

HILDA, hamlet   (M-8)
Named after the first child born there. (1910)

HILL END, locality   (K-5)
A range of hills terminated near the settlement. (1902)

HILL SPRING, village   (O-6)
A spring on the hill was piped to the village at the time it was named. (1911)

HILLCREST, locality, mountain (7,101 feet) and HILLCREST MINES, hamlet   (N-5)
After Charles P. Hill, managing director, Hillcrest Coal and Coke Company. This area in the Crowsnest Pass was the scene of one of the worst mining disasters in Canada when, on June 19, 1914, an explosion took 189 lives.

HILLIARD, hamlet   (I-6)
After one Hilliard McConkey. (1905)

HILLSDOWN, locality   (K-6)
North and south are "hills" with "downs" on the east and west. (1902)

HINDVILLE, locality   (J-8)
After Thomas Hind, first postmaster. (1909)

HINES CREEK, village (F-2)

"In the 1920's Mr. Carl Leonard opened a trading post in the vicinity of a creek called Hines. In connection with the trading post, he applied for a post office which he named Hines Creek. In 1930 when the N.A.R. was extended from Fairview to the present site that was in the Callagan school district (named in honour of the engineer in charge of railroad construction) Mr. Leonard moved his log building trading post with the Hines Creek Post Office to the new town and there the name Hines Creek prevailed." (S. Velichka, Municipal Secretary, letter, Sept., 1970)

HINTON, town (I-3)

After W. P. Hinton, sometime general manager, Grand Trunk Pacific Railway. The name Hinton, in the original derivation appears in many place names in England. e.g. Hinton Ampner (Hampshire) and Cherryhinton (Cambs). It has at least two sources: 1. Old English *Hea-tun* 'tun' situated on high land. 2. *Higna-tun* the monks' or nuns' tun. e.g. Monks" (or nuns') homestead, enclosure, village. (Ekwall)

HINTON TRAIL, locality (G-1)

After an old pack trail from Hinton on the G.T.P. to the Grande Prairie district; it afforded a short cut to the Peace River area. (1923)

HOADLEY, locality (J-5)

The name was changed from Haverigs, in 1924, to honour Hon. George Hoadley (1866-1945), Minister of Agriculture, Alberta in the United Farmers Government (1921-1935). A former Conservative, he became disenchanted with them and espoused the U.F.A. cause.

HOBBEMA. hamlet (J-6)

After Meyndert Hobbema (1638-1709), Dutch painter.

HOFFMAN, mount (6,600 feet) (M-5)

After member of survey party, later, hotel proprietor in Olds. (1896)

HOLBORN, locality (J-5)

After an early settler. (1913)

HOLDEN, village (J-6)

After J. B. Holden (1876-1956), former member of the Alberta Legislative Assembly. Vermilion Valley Post Office was changed to Holden, in 1907.

HOLLEBEKE, mountain (7,884 feet) (N-5)

After a village southeast of Ypres, Belgium, (1917)

HOLMES, lake (A-7)

In honour of the distinguished English geologist and petrologist, Sir Arthur Holmes. He was one of the first to postulate a logical hypothesis of continental drift; also a highly praised textbook author and teacher. (1958)

HOMEGLEN, locality (J-6)

Name suggested by James Burns, first settler. Descriptive. (1909)

HONDO. locality (G-5)

There are places in California and Texas bearing this name. (1914)

HONEY, lake (H-7)
After Leading Sergeant Hedley Arthur Honey, M.I.D., Edmonton, killed in World War II. (1951)

HOOD, mount (9,425 feet) (M-4)
After Rear Admiral Hon. H. L. A. Hood, who participated in the Battle of Jutland, 1916, and went down with H.M.S. *Invincible,* (see also Invincible, mount). (1922)

HOOGE, mountain (10,550 feet) (K-3)
After the village of the same name two miles east of Ypres where the Canadians regained ground on June 2, 1916. (1920)

HOOHEY, creek (A-4)
After Joe Hoohey, local trapper. (1963)

HOOKER, mount (10,872 feet), and icefield (K-2)
This mountain near Athabasca Pass was named by David Douglas in 1827, "in honour of my early patron, the Professor of Botany in the University of Glasgow." This was Sir William Jackson Hooker (1785-1865), noted English botanist, who was appointed Director of the Royal Botanical Gardens, Kew, in 1841.

HOPE VALLEY, locality (J-8)
Descriptive of the optimism of the inhabitants and of the situation of the original post office in a valley. (1911)

HORBERG, lake (A-7)
Named after a distinguished American geomorphologist, Leland Horberg, who died in 1955. (1958)

HORNBECK, hamlet (I-3)
The name is derived from that of an old-time settler in the Big Eddy area of the McLeod River. (1909)

HORNE, lake (H-7)
After Warrant Officer A. M. Horne, D.F.C., Edmonton, killed in World War II. (1951)

HORSE HILL, hamlet (I-6)
After the nearby Horse Hills where the horseguard or wintering ranch of the Hudson's Bay Company, Edmonton, was formerly situated.

HORSESHOE, ridge (N-5)
Descriptive. (1959)

HOSELAW, locality and lake (H-8)
After Hoselaw Loch, Roxburghshire, Scotland. (1913)

HOTCHKISS, hamlet and river (E-3)
After Cyprus Percival Hotchkiss, D.L.S. (1915)

HOUCHER, lake (K-8)
Probably after one Mr. Houcher of Czar.

HOUSE, mountain (3,950 feet) (G-4)
Translation of Indian *waskahegan*. The summit resembles the roof of a house.

HOWARD, mount (9,100 feet) (M-5)
After one Edward Howard who was the local forest ranger in the area. He retired in 1938. (1939)

HOWARD DOUGLAS, creek and mount (9,200 feet) (L-4)
After Howard Douglas, sometime superintendent, Banff National Park. (1904)

HOWIE, locality (M-7)
After James Howie, first postmaster. (1913)

HOWSE, pass, peak (10,800 feet), and river (K-3)
After Joseph Howse, fur trader and explorer (1774-1852). A native of Gloucestershire, England, he entered the service of the Hudson's Bay Company and for much of the decade of 1799-1809, he was in charge at Carlton House. In 1809, he made a journey to the Rockies and the following year led the first Hudson's Bay Company party over the pass that now bears his name. In the course of this journey, he explored parts of the Columbia and Kootenay Rivers and wintered with the Flathead Indians in what is now American territory. Although this venture was profitable it was never repeated and the route was closed by the Peigan Indians. Although Howse led the first Hudson's Bay Company party over the pass, it was Thompson who first crossed it; it appears on Thompson's map of 1814 as Howse Pass. Howse was appointed a councillor of Rupert's Land in 1815 but retired to England to become a Fellow of the Royal Geographical Society. He published *A Grammar of the Cree Language* in 1844.

HUALLEN, locality (G-2)
After Hugh Allen (1889-1972) former M.L.A. for Peace River and Grande Prairie, (1926-1935). In 1934, he became Minister of Municipal Affairs and Lands and Mines and held the post until his defeat in 1935.

HUBBLES, lake (I-5)
After one Mr. Hubble who started a resort and beach there. (1950)

HUESTIS, mount (10,086 feet) (L3)
Named after E. S. Huestis (1900-   ), former Deputy Minister of Lands and Forests for Alberta. He was interested in conservation throughout his career.

HUGGETT, locality (J-5)
After J. Huggett, first postmaster. (1925)

HUGHENDEN, village and lake (K-7)
After Hughenden, Buckinghamshire, England, estate of Benjamin Disraeli, first Lord Beaconsfield (1804-1881). (1909)

HUMMOCK, lake (K-6)
From isolated small hills on its margin, principally on west side. (1893)

HUNGABEE, glacier and mountain (11,447 feet) (L-4)
Stoney Indian word meaning "chieftain"; on S. E. S. Allen map, 1894; refers to the "dominating" aspect of the mountain.

HUNT, creek (J-3)
Athabasca River; named after a local resident.

HUNTER, mount (8,554 feet) (J-2)
After Flight Lieutenant R. H. Hunter, D.F.C., Westlock, killed in World War II. (1948)

HUNTING, hill (M-7)
Know in Cree as *onachewassawpewin*. The Indian hunters, used to watch for buffalo from the summit (Steele). In Blackfoot, it was known as *sahami-sapikawaghway*.

HUSSAR, village (L-6)
According to the Secretary-Treasurer of the village N. L. Kropinak, (letter, January, 1972), the Canadian Pacific Railway, by arrangement with the Canadian Government had taken over a large tract of land for irrigation purposes and when the ranch leases which had formerly occupied the land were cancelled in 1911, settlers began to arrive.

Mr. Kropinak continues: "Next was the sale by the Canadian Pacific Railway of a large tract of land, situated just south of the townsite to a German syndicate known as the German Canadian Farming Company. To this company, is attributed the naming of Hussar, as one of the founders of the company was a Lieutenant of a German Hussar Regiment; the name meaning a light armed cavalry soldier. But as this name is also used in the English Cavalry, the Canadian Pacific Railway may have named the village from the English origin. The colony of Germans began operations in 1913."

HUTTON, lake (A-7)
After Sir James Hutton (1726-1797), Scottish geologist. He was the first geologist to postulate the modern theories of metamorphism and sedimentation. He also formulated the concept of "the present is the key to the past."

HUTTON, locality (L-7)
After the manager of the Northern Crown Bank, Calgary, through whose effort a loan was granted to buy a townsite; name changed from Fieldholme, 1911.

HUXLEY, hamlet (K-6)
After Thomas Huxley (1825-1895), noted English naturalist. (1907)

HYTHE, village (G-1)
Named after the town of Hythe, England the home of Mr. Hartley, first postmaster. Land was surveyed, 1909, and the first settlers arrived that year. The name is from the Old English and means a landing place. Hythe, Kent, England is mentioned in Domesday Book (*Hede* then Hythe) and was one of the Cinque Ports, (Ekwall).

— I —

IDAMAY, locality (L-8)
Probably named after the daughter, Ida May, of Jacob Gerig, the postmaster when the original post office was opened in 1929.

IDDESLEIGH, locality (M-7)
After Sir Walter Stafford Northcote, Earl of Iddesleigh; Governor, Hudson's Bay Company, 1869-74. (1914)

ILLINGWORTH, locality (N-7)
After W. J. Illingworth, sometime director of the Canadian Pacific Railway.

INDEFATIGABLE, mountain (8,700 feet) (M-4)
Kananaskis River; after a battle cruiser engaged in the Battle of Jutland, 1916. She was built in 1909 and destroyed by German gunfire at that battle. (1922)

INDUS, hamlet (L-6)
Named after the Indus River, flowing through Pakistan, formerly part of India. (1914)

INFLEXIBLE, mount (9,800 feet) (M-4)
Kananaskis Range; after a battle cruiser engaged in the Battle of Jutland. (1922)

INGLISMALDIE, mount (9,885 feet) (L-4)
South of Lake Minnewanka and named by George A. Stewart, superintendent of Rocky Mountains Park (now Banff National Park) in 1886 or 1887, after Inglismaldie Castle, Kincardineshire, Scotland, seat of the Earl of Kintore, who visited Banff at that time.

INLAND, locality (I-7)
A descriptive name suggestive of its distance from the sea. (1911)

INNISFAIL, town (K-5)
Named by Mrs. Estella Scarlett, a former resident. A newspaper clipping reads: "In 1887 my father and mother, Mr. and Mrs. W. Wildman, brother Marmaduke and myself, Estella, came to what was then Poplar Grove. My father homesteaded in the Little Red Deer Settlement that year. The first postmaster in Poplar Grove was Norman Stiles. When the new post office was built in 1891 Mr. Stiles asked me to suggest a new name for it. Mr. Stiles and I had gone to the same school in Newmarket, Ontario. My grandmother was born in Innisfail, Ireland. I had always thought that this was a pretty name so I asked Mr. Stiles to call the new post office by this name. This name was accepted by the Department of Postal Affairs in the same year." (Taken from a clipping sent by the Municipal Secretary, G. Redlich, with a letter dated October, 1970. No date is given on the clipping). "Innis" in Gaelic means island.

INNISFREE, village (I-7)
After the summer residence of Sir Edmund Walker, sometime president, Canadian Bank of Commerce. It was called Del Norte Post Office until 1909.

INTERSECTION, mountain (8,044 feet) (I-1)
It is at the intersection of the Continental Divide with the 120th Meridian.

INVERNESS, river (G-4)
Swan River, Lesser Slave Lake; after Inverness, Scotland.

INVERSNAY, locality (N-7)
After Inversnaid, Scotland. (1912)

INVINCIBLE, mountain (9,000 feet)   (M-4)
Kananaskis River; after a battle cruiser engaged in the Battle of
Jutland, 1916 and destroyed at that engagement. (1922)

IOSEGUN, lake, river and hamlet   (H-3)
From an Indian name meaning "tail."

IPIATIK, lake and river   (G-7)
Cree Indian for "look-out."

IRETON, locality   (J-6)
After Henry Ireton (1611-1651). Ireton was a general in the army of the
Parliamentary forces under Oliver Cromwell during the Civil War in
England, (1643-1646). He was also Cromwell's son-in-law.

IRMA, village   (J-7)
After the daughter of W. Wainwright, second vice-president, Grand
Trunk Pacific Railway. See also Wainwright, town. (1909)

IRON, lake and creek   (J-8)
Translation of Cree *pi-wa-pisk-oo* (Tyrrell). After a large piece of
meteoric iron found on a mound near the lake.

IRON SPRINGS, hamlet   (N-6)
After mineral springs in the Blackspring Ridge. (1908)

IRRICANA, village   (L-6)
Both the Canadian Pacific and the Grand Trunk Pacific Railways
built railroads through here in 1908 and 1909. The C.P.R. also dug a
canal from the Bow River to within three to five miles west of this
village and a tributary past the east side within 1,000 yards. No water
was ever turned into this stretch and years after it gradually was filled
in. It was from this that the early settlers of the village derived the name
—an abbreviation of irrigation and canal. (Letter from J. G. Bell,
Secretary-Treasurer, August, 1970). The village is on or near the
site of "Slaughter Camp" of Captain Palliser, August, 1859, where the
expedition killed seventeen buffalo.

IRVINE, town   (N-8)
After Colonel A. Irvine, Commissioner, Royal North-West Mounted
Police, 1880-1886; member of the Council of the North-West Territories.
Appointed, 1892, Warden of Stony Mountain Penitentiary, Manitoba.

ISAAC, creek   (I-2)
After one Isaac Plante who had a trap line near the creek. (1947)

ISABELLA, lake   (K-3)
Named in 1898 by C. S. Thompson after his sister.

ISHBEL, mount (9,440 feet)   (L-4)
After Ishbel MacDonald, daughter of British Prime Minister Ramsey
MacDonald (1866-1937).

ISLAY, hamlet   (I-8)
The first family, the Gilchrists, who settled here came from Victoria
county, Ontario and originally from Islay, Scotland. It was formerly
known as Island Lake. (1905)

ISLE, lake   (I-5)

Shown on some of the old maps as Lac des Isles or Lac des Islets
from islands in the lake. Hector notes (March 4, 1859) en route to
Edmonton: "Ten miles after crossing Pembina River, having passed over
a ridge of land that forms the watershed of the Saskatchewan, and
which is within a few miles of Pembina River, we reached a series of
large lakes, on the ice of which we travelled very fast. The largest of
these, *Lac des Isles*, is 13 miles long from east to west." The lake also
appears on the Palliser map of 1865.

ISOLA, peak (8,182 feet)   (N-5)

An isolated mountain. (1919)

ISPAS, locality   (I-7)

After the birthplace in Bukovina, Romania, of N. Pawlink, the first
postmaster. (1911)

— J —

JACKPINE, mountain (8,400 feet), pass (3,694 feet) and river   (I-1)

Named for the jackpine on its slopes.

JACKSON, locality   (K-6)

After G. T. Jackson, former station agent and Mayor of Lacombe.

JACKSON, creek   (I-2)

Wildhay River; after Pilot Officer H. N. Jackson, D.F.C., Edmonton,
killed in World War II. (1948)

JACOB, creek and Indian Reserve   (L-5)

After a Stoney Indian chief who signed Indian Treaty No. 7, 1877.

JACQUES, ROCHE, mountain (8,540 feet), range, pass and creek   (J-2)

It appears on the Palliser map, 1865; probably named after Jacques
Cardinal (q.v.), North West Company employee, who was in charge
of a horseguard near Snaring River. David Douglas relates that as he
came down the Athabasca Pass in 1827, he met "old Jacques Cardinal"
with horses for the fur traders.

JAMES, pass and river   (K-4)-(K-5)

After James Dixon, Stoney chief, one of the signatories of Treaty No.
7 of 1877.

JAMES RIVER BRIDGE, locality   (K-5)

See James, pass and river.

JARVIS, lake and creek   (I-2)

North of Brûlé Lake and named after E. W. Jarvis, C.E., C.P.R.
survey. (1873).

JASPER, town, lake and national park   (J-2)

After Jasper Hawes who was in charge of the North West Company's
trading post of the same name on the west side of Brûlé Lake in 1817.
The post was in existence in 1814 when François Decoigne was in
charge; later the post was removed to the shore of Jasper Lake. Jasper

House was originally built by the North West Company on the north end of Brûlé Lake about 1813. Some time between 1827-1829 it was rebuilt near the site of a marker on the highway some twelve miles east of the present town of Jasper. For half a century it was the main support of a trade route over the mountains via the Whirlpool River and Athabasca Pass to the Columbia. It was also an important point for the route through the Yellowhead Pass. Paul Kane in his journey describes Jasper House as "three miserable log huts in the mountains." Jasper House was abandoned in 1884. Lewis Swift who arrived in the early 1900's was the first permanent resident. Jasper town was formerly known as Fitzhugh but the name was changed.

JAYDOT, locality   (O-8)
After a nearby ranch. (1922)

JEFFREY, locality   (I-6)
After one Jeffrey Garon, one time postmaster. (1906)

JELLICOE, mount (10,065 feet)   (M-4)
After Admiral Lord Jellicoe (1859-1935), Commander of the Grand (British) Fleet, 1914-1916. (1918)

JENNER, locality   (M-7)
After Dr. Edward Jenner (1749-1823), famous English physician who discovered vaccination for the prevention of smallpox. Prior to 1913 known as Websdale Post Office.

JERRAM, mount (9,800 feet)   (M-4)
After Admiral Sir Thomas Jerram who commanded the Second Battle Squadron, 1915-1916, leading it at the Battle of Jutland, 1916. (1922)

JESSIE, mount (8,702 feet)   (I-1)
Smoky River; after Miss Jessie Campbell, sister of A. J. Campbell, D.L.S. (1925)

JOB. creek and pass   (J-3)
Named by A. P. Coleman after a Stoney Indian, Job Beaver, a famous hunter and guide, who was most enterprising in chopping trails into new valleys.

JODOIN, creek   (B-6)
After Able Seaman Lawrence James Jodoin, M.I.D., Edmonton, killed in World War II. (1950)

JOFFRE, mount (11,316 feet) and locality   (M-4)
After Marshal J. J. C. Joffre (1852-1931), Commander in Chief, French Armies, 1915-1917. (1918)

JOHNSON, lake   (A-7)
West of Lake Athabasca; named after P. N. Johnson, former Director of Surveys for Alberta.

JOHNSON, lake   (C-6)
Southwest of Lake Claire; after a trapper by the name of Johnson who made his headquarters on the banks of this small lake. (1963)

JOHNSON, lake   (D-7)
Northeast of McClelland Lake; after Sergeant Gordon Fraser Johnson, M.I.D., Calgary, killed in World War II. (1950)

JOHN WARE, ridge   (M-5)
After John Ware (d. 1905), pioneer negro rancher. John Ware was born in the southern United States and came north to Alberta on a cattle drive in 1882. For several years he worked on the Bar U and Quorn Ranches and then went ranching for himself on Sheep Creek near Millarville. He was one of the best known cattlemen of the ranching era in southern Alberta and tales of his feats of horsemanship are almost legendary. He often referred to himself as a "Smoked Irish-man". Formerly known as Nigger John Ridge, the feature was re-named in 1970.

JOLI FOU, rapides du (rapids)   (F-7)
Athabasca River, above House River; commemorates an unskilled steersman who ran his boat against the most conspicuous rock in the channel.

JONAS, pass and creek   (K-3)
After Jonas, a chief of the Morley band of Stoneys; in 1893 he gave Coleman information respecting trails from the North Saskatchewan to the Athabasca. (1893)

JOUSSARD, hamlet   (G-4)
After the Rev. C. Joussard, O.M.I. (1851-1932); formerly Indiana.

JOYCE, river   (K-4)
North Ram River; after Squadron Leader R. G. Joyce, A.F.C., M.I.D., Calgary, killed in World War II. (1950)

JUDAH, locality   (F-3)
After N. F. Judah, former auditor of the Edmonton, Dunvegan and British Columbia Railway. (1916)

JUDSON, locality   (N-7)
After Judson Bemis of the Bemis Bag Company. (1914)

JUMPING BUFFALO, hill   (M-6)
Translation of Blackfoot *oteschiksisapaghkioteseh* (Nelson).

JUMPINGPOUND, creek, locality and mountain (7,300 feet)   (L-5)
Bow River; in Blackfoot *ninapiskan*, "men's pound"; in Stoney, *to-ko-jap-tap-wap-ta* (Tyrrell). From a high steep bank near its mouth where the buffalo were driven over and killed—a buffalo "pound."

JUNCTION, mountain (8,800 feet) and creek   (M-5)
Two branches of the Sheep River join here. (1895-6)

JUNO, locality   (N-7)
After the mythological queen of the sky. (1894)

JUTLAND, mountain (7,900 feet) and creek   (O-5)
Castle River; after the naval Battle of Jutland, 1916. This battle, which ended in a draw, was the only time in World War I when the entire British and German fleets were engaged. (1917)

KAHWIN, locality (I-6)
Sioux Indian for "no", expressive of the opposition to the original
name proposed, the Russian one "Ostasik." (1912)

KAKWA, mountain (7,531 feet), river and falls (I-2)
Cree Indian for "porcupine."

KALELAND, locality (I-7)
Probably named by Swedish settlers; Kalle's land, i.e., Kalle's farm.

KANANASKIS, range, lake, river, hamlet (M-4)
Palliser says he named Kananaskis Pass after "an Indian of whom
there is a legend, giving an account of his most wonderful recovery
from the blow of an axe, which had stunned but failed to kill him,
and the river which flows through this gorge also bears his name."
(1858)

KANATA, locality (K-6)
The same word as "Canada" which is derived from it. "Kanata" is a
Huron word meaning a collection of dwellings. The name of the
Alberta locality refers to a dwelling of a father, three sons and a
son-in-law who squatted there. (1908)

KANE, mount (10,000 feet) and glacier (K-2)
After Paul Kane (1810-1871), the Canadian artist who travelled from
Toronto to the Pacific Coast in the years 1845-1848, sketching the
Indians and scenery as he went. He recorded his impressions in
Wanderings of an Artist Among the Indians of North America which
was published in 1859. He also left behind a large collection of
sketches and paintings, showing an unrivalled record of the early west.

KANGIENOS, lake (L-5)
The local name is *mnaysto* or "narrow."

KAPASIWIN, summer village (I-5)
Cree Indian for "camp." Established in 1918, it is the oldest summer
village in Alberta.

KASHA, locality (K-5)
After one J. Kasha, owner of land on which station was situated.
(1924)

KATAKA, mountain (8,600 feet) (J-2)
Indian for "fort"; descriptive. (1916)

KATHLEEN, hamlet (G-3)
After a relative of W. R. Smith, former general manager of the
Edmonton, Dunvegan and British Columbia Railway. (1915)

KATHRYN, locality (L-6)
After Kathryn McKay, daughter of Neil McKay, local landowner.
(1913)

KAUFMANN, peaks (10,150 feet) (K-3)
The name is on Collie's map, in the *Geographical Journal*, of 1903. After Christian Kaufmann, Swiss guide, who was with James Outram when the mountain was first climbed.

KAVANAGH, hamlet (J-6)
After Charles Edmund Kavanagh, at one time superintendent of Railway Mail Service, Winnipeg. (1911)

KAWAGASUM, butte (H-7)
After an old Indian of that name who used to camp on the top when he was in the neighbourhood and there is a tradition that he is buried up there, but no one seems to know the spot. The name is Cree for "he that gives a crooked (uncertain) light." The hill is the highest point for miles around.

KEARL, lake (E-7)
After Flight Lieutenant E. E. Kearl, D.F.C., Cardston, killed in World War II. (1950)

KEEPHILLS, locality (I-5)
The name was suggested by George H. Collins, postmaster, after a place in Buckinghamshire, England. (1909)

KEHIWIN, Indian Reserve, creek and lake (I-7)
After Chief Keheewin, who signed the treaty of 1876. The chief was named after the "eagle" (*kehew* in Cree). As a young man he distinguished himself by his bravery in many fights with the Blackfoot and became a chief early in life. Later, he joined the Roman Catholic Church and was known as a good Christian. He was also well looked upon by the Hudson's Bay Company factors. He died in 1887 at Onion Lake, Saskatchewan.

KEHO, lake (N-6)
Incorrectly named after Dan Keough, a wolfer who mined coal in the vicinity and sold it at Forts Macleod and Whoop-Up about 1873-1875.

KEITH, locality (L-5)
Named by Lord Strathcona after Keith, Banffshire, Scotland. (1884)

KEITH, lake (H-7)
After Flying Officer G. N. Keith, D.F.C., Taber, killed in World War II. (1951)

KELSEY, locality (J-6)
After Moses S. Kelsey, who came from Millbank, South Dakota, and homesteaded in 1901, on the quarter section on which the station was located later. (1916)

KEOMA, locality (L-6)
Indian for "over there", "far away." (1910)

KERENSKY, locality (I-6)
After Alexander Kerensky (1881-1971). Immediately following the abdication of Tsar Nicholas II he was President of Russia from July to November, 1917 when his administration was ousted by the Bolsheviks under Lenin. (1920)

KERR, mount (8,400 feet) (J-2)
After Private J. C. Kerr, V.C., 49th Battalion, C.E.F. of World War I, Edmonton, Alberta. (1951)

KETTLE, lake (I-5)
After the people who owned the land on which the lake is located. (1950)

KEVISVILLE, locality (K-5)
After Charles W. Kevis, first postmaster. (1910)

KEW, locality (M-5)
An oldtimer's (Quirk) cattle brand was "Q."

KICKING HORSE, pass (5,339 feet) (L-3)
On the Alberta-British Columbia Boundary. Dr. Hector, geologist and surgeon of the Palliser Expedition, was kicked by his horse and the name was given by his men. Hector (August 29, 1858) says that ". . . one of our pack horses to escape the fallen timber, plunged into the stream, luckily where it formed an eddy, but the banks were so steep that we had great difficulty in getting him out. In attempting to recatch my own horse which had strayed off while we were engaged with the one in the water, he kicked me in the chest but I had luckily got close to him before he struck out so that I did not get the full force of the blow. However it knocked me down and rendered me senseless for some time." Later he notes: "After travelling a mile along the left bank of the river from the N.W. which because of the accident the men had named the Kicking Horse River, we crossed to the opposite side . . ." Later Hector (when at the summit of Bow Pass) notes: "The altitude of this point is about 6,350 feet above the sea, being much higher than the height of land either of the Vermilion or Kicking Horse passes." This is his first reference to the name of the Pass.

KIDD, mount (9,605 feet) (L-4)
Named by Dr. D. B. Dowling, geologist, 1907, after Stuart Kidd, manager at Scott and Leeson's trading post, Morley, then at Brazeau Trading Co., Nordegg. (1904)

KILLAM, town (J-7)
After Hon. A. C. Killam (1849-1908), first Chairman of the Railway Commission of Canada. Incorporated as a village on December 29, 1906 and as a town, May 1, 1965. There were five streets: Stanley, Minto, Dufferin, Monck, Aberdeen and three avenues: Lansdowne, Lorne, Lisgar, in honour of the first eight Governors General of Canada, 1867-1904. (1906)

KILLARNEY, lake (K-8)
Probably after the town of the famous lakes, Kerry, Ireland.

KILLARNEY LAKE, locality (K-8)
See Killarney, lake

KILPATRICK, creek (A-6)
After Lieutenant Vernon Francis Kilpatrick, M.I.D., Calgary, killed in World War II. (1950)

KILSYTH, locality and creek (H-5)
Probably after Kilsyth, Stirlingshire, Scotland. (1914)

KIMBALL, locality (O-6)
After one Heber C. Kimball, whose grandsons were early settlers; prior to 1903 it was named Colles.

KIMIWAN, lake (F-3)
Cree for "rain".

KING ALBERT, mount (9,800 feet) (M-4)
After King Albert of Belgium (1875-1934). King Albert was a hero in the eyes of his people in World War I. He died while mountain climbing in 1934. (1918)

KING EDWARD, mount (11,400 feet) (K-3)
After King Edward VII (1841-1910); succeeded to the throne, 1901. (1907)

KINGMAN, hamlet (J-6)
After F. W. Kingsbury, former postmaster. In 1897 a post office was asked for by Norwegian settlers of the area and called "Northern". It served a large area and was at Jenning's farm. Other post offices opened up as settlers came in and one seven miles south of Northern had Mr. F. Kingsbury as postmaster. It was intended to call the settlement "Kingsbury" but there was already a town by that name and so Kingman seemed a fair compromise. (1907)

KINIKINIK, locality, lake (H-6)
An Indian name for the Common Bearberry (*Arctostaphylos uva-ursi*). The Indians used the berries of this tough little trailing shrub to make a kind of pemmican and the dried leaves to smoke in their pipes. (*Wild Flowers of Alberta*—R. G. H. Cormack, 1967). (1917)

KININVIE, station. (M-7)
After Kininvie House, Banffshire, Scotland. (1884)

KINNAIRD, lake (H-7)
After D. G. Kinnaird, homesteader. (1921)

KINROSS, mount (8,400 feet) (J-2)
After Private C. J. Kinross, V.C. 49th Battalion, C.E.F., World War I, Calgary, Alberta. Died 1957. (1951)

KINSELLA, hamlet (J-7)
After the former private secretary to the vice-president, Grand Trunk Pacific Railway. (1910)

KINUSO, village (G-4)
Cree for "fish"; formerly Swan River. (1915)

KIPP, locality (N-6)
Named after Fort Kipp, located in the river bottom at the junction of the Oldman and Belly Rivers. It was built by Joseph Kipp (1847-1913), who came to Canada to sell whisky to the Indians in exchange for buffalo robes. The post was not fortified.

KIRBY, lake   (G-7)
After Flight Sergeant Erlyn E. Kirby of Waskatenau, Alberta. (1963)

KIRKCALDY, locality   (M-6)
After Kirkcaldy, Scotland. (1911)

KIRKPATRICK, locality   (L-6)
After Major W. M. Kirkpatrick, former foreign traffic manager of the Canadian Pacific Railway. (1921)

KIRON, locality   (J-6)
There is a place of this name in Iowa. Two early residents of the Iowa town were impressed by the name Kirin in Manchuria and so named their town by adaptation. (1916)

KIRRIEMUIR, locality   (K-8)
After Kirriemuir, Forfarshire, Scotland. (1914)

KISKIU, creek   (H-2)
Indian name for "bob-tail" describing the flats where the creek enters the Little Smoky River. (1947)

KITCHENER, mount (11,500 feet)   (K-3)
After Horatio Herbert, 1st Earl Kitchener of Khartoum and of Broome, (1850-1916). He obtained his title from his reconquest of the Sudan in 1897. He was Secretary of State for War, 1914-1916. Kitchener lost his life while on a secret mission to Russia when the cruiser on which he was travelling struck a mine. (1916)

KITSCOTY, village   (I-8)
After Kitscoty, Kent, England; the name is said to mean "The Tomb in the Woods", (Celtic). "Our village would seem to have been given its name by one of the contractors who built the railroad. One was Scotch, one was English (George Still). They took turns at naming the places. It would seem that the Englishman named Kitscoty." (Marguerite E. Sheppard, Secretary, Village of Kitscoty, letter, August, 1970).

"North of Aylesford in Kent, about a mile and a half, stands a famous cromlech known as Kit's Coty House. This relic of an unknown past, set on a close-cut green in the midst of a cornfield, consists of four great, irregular slabs of stone, three upright and the fourth and largest balanced above them, the total weight of the four being estimated at about thirty tons. How they were erected by primitive man must puzzle everyone who sees them." (*Highways and Byways of Kent*). (1905)

KLESKUN, creek and **KLESKUN HILL**, locality   (G-3)
Beaver Indian for "white mud". The hill is visible for a long distance.

KNAPPEN, locality   (O-7)
After the Knappen family, early residents. Mr. Herb Knappen was printer and newspaper man from Minnesota and then farmed in the area. (*Milk River Country*, A. A. Campbell, 1959). (1913)

Captain John Palliser (1817-1907) and Dr. James Hector (1834-1907). They recorded many existing names and bestowed names upon many features.

Edith Cavell (1865-1915), with her friends Don and Jack, in Brussels, 1914.

Charles Ora Card (1839-1906), after whom the Town of Cardston was named. (Alberta Provincial Library)

Count A. E. W. Gleichen (b. 1863). The Town of Gleichen was named after him. (Alberta Provincial Library)

*Bishop Emile Grouard (1840-1931). He travelled exten-
sively in northern Alberta.*

(Provincial Archives of Alberta—Oblate Archives)

Father Albert Lacombe (1827-1916)
(Provincial Archives of Alberta — Ernest Brown Collection)

Raymond Knight after whom the Town of Raymond was named.

KNIGHTSBRIDGE 7972.

28, HYDE PARK GATE,

LONDON, S.W.7.

3l May, 1958

My dear Premier,

      I am indeed obliged to you for
sending me such a remarkable photograph of the
range of mountains named after me, on behalf
of the people and the Government of Alberta.
It is a source of great pleasure to me that
my name should so have been honoured in your
famous Province.

      With good wishes,

        I remain,

          Yours very sincerely,

            Winston Churchill

The Honourable Ernest C. Manning, M.L.A.,
Premier of the Province of Alberta.

Letter from Sir Winston Churchill acknowledging the naming of the Winston Churchill Range.

                      (Alberta Provincial Library)

The Winston Churchill Range.

(Alberta Government Photograph)

Armand Trochu (1857-1930), one of the founders of the Town of Trochu.

(Glenbow-Alberta Institute)

Carl Stettler (1861-1919), who hailed from Switzerland and founded the Town of Stettler.

(Alberta Provincial Library)

KNEE, hills (L-6)
So named because of their shape. In Cree *mi-chig-wun*; in Stoney, *che-swun-de-ba-ha*, (Tyrrell).

KNEE HILL VALLEY, locality (K-6)
See Knee, hills. (1894)

KNEEHILL, locality and municipality district (L-6)
See Knee, hills.

KNEEHILLS, creek (L-6)
See Knee, hills.

KNIGHT, mount (9,535 feet) (J-2)
After one Richard H. Knight, superintendent of Jasper Park until his death in 1931. (1954)

KNIGHTS, creek (B-6)
After Flight Lieutenant J. K. Knights, D.F.C., Calgary, killed in World War II. (1950)

KNOB HILL, locality (J-5)
From the many knobs and hills in the vicinity. (1914)

KOOTENAY, plains (K-3)
Hector says: "This plain, which is 7 or 8 miles long, and 2 to 3 wide, is called the Kootanie Plain, as at the time that the Kootanie Indians exchanged their furs with the traders of the Saskatchewan forts, before there was any communication with them from the Pacific coast, an annual mart was held at this place, to which the Kootanie Indians crossed the mountains, while the traders came from the Mountain House." (1858)

KRAKOW, locality (I-6)
Named by Austrian settlers after a city in what is now Poland and formerly part of the Austro-Hungarian Empire.

KSITUAN, river, lake, locality (F-2)
Indian name meaning "swift current."

— L —

LA BICHE, river (G-6)
See Biche, Lac la, lake.

LAC LA BICHE, town (H-7)
See Biche, Lac la, lake.

LAC LA NONNE (I-5)
See Nonne, Lac la, lake.

LACOMBE, town and county (K-5)
After Father Albert Lacombe (1827-1916), Roman Catholic missionary of the Oblate Order, who came to Alberta in 1852 and spent the greater part of his life here in evangelical work among the Indians and Metis, dying at Midnapore. In 1874 his standard *Dictionnaire de*

la langue des Cris, was published at Montreal, a work begun during his first winter 1852-1853 at Edmonton. During the Riel Rebellion of 1885 he kept the Blackfoot Indians neutral. A centennial history of Lacombe quotes: "Railroad officials decided this locality had promise of being a community centre so a spur siding was built and a box car placed in position as a station. Catalogued as Siding No. 12 it was quickly renamed Barnett Siding by local residents, in tribute to Ed Barnett, who nine years previously had pioneered the site." However, Father Lacombe's name had precedence and it was chosen for the community.

LA COULOTTE, peak and ridge   (O-5)
After a place on the outskirts of Lens, France. (1917)

LA CRÈCHE, mount (7,641 feet)   (H-1)
A mountain goat cradle or nursery. (1925)

LACROIX, lake   (H-7)
French translation of Cree Indian name, *ayamihewattik sakahegan* or "Cross lake"; referring to a cross erected by the Indians near the lake.

LAFOND, locality   (I-7)
After C. B. Lafond, first postmaster. (1907)

LAFORCE, creek   (H-2)
Beaverdam creek; after Private Alphonse Joseph Laforce, M.M., Legal, killed in World War II. (1951)

LAGRACE, mount (9,406 feet)   (J-3)
After an Indian hunter, who accompanied Lord Southesk in 1859 (see Southesk, mountain). Southesk speaks of him: "Then Lagrace, that original and amusing old man in a purple cotton shirt, tight but very long and wrinkled trousers, a white blanket skull-cap enriched with peak and ears, and decorated with streamers of scarlet cloth, beneath a battered eagle-feather which probably once adorned some Indian horse's tail—that keen-witted ancient traveller who did everything differently from other men—led when they drove, woke when they slept, drank cans of strong tea at dead of night, walked out alone and slew queer animals with sticks and stones while all the rest were at their meals—that quaint old jester who enlivened our halts, after the weariest marches on the dullest days, by all manner of strange devices—scalp-dances round the kettle lid, Cree war-songs, sudden wrestling matches with Antoine (in which this old aggressor always got the worst), jokes in the most astonishingly broken English —to whom or what shall be he likened, with his brown parchment skin, his keen aquiline nose, his piercing black eyes, long wild locks, and half-mockingly smiling, small and thin-lipped mouth? I know not unless Mephistopheles have an American twin-brother." (*Saskatchewan and the Rocky Mountains,* 1875). (1925)

LAKE ISLE, locality   (I-5)
Changed from Shearwater. (1915) See Isle, lake.

LAKE LOUISE, hamlet (L-4)
Formerly known as Holt City (1883); then Laggan (1883-1914), which was named by Lord Strathcona after Laggan, Inverness, Scotland. Laggan was changed to Lake Louise, 1916, after H. R. H. Princess Louise (1848-1939). See Louise, lake.

LAKE MAJEAU, locality (I-5)
After one Majeau of Lac la Nonne, the first white settler in the district.

LAKE SASKATOON, locality (G-2)
Beaverlodge until 1912; after the saskatoon berry.

LAKEVIEW, ridge (O-5)
A name descriptive of its commanding view of Waterton Lakes. (1917)

LAMBE, mount (10,438 feet) (K-3)
After Lawrence M. Lambe; graduate of the Royal Military College, 1883; vertebrate paleontologist to the Geological Survey of Canada. (1920)

LAMERTON, locality (K-6)
After Lamerton, Devonshire. England. The name originated in Saxon times as *Lamburnan* in which form it is recorded ca. 970; *tun* (habitation) on Lumburn Water. In 1242 the present form is recorded, (Ekwall). (1914)

LAMONT, town, creek, island (I-6)
After the Hon. Mr. Justice Lamont, formerly of the Supreme Court of Canada. The island in Astotin Lake and the creek take their names from the town. (1906)

LAMOUREUX, hamlet (I-6)
After two brothers Joseph and François (Frank) Lamoureux who hailed from near Montreal. After extensive wanderings in the western United States and Canada they arrived in the area in 1872. (1896)

LANDELS, river (F-8)
After one A. F. Landels, Calgary.

LANDONVILLE, locality (I-8)
After J. H. Landon, first postmaster. (1908)

LANE, lake (H-7)
After Brigadier John Lane, D.S.O., Edmonton, killed in World War II. (1951)

LANFINE, locality (L-8)
After Lanfine House, Ayrshire, Scotland, near former home of William Davidson, first postmaster. (1912)

LANGDON, hamlet (M-6)
After Langdon of Langdon and Shepard, sub-contractors who built part of the Canadian Pacific Railway in the vicinity of Langdon and Shepard stations.

LAPENSÉE, mount (10,190 feet)   (J-3)
    After Olivier Roy Lapensée, member of 1814 party, who crossed the
    Athabasca Pass from Astoria; drowned May 25, 1814, in the Athabasca
    River, below Brûlé Lake. (1921)

LARKSPUR, locality   (H-6)
    Named as wild larkspur grew plentifully in the surrounding district.

LARMOUR, locality   (N-8)
    After one R. E. Larmour sometime general freight agent, Canadian
    Pacific Railway. (1909)

LAST, hill   (K-5)
    Medicine River; Last Hill on Palliser map, 1859; descriptive.

LASTHILL, creek   (K-5)
    See Last, hill.

LATHOM, locality   (M-7)
    After Edward George Bootle Wilbraham, Earl of Lathom (1864-1910);
    director of the Oxley Ranch Company; he travelled over the Canadian
    Pacific Railway with other directors in 1883. (1884)

LATORNELL, river   (H-2)
    After Lieutenant-Colonel A. J. Latornell, Edmonton city engineer and
    D.L.S., killed in World War I.

LAURIE, mount (7,200 feet)   (L-5)
    After John Laurie who founded the Indian Association of Alberta and
    did much for the Indians of the Province. In 1948 John Laurie was
    made Chief White Cloud of the Stoneys. In 1949 the Sarcees gave him
    the name of Sitting Eagle. In 1951 the Blood tribe made him honourary
    Chief Red Crow. He was awarded an honourary doctorate by the Univer-
    sity of Alberta and completed a Stoney dictionary before he died.
    He is buried in the Indian cemetery at Morley, Alberta. (1961)

LAUT, mount (7.900 feet)   (I-2)
    After Wing Commander A. Laut, M.I.D., Crossfield, killed in 1943.
    (1949)

LAVESTA, locality   (J-5)
    After Vesta McGee, daughter of the first postmaster. (1911)

LAVOY, village   (I-7)
    After Joseph Lavoy, early settler. Dinwoodie Post Office until 1906.
    (1905)

LAWRENCE, river   (C-4)
    After a pioneer in the Fort Vermilion district. This was Sheridan
    Lawrence (1870-1952), known as the "Emperor of the Peace." A native
    of the Eastern Townships. Quebec. he came to Fort Vermilion in 1886
    where he homesteaded. He engaged in farming and trading. He resided
    at Fort Vermilion for over fifty years, retiring to Peace River where he
    died in 1952.

LAWSON, mount (9.210 feet) and lake   (M-4)
    Kananaskis River; after Major W. E. Lawson, topographer with Geo-
    logical Survey, killed in France. (1922)

LAWSONBURG, locality (L-7)
After Mrs. L. L. Lawson, former postmistress. (1909)

LEAH, peak (9,191 feet) (J-3)
Named by Mrs. M. Schäffer, author of *Old Indian Trails*, 1911, after the wife of a Stoney Indian, Samson Beaver (see Samson, peak). (1911)

LEASOWE, locality (J-6)
Originally Middleton; name Leasowe suggested by one Christie after Leasowe, Chester, England, (1914)

LEATHER, peak (7,500 feet) (J-2)
It commemorates a former name for the Yellowhead Pass. The name refers to the dressed moose or caribou skins for the trading posts in the New Caledonia Department (now British Columbia). These were obtained in the Saskatchewan Department (part of which is now Alberta) and were used for moccasins, bags and ropes. See also Tête, Roche, mountain and Yellowhead, mountain and pass.

LEAVITT, hamlet (O-6)
After William Leavitt, first postmaster. (1900)

LEBEAUS, lake (H-6)
After Mr. Lebeau who homesteaded there and was formerly Reeve of the municipality of Pibrock. (1952)

LECTERN, peak (9,095 feet) (J-2)
It resembles a church lectern. (1917)

LEDUC, town and county (J-6)
After Reverend Hippolyte Leduc, O.M.I. (1842-1918), who served the Edmonton area from St. Albert. The name was first used to identify the telegraph station established at this point in 1876 when it was the western terminal of the telegraph line from Fort Garry, the famous Dominion Telegraph. Leduc was incorporated as a village in 1899 and a town on December 15, 1906. It gained fame in 1947 as an oil centre when Imperial Leduc No. 1 came into production setting off the Alberta oil boom.
Father Leduc was born in Evron, France and was ordained priest in the Oblate Order in 1864. In 1865 he went to Pembina and two years later was at St. Albert and Edmonton. He also served at Calgary and Lac Brochet. He died in Edmonton in 1918.

LEE, creek (O-6)
After W. S. Lee, early settler; Lariat Cross or Lee Creek on the Department of the Interior map, 1883. In Blackfoot, *sakemapeneu* "rope across", the Indians used to stretch a rope across, in high water, to ford the creek, (Steele).

LEEDALE, locality (K-5)
For William H. Lee, former postmaster, 1922-25; Wittenburg Post Office until 1917.

LEFROY, mount (11,220 feet) and glacier (L-4)
Named by Hector in 1858, after Major-General Sir John Henry Lefroy (1817-90). He observed the magnetic declination at a number of points

in Canada, at Cape of Good Hope and St. Helena. With the exception of a short interval, he was head of the Toronto Observatory from 1842 to 1853.

LEGAL, village (I-6)
Founded as a French Canadian settlement in 1898, it is named after Monsignor Emile Joseph Legal (1849-1920), first Roman Catholic Bishop of Edmonton. He first came to Alberta in 1881 and spent many years in missionary work in what is now the Province, being consecrated in 1912. He was the author of *Short Sketches of the History of the Catholic Churches and Missions in Central Alberta*. It is said that the patron saint of the new mission was St. Emile (after Bishop Legal's first name).

LEGEND, lake (N-7)
A Chipewyan Indian legend states that there is, or was, in the lake, a great fish, which sometimes swallowed canoes.

LE GOFF, locality (H-8)
After Father Le Goff, stationed here at the time of the North-West Rebellion, 1885. (1913)

LEIGHMORE, locality (G-1)
An error for Teighmore, Channel Islands, former home of one time postmaster, G. J. Beadle. (1922)

LEIGHTON, locality (I-8)
The name was suggested by J. V. Armstrong, an early settler, after a place of the same name in England. The name originally means the *tun* (habitation) of "Leigh", (Ekwall). (1911)

LEMAN, mount (8,956 feet) and lake (M-4)
After General G. Leman, defender of Liége, Belgium, during First World War. (1918)

LENARTHUR, locality (E-7)
A compound of the names of Dr. J. K. McLennan and J. D. McArthur, vice-president and president respectively of the Alberta and Great Waterways Railway now Northern Alberta Railways. (1917)

LENZIE, locality (N-6)
After a part of Kirkintilloch, Scotland. (1916)

LEO, locality (K-6)
After a grandson of O. L. Longshore, first postmaster, who came from Oklahoma in 1906. (1908)

LESLIEVILLE, hamlet (K-5)
After Leslie Rielly, whose family settled the area in 1903. (1906)

LESSARD, locality (H-8)
After Prosper Edmond Lessard (1873-1931). He was elected in 1909 to the Alberta Legislature and was Minister Without Portfolio from 1909-1910. He was re-elected in 1913 and 1917 but defeated in 1921. In 1925 he was called to the Senate. (1921)

LESSER SLAVE, lake   (G-4)-(G-5)
Sir Alexander Mackenzie heard of this lake in 1792 from Indian
hunters, who told him that the Cree name meant Slave Lake, after the
original Indian inhabitants. The term "Lesser" distinguishes it from
Great Slave Lake, Northwest Territories.

LESSER SLAVE LAKE, provincial park   (G-5)
See Lesser Slave, lake.

LETHBRIDGE, city and county   (N-6)
After William Lethbridge (1824-1901); first president of North West
Coal and Navigation Company, Limited; prior to 1885 called Coal Banks;
in Blackfoot, *achsaysim* or "steep banks." Mr. Lethbridge was a partner
in W. H. Smith and Son, booksellers, London, England. According to
J. D. Higinbotham's book *When the West Was Young* (1933), the area
was known to the Blackfeet as *si-ko-ko-to-ki, meaning* "the place of
the black rocks", the word refering to the coal outcroppings along
the river. Coal was sometimes used by them as fuel. It was also known
as "Medicine Stone" from a large granite boulder opposite the old Galt
Hospital on which the Bloods placed offerings. Later the whites called
it Coalbanks. It was called Coalhurst by the postal authorities even after
the residents started calling it Lethbridge as there was already a Lethbridge in Ontario. The name was officially changed to its present one
on October 14, 1885.

LEVAL, mount (8,900 feet) and creek   (M-4)
After Gaston de Leval, the Belgian lawyer who defended Edith Cavell.
(1918) See also Edith Cavell, mountain.

LEVERING, lake   (J-6)
After Bishop J. Mortimer Levering of the Moravian Church, who paid an
official visit to the district in 1904.

L'HIRONDELLE, hamlet   (F-4)
Named after a pioneer farmer and trader in the district.

LICK, peak (9,440 feet) and creek   (J-2)
From a salt deposit or "lick" near the creek, to which wild animals
resort to obtain salt. (1921)

LIÉGE, river   (E-5)
After the City of Liége, Belgium. (1914)

LILLIPUT, mountain (8,200 feet)   (L-4)
Rock pillars on it resemble a crowd of little people. (1918)

LIMON, lake   (C-7)
Limon is French for "mud", which was the former name of the lake.
(1918)

LINARIA, locality   (H-5)
After the flaxseed or linaria. (1918)

LINDALE, locality   (J-5)
After C. Lindell, first postmaster. (1914)

LINDBERGH, hamlet (I-8)
After Charles Lindbergh (1902-), American flyer, who in 1927 was the first to fly solo from west to east across the Atlantic Ocean. For this he won the Raymond Orteig prize. Sir Henry Thornton, president of the Canadian National Railway named the station for him in 1927.

LINDEN, village (L-6)
Named after Linden school established in 1904 northeast of the present site of the village. It is not certain how the name Linden was chosen.

LINDGREN, lake (A-7)
Named for Waldemar Lindgren (1860-1939), American geologist, who was noted for his petrological and mineralogical work on ore deposits. (1958)

LINDSAY, mount (9,000 feet) (J-3)
Named by the Earl of Southesk, 1859, after his friend Sir Coutts Lindsay, of Balcarres, Fifeshire, Scotland. See also Southesk, mount.

LINEHAM, creek and mount (8,000 feet) (M-5)
After John Lineham, a rancher. A native of Perth, Ontario he came west in 1878. He was first returned to the Legislative Assembly of the North-West Territories in 1888.

LION, LIONESS, peaks (K-3)
Probably descriptive, Northeast of Mount Cline (q.v.) (1959)

LIPSETT, mount (8,400 feet) (M-5)
After Major-General L. J. Lipsett, C.M.G., Canadian Expeditionary Force. (1918)

LISBURN, locality (I-5)
Known as Merebeck Post Office until 1916; presumably after Lisburn, Antrim, Ireland.

LISTENING, mountain (10,300 feet) (K-2)
From its resemblance to an ear. (1921)

LITTLE, mount (10,293 feet) (L-4)
Bow Range; after George F. Little, Bowdoin College, Brunswick, Maine, a member of the party who made the first ascent.

LITTLE BOW, river (M-6)-(N-6)
In Blackfoot, na-muhtai (Dawson); name is Blackfoot for "bow."

LITTLE PLUME, creek (N-8)
After a chief of the South Peigan Indians and a friend of the white man.

LITTLE RED DEER, river (K-5)-(L-5)
It appears as "Little Red or La Biche" on Arrowsmith map of 1859. It is known in Blackfoot as asino-ka-sis-ughty (Nelson); was-ke-sis-si-pi-sis in Cree and pachidi waptan in Stoney (Tyrrell).

LITTLE ROCK ISLAND, lake (I-8)
Named by Metis because of numerous small rocks found on the island in the lake. (1950)

LITTLE ROLLING, hills   (M-7)
   Translation of Blackfoot name, *pekisko* or hilly country (Steele).
   Descriptive.

LITTLE SMOKY, river, hamlet   (I-2)-(H-3)
   The Smoky Rivers in northwestern Canada usually derive their name
   from coal beds, which have become ignited and sometimes burn for
   many years. The hamlet takes its name from the river.

LIVINGSTONE, range, mount (10,310 feet) and river   (N-5)
   The range was named by Captain Blakiston of the Palliser Expedition in
   1858; name spelled by him without the final "e". After David Livingstone (1813-1873), noted explorer and missionary in Africa.

LIVOCK, river   (F-6)
   After Chief Factor W. T. Livock, Hudson's Bay Company, in charge
   of all transport down the Athabasca River from 1890 to 1911.

LLOYD, creek   (J-5)
   After Flight Lieutenant Lloyd George Anderson of Craigmyle, killed
   in World War II. (1950)

LLOYDMINSTER, city   (I-8)
   The Border City, so called because it is astride the Alberta-Saskatchewan
   border, takes its name from the Reverend (later Right Reverend) George
   Exton Lloyd (1865-1940). Lloyd was chaplain to the All British Colony,
   familiarly known as the Barr Colony after its first leader, the Reverend
   I. M. Barr (1849-1937), who withdrew from active leadership of the
   enterprise. The colony consisted of some 2,000 souls from the British Isles
   who settled on a large tract of land reserved for them, largely through
   Barr's negotiations. Dissatisfaction with Barr's leadership ultimately led
   to his relinquishing control of the affairs of the colony and Lloyd
   succeeded him.
       A settlement had grown up on the Fourth Initial Meridian (110°
   west longitude) and of the naming of it Lloyd: "declared that by a
   unanimous vote it was decided to name the area forming the British
   Colony, Britannia Colony and the first town was to be named Lloydminster by which name it has ever since been known. The address had
   been sent to the postal authorities who had approved it." In his letters to
   his employers the Colonial and Continental Church Missionary Society
   from Britannia, N.W.T., Lloyd is almost modest: "the name of the first
   town was decided to be Lloydminster but as this sounds somewhat
   personal I am not saying much about it."
       Being astride the border brought some problems for Lloydminster.
   At first it was in two halves each half controlled by the appropriate
   municipal legislation of the province concerned. Ultimately a charter
   was worked out based on Saskatchewan municipal legislation and
   confirmed by complimentary orders in council of both provinces.
       George E. Lloyd ultimately became Bishop of Saskatchewan. He
   died in Victoria in 1940.
       The name Lloydminster means literally "Lloyd's monastery." Min-
   ster was the old English word for monastery. Thus Westminster means

"western monastery." (Most of the foregoing information is from *Issac M. Barr and the Britannia Colony,* unpublished Master's Thesis of the writer, 1964, p. 129).

LLYSYFRAN, peak (10,304 feet)   (K-3)
Named by Mrs. M. Shäffer, author of *Old Indian Trails,* 1911, after a "family name" of her companion, Miss Mary Vaux. See Mary Vaux, mount.

LOAF, mountain (8,658 feet)   (O-5)
Castle River; probably descriptive. (1915)

LOBSTICK, river, locality   (I-4)
Lobstick Creek on Palliser map, 1865; after a tall lobstick on its bank which marked the point at which the trail strikes the creek; in Cree *mistikipikwam-akesot* (Steele). A lobstick is a jack pine or lodgepole pine with the lower branches cut off, causing the upper ones to bush out and give a distinctive appearance. This was a common landmark in fur trade days.

LOCHINVAR, locality   (K-6)
It may have been named after Lochinvar, Kirkcudbrightshire, Scotland, or possibly after the hero of Scott's well known poem. (1917)

LOCKHART, locality   (K-5)
After James Lockhart, first postmaster. (1959)

LODGEPOLE, hamlet   (J-4)
Southwest of Drayton Valley in the Pembina oil field. So named because of a few lodgepole pines near the site. (1955)

LOGAN, river   (G-7)
After Major R. W. Logan, D.L.S.; served with Royal Air Force in the First World War.

LOMOND, village   (M-6)
"According to the old timers in the village of Lomond, the origin of the name of our village came from Lomond Dugal McCarthy, who homesteaded on the town-site." (Mrs. Marion Root, Secretary, Village of Lomond, August, 1970.)

LONE, mountain (7,950 feet) and brook   (O-5)
Blakiston brook; descriptive.

LONGVIEW, village   (M-5)
"Longview was originally located 8 miles east of the present location, which consisted of a post office and a store, which was owned by a Mr. Long. Because of development he moved his store to the present location of Longview and the name came with him, not only because of the store but also there is a long view from the village." (E. Malmberg, Secretary-Treasurer, Village of Longview, September, 1970)

LONIRA, locality   (I-4)
Name given by one Mr. Bowan, postmaster, from London and Iroquois, Ontario, home of himself and his wife respectively. (1921)

LOOKOUT, butte   (N-6)
In Blackfoot, *ickkemochsoking* or "salt" butte, (Steele).

LOOMIS, mount (9,100 feet) and creek (M-5)
In honour of Sir F. O. W. Loomis (1870-1937). In 1914 he went overseas commanding the 13th Battalion, C.E.F. In 1916 he was promoted Brigadier-General and became Commander of the 3rd Canadian Division. He was made Major-General in 1918 and retired in 1919. He received the D.S.O., 1916 and bar, 1918; C.M.G., 1917 and K.C.B., 1919. (1918)

LOOP, ridge (N-5)
After a "loop" in the railway track in the Crowsnest Pass.

LORETTE, mountain (8,100 feet) and creek (M-4)
After Lorette Ridge, France. (1922)

LOUGHEED, mount (10,190 feet) and village (M-4) (J-7)
Both mountain and village are named after the Honourable Sir James Lougheed (1854-1925). A native of Ontario he studied law and was called to the Ontario bar and to the bar of the North-West Territories in 1877. In 1885 he was Queen's Counsel for the North-West Territories. He practised law in Toronto and Calgary and in the latter city was counsel for the Canadian Pacific Railway. He was a director of the Canada Life Assurance Company and from 1914-1918 was chairman of the Military Hospitals Commission. Lougheed had been called to the Senate in 1889 and was Conservative leader there from 1906-1921. He was made a Privy Councillor in 1911 and for seven years was Minister Without Portfolio. From 1918-1920 he was Minister of Soldiers' Civil Establishment, Minister of the Interior and Superintendent General of Indian Affairs. He was Minister of Mines from 1920-1921. In 1916 he was created K.C.M.G.

His grandson, Honourable Peter Lougheed became Premier of Alberta as a result of the Alberta Provincial Election of August 30, 1971.

Mount Lougheed was named Wind Mountain by Bourgeau (see Bourgeau, mount) in 1858, as it was a high peak on which the clouds were gathering and curling about; it received its present name in 1928.

LOUIS, mount (8,800 feet) (L-4)
After Louis B. Stewart (1861-1937), D.L.S., D.T.S., Professor of Surveying and Geodesy, University of Toronto. He surveyed the Banff National Park with his father George A. Stewart, C.E. (1904) See also Stewart, mount.

LOUIS BULL, Indian Reserve (J-6)
After an Indian chief of this name; originally part of Ermineskin Reserve.

LOUISE, lake and creek (L-4)
The "Gem of the Rockies" is named for Her Royal Highness Princess Louise Caroline Alberta (1848-1939), fourth daughter of Queen Victoria and wife of the Marquis of Lorne, later Duke of Argyll, who was Governor General of Canada from 1878-1883.

The lake was discovered in 1882 by Tom Wilson, who first called it Emerald Lake, but in 1884 it received its present name. The story is that Wilson, who was camped near Laggan (the former name for Lake Louise station) heard the sound of an avalanche. Some Indians told him that this was the thunder from the big snow mountain above the

Lake of Little Fishes, as they called it. Wilson was determined to explore and the following day accompanied by one of the Indians visited the lake. The wonder of the scene made him breathless.

LOUSANA, hamlet   (K-6)
W. G. (Judge) Biggs a settler from the State of Louisiana, U.S.A., and owner of land in the vicinity, suggested the name, but the Post Office Department dropped the second "i" to avoid confusion. (1912)

LOVETT, river
See Lovettville, locality.

LOVETTVILLE, locality   (J-3)
After A. H. Lovett, K.C., Montreal, president of the North American Collieries. Fergie was the name of the post office until 1915, after a well known mining engineer.

LOW, mount (10,075 feet)   (K-3)
After Albert Peter Low, Director of Geological Survey and Deputy Minister of Mines (1906-1907). He commanded an expedition in the *Neptune* to the northwestern portion of Hudson Bay and to Ellsmere Island, 1903-1904. (1920)

LOWER ROWE, lake   (O-5)
After Lieutenant Rowe, R.E., surveyor, British Boundary Commission, 1872-76. (1960)

LOYALIST, locality, creek   (K-8)
Consort, Loyalist, Veteran, Throne, Coronation were adjacent Canadian Pacific Railway stations named in Coronation year, 1911, (of King George V). Formerly known as Vallejo.

LUBICON, lake and river   (F-4)
After an Indian family, who resided in the locality in the autumn and winter. (1911)

LUCAS, island   (B-7)
After Right Reverend J. R. Lucas, (d. 1938), Bishop, 1913-1926, Anglican Diocese of Mackenzie River. (1922)

LUCERNE, peak (7,600 feet)   (J-2)
This peak on the Alberta-British Columbia boundary overlooks Lucerne, B.C., which in turn was named after Lucerne, lake and canton, Switzerland. (1918)

LUCKY STRIKE, locality   (O-7)
When the former post office opened, those who obtained land in the vicinity were considered to be fortunate; named by a Mr. Jochem. (1910)

LUNDBRECK, hamlet, falls   (N-5)
Compound of Lund and Breckenridge after Breckenridge and Lund Coal Company which operated collieries and sawmills here. (1904, 1964)

LUNDINE, creek   (J-4)
After a trapper of this name who was a permanent resident of the area.

LUNETTE, peak (11,150 feet)   (M-4)
South of Mount Assiniboine; a descriptive name.

LUNNFORD, peak (11,150 feet)   (M-4)
After E. L. Lunn, first postmaster. (1910)

LUSCAR, locality, mountain (8,500 feet) and creek   (J-3)
After Luscar Colliery, which was named after Luscar, Fifeshire, Scotland. (1922)

LUZAN, locality   (I-6)
The name was suggested by Simon Iconiuk, former postmaster, after Luzan, Romania. (1913)

LYALL, mount (9,680 feet)   (L-4)
After Dr. David Lyall, R.N., surgeon and naturalist, British Boundary Commission, Pacific to the Rockies, 1858-62. Lyall was surgeon with Belcher on the Arctic expedition from 1852-1854. He was appointed to H.M.S. *Plumper*, well known as a survey ship on the Pacific coast. In 1861 he was appointed Inspector of General Hospitals and Fleets. He retired in 1873.

Lyall owed his appointment to the Boundary Commission to the good offices of Sir William Hooker, Director of the Royal Botanic Gardens at Kew. He collected and sent some 1,375 species of plants to England. Some new plants he discovered he named for himself and members of the Commission. (1917)

LYALTA, locality   (L-6)
Compound of Lyall and Alberta; suggested by A. Harry Parsons of Lyall Trading Company; formerly Lyall. (1914)

LYAUTEY, mount (9,900 feet) and glacier   (M-5)
After General Herbert Lyautey, Minister of War, France, 1916. (1918)

LYCHNIS, mountain (9,250 feet)   (L-4)
After the wild flower commonly known as alpine campion. (1911)

LYELL, mount (11,495 feet) and icefield   (K-3)
Named by Hector in 1858, after Sir Charles Lyell (1795-1875), a noted British geologist. The icefield which takes its name from the mountain was named in 1964.

LYNDON, locality and creek   (N-6)
After Charles A. Lyndon, settler, 1881.

LYNX, mountain (10,471 feet)   (I-1)
So named because a dead lynx was found on the mountain. (1911)

LYON, creek   (N-5)
After Lieutenant-Colonel H. E. Lyon, early settler; sometime postmaster, Blairmore. During the First World War, he raised an infantry battalion in the Crowsnest Pass area.

LYS, ridge   (O-5)
After River Lys, flowing through Armentières, France. (1917)

— M —

MACBETH, locality (M-7)
After Hugh Macbeth of the North West Coal and Navigation Company; purser on the *Alberta* plying between Lethbridge and Medicine Hat; died 1923. (1912-1914)

MACCARIB, mountain (9,020 feet), pass and creek (J-2)
Quinnipiac Indian for "caribou"; caribou were seen below the peak. (1916)

MACHRAY, mount (9,020 feet) (J-2)
After Most Reverend Robert Machray, D.D., (1831-1904), Archbishop of Ruperts Land, first Anglican Primate of Canada. (1923)

MAGEE, lake (K-6)
After an old settler who lived nearby.

MAGNOLIA BRIDGE, hamlet (I-5)
There are over twenty-five places of the name in the United States; after the magnolia tree, in turn, named after Pierre Magnol, Professor of Botany at Montpellier, France, in the seventeenth century.

Some of the settlers who had lived near Magnolia Bluffs, Washington, saw a resemblance in the two places and named the new settlement, Magnolia. (1908)

MAGRATH, town (O-6)
After Charles A. Magrath (1860-1949). A native of Ontario, Magrath became a surveyor and from 1878-1885 was Dominion Topographical Surveyor in the North-West Territories. From 1885-1906 he was manager of the Canadian North West Irrigation Company. In 1891, he became the first Mayor of Lethbridge and that same year was elected to the North-West Territories Assembly, and was again elected in 1894. From 1908-1911, he was Member of Parliament for Medicine Hat. He served on the International Joint Commission from 1911-1914 and was Chairman from 1914-1936. He was also a member of the Royal Commission on Newfoundland in 1933. (1900).

MAHASKA, locality (I-4)
After a county in Iowa, in turn, after an Indian Chief, of the early nineteenth century. (1913)

MAHOOD, mount (9,500 feet) (J-2)
After a Canadian Pacific Railway engineer. (1924)

MAJEAU, lake (I-5)
After one Majeau of Lac la Nonne, the first white settler in the district.

MAJESTIC, mountain (10,128 feet) (K-2) and locality (L-8)
An imposing peak; locality (1916, 1914)—descriptive.

MAKAOO, Indian Reserve (I-8)
After an Indian chief of the name. (1879)

MAKEPEACE, locality (M-6)
After William Makepeace Thackeray (1811-1863), the novelist. (1913)

MAKWA, ridge and creek (J-2)
Indian for "loon." (1916)

MALCOLM, creek (I-2)
After Malcolm Moberly who owned land at the mouth of the creek. (1953)

MALEB, locality (N-7)
A combination of the initials of the names of Mr. and Mrs. Bowen: Morley, Amy, Lorne, Elizabeth, Bowen; Mr. Bowen settled here in 1910. (1911)

MALIGNE, river, lake and mountain (10,475 feet) (J-2)—(J-3)
Father de Smet refers to it as the "Maline" River, (French for "bad"). The name was originally applied to the river which became so known in 1846. H. A. F. McLeod, who explored the lake in 1875 on Canadian Pacific Railways surveys, named it Sorefoot Lake. The mountain was named in 1911.

MALLAIG, hamlet (H-7)
After a town in Inverness, Scotland, associated with Bonnie Prince Charlie.

MALLARD, peak (9,300 feet) (K-2)
From a rock bearing a fancied resemblance to a mallard duck. (1921)

MALLOCH, mount (10,067 feet) and creek (K-4)
After George Malloch, Canadian geologist, who mapped the area overlooked by the peak and also climbed it. He died on Wrangel Island, Alaska in 1914. (1920)

MALMO, locality (J-6)
Named by settlers from Malmo, Nebraska, which in turn takes its name from Malmo, Sweden. (1911)

MALOY, locality (H-7)
There is a place of the name in Iowa. (1915)

MAMAWI, lake and creek (C-7)
A Cree Indian name; Father Lacombe gives the meaning of *mamawi* as "the river flows this way."

MA-ME-MO BEACH, summer village (J-5)
From the Cree (original) *mee-mee-o*. The name means place of lots of shore birds. Ma-Me-O is a corrupted form.

MANAWAN, lake (I-5)
Indian for "egg gathering place." Descriptive.

MANGIN, mount (10,030 feet) and glacier (M-4)
After General Mangin, France, who distinguished himself in "The Labyrinth", 1915, and in the Battle of Verdun, 1916. Because of his hatred of the Germans he was known as "The Butcher."

MANIR, locality (F-2)
After Madame Manir Polet, Belgian painter, and for fifteen years a resident of Alberta. (1916)

MANLY, locality (I-5)
Formerly known as Manly Corner, it is at the junction of Highways Nos. 16 and 43. In 1907 when pioneers arrived there, the corner was near the site of the Manly School, general store and post office. It is four miles from Carvel Post Office. It may have been the name of the former home in England, of some of the first families. (1956)

MANNING, town (E-3)
Named after the Honourable E. C. Manning, (1908-), Premier of Alberta, 1943-1968; appointed to the Senate of Canada, 1970. The name "Manning" was chosen as a result of objections of the postal authorities to the name Aurora because of possibility of confusion with the Ontario town of that name. The original name is perpetuated in various businesses such as Aurora hotel and theatre. The change to "Manning" was voted at a public meeting held in 1947.

MANNVILLE, village (I-7)
For Sir Donald D. Mann (1853-1934), one of the builders and vice-president of the Canadian Northern Railway; he was associated with Sir W. Mackenzie.

MANOLA, hamlet (I-5)
For the daughter of James Albert McPhee, an early settler. In 1908, residents wished to have improved mail service and ascertained that Mrs. Robert McPhee would accept the position of postmistress and they petitioned the government for establishment of the office. Mrs. McPhee was requested by the Post Office to suggest three names. California had been her former home and she chose three names from that state; Eureka, Orlando and Manola. The first two were eliminated as there were already post offices with those names, so Manola, it became. Mrs. McPhee's second daughter was given this as a Christian name. Manola is of Spanish origin.

MANX, peak (9,987 feet) (J-2)
The shape of the contours resembles the coat of arms of the Isle of Man. (1916)

MANY ISLAND, lake (M-8)
A translation of the Cree Indian name *aka-amuskieskway* or *aka-maywass*, meaning "many lizards", or "many islands."

MANYBERRIES, creek and hamlet (N-8)
A translation of the Blackfoot name, *akoniskway*, and refers to the saskatoons and chokecherries which grow in profusion in the area. An attempt was made to change the name to Polestar. (1911)

MAPLE LEAF, hill (M-5)
Sitook-spagway; Indian term meaning "middle heights." The term *sitook-spagway* is used only on topographical maps and by some geologists. It was used on Dawson's map of 1884 but in his report he calls it *sitook-sparkoy.*

MARGARET, lake (L-3)
Named by one Thompson before 1898, after a daughter of Reverend H. P. Nichols, Holy Trinity Church, New York.

MARGIE, locality (G-7)
After the wife of J. W. Judge, assistant superintendent of the Alberta Great Waterways Railway. (1916)

MARGUERITE, river (B-7)
After Marguerite, sister of F. V. Seibert, D.L.S.

MARIE, lake and creek (H-8)
A corruption of Cree name *methai(merai)*, fish.

MARIE-REINE, hamlet (F-3)
The name was derived from the name of the district and is a religious name meaning "Mary Queen of Hearts." (1955)

MARKERVILLE, hamlet (K-5)
After C. P. Marker, LL.D., Dairy Commissioner for Alberta (1905-1934). (1902)

MARLBORO, hamlet (I-3)
From marl deposits in the vicinity, used for making cement. A cement plant was erected here in 1912. (1912)

MARLBOROUGH, mount (9,700 feet) (M-4)
After a battleship engaged in the Battle of Jutland, May 31, 1916; she was launched in 1912 and scrapped in 1930. (1918)

MARMOT, creek (A-2)
Named after a family of marmots that lived opposite the campsite on the creek and gave a group of geologists many pleasing and diverting moments in observing their habits.

MARSH, creek (I-3)
Surrounded by a marsh. (1946)

MARSTON, creek (M-5)
After E. Marston, who owned a ranch on this creek at the time it was named.

MARTEN, mountain, lake and creek (G-5)
Lesser Slave Lake; after an oldtimer of this name.

MARTIN, lake (G-2)
In honour of Pilot Officer S. S. Martin, D.F.C., Calgary, killed in World War II. (1947)

MARTINEAU, river (H-8)
Flowing from Primrose Lake into Cold Lake. After A. Martineau, former Hudson's Bay Company manager at Cold Lake. (1909)

MARVEL, peak (8,900 feet), lake, creek and pass (M-4)
Descriptive of the peak. (1917)

MARWAYNE, village (I-8)
Named by Fred Marfleet, one of the earliest settlers in this district. He came to this country from Wainfleet, Lincolnshire and the name Marwayne was chosen as a combination of his name Marfleet and Wainfleet-Marwain, but it was decided that it would be spelled Marwayne, (Mrs. I. Wellman, Secretary-Treasurer, Village of Marwayne, letter August, 1970). (1906)

MARY VAUX, mount (10,502 feet) (J-3)
Named in 1911, by Mrs. M. Schäffer, and mentioned in her book *Old Indian Trails* (1911), after Miss Mary Vaux, who, like the other members of her family, had taken a great interest in the Canadian Rockies.

MASINASIN, locality (O-7)
The Cree name meaning "writing on stone," referring to pictographs cut in the sandstone cliffs in the valley of the Milk River. (1909)

MASSACRE BUTTE, hill (N-6)
Named for a massacre that occurred in 1867 when an immigrant group of twelve men, women and children were massacred by a war party of Blood Indians. The party, led by a Blood warrior Medicine Calf, struck while the group was in night camp. The only victim to be identified was a man named John Hoise. The victims were part of Captain Fiske's expedition from Minnesota and had left the main party in Montana.

MASSIVE, mountain (7,990 feet) (L-4)
Descriptive of the mountain.

MASTODON, mountain (9,800 feet) and glacier (J-2)
From the fancied resemblance of the mountain to that extinct form of elephant. (1922)

MATCHAYAN, lake (I-5)
Shown as Little Manito on Palliser map, 1865. Cree Indian name meaning "bad spirit."

MATKIN, mount (7,934 feet) (O-5)
After Sergeant Philip K. Matkin R.C.A.F., Cardston, Alberta. Killed in World War II. (1962)

MATTHEWS, lake (H-7)
After Flying Officer L. W. Matthews, D.F.M., Calgary, killed in World War II. (1952)

MATTOYEKIU, lake (M-6)
Indian name meaning "grassy lake."

MATTS, creek (K-5)
After Matthew Bradshaw, long time resident of the Rocky Mountain House district who had a cabin beside the creek and stocked the stream with beaver. (1956)

MAUDE, mount (9,980 feet), lake and brook (M-4)
After Major General Sir F. S. Maude (1864-1917), captor of Bagdad. He was military secretary to the Governor General of Canada, 1901-1904. (1918)

MAUGHAN, locality (I-7)
After A. Maughan, first postmaster. (1907)

MAUNSELL, locality (N-5)
After Edward Maunsell, early rancher, and a member of first Mounted Police Force which travelled from Fort Garry to Fort Macleod in 1874. He died on November 11, 1923.

MAURICE, lake   (G-3)
   North of Snipe Lake. After former Mayor Verner Maurice of High
   Prairie. (1949)

MAWDSLEY, mount (7,000 feet)   (I-2)
   After an Indian by the name of Mawdsley who lived in this vicinity.
   (1953)

MAY, lake   (A-2)
   After Captain Wilfred Reid (Wop) May, D.F.C., (1896-1952), of
   Edmonton; famous northern bush pilot. "Wop" was a nickname.

MAY, mount   (I-1)
   The mountain has two peaks, George peak, 8,038 feet, and Francis
   peak, 8,019 feet. After Private Francis Loren May and Lieutenant George
   Geoffrey May, Ottawa, who were killed in action, 1916-1917. (1926)

MAYBUTT, locality   (N-6)
   For May Butt, wife of Mr. Fisher, original owner of the townsite. (1912)

MAYCROFT, locality   (N-5)
   After Mrs. A. C. Raper, wife of the first postmaster. Her Christian name
   was May. (1910)

MAYERTHORPE, town   (I-4)
   After R. I. Mayer, the first postmaster. The original post office was
   located three miles west of the present site on the homestead of a settler
   of Scandinavian descent named "Mayer." It was given the name
   Mayerthorpe—"thorpe" being the Scandinavian for village (more likely
   hamlet). In 1919 L. O. Crockett was instrumental in having the land on
   which the village was to be located surveyed and the settlement was
   named "Little Paddle." The name was changed to "Mayerthorpe" when
   the Federal Government closed the original Mayerthorpe Post Office
   and opened one at the new location. (1915)

MAYTON, locality   (L-5)
   The first settlers came from May City, Iowa.

MAZEPPA, locality   (M-6)
   After the Cossack hetman, the hero of Byron's poem, *Mazeppa*. (1912)

McBEATH, mount (9,334 feet)   (J-3)
   Medicine Tent River; after a member of Lord Southesk's party, 1859,
   one Morrison McBeath. (1925)

McCONACHIE, lake   (F-6)
   After Grant William McConachie (1909-1965), Edmonton; former bush
   pilot, later associated with Canadian Pacific Airlines. (1954)

McCONNELL, mount (10,200 feet), and creek   (L-5)
   Named by Dr. G. M. Dawson in 1884, after R. G. McConnell, his
   assistant in 1882; later Deputy Minister, Department of Mines.

McCORD, mount (8,240 feet)   (J-2)
   North of Miette Pass; after William C. McCord, head of Canadian Pacific
   Railway trail-making party, 1872. (1923)

McCOWAN, lake (A-7)
After Dan McCowan (1882-1956), writer on natural history particularly about northwestern Canada. (1959)

McDONALDVILLE, locality (J-8)
After Adam McDonald, early settler. (1908)

McDONELL, peak (10,700 feet) (J-2)
A peak of Mount Fraser; after Simon Fraser's wife, daughter of Colonel Allan McDonell, of Dundas County, Ontario. (1922)

McDOUGALL, mount (8,500 feet) (M-4)
This mount was named by Dawson in 1884 for the Reverend George Millward McDougall (1820-1876), Methodist missionary to the Stoneys and his sons Reverend John McDougall (1842-1917) and David George McDougall (1845-ca. 1930). After George McDougall's death in a blizzard John McDougall carried on his work.

McGILLIVRAY, ridge (K-2)
Gabriel Franchère says that it was named McGillivray's Rock by "J. Henry." In his diary. October 10th, 1823, John Work says "after William McGillivray." William McGillivray, elder brother of Simon McGillivray and uncle of Duncan McGillivray, was one of the leading members of the North West Company. He is also commemorated by Fort William (now part of Thunder Bay). Ontario. He was a member of the House of Assembly of Lower Canada in 1808-1809 for Montreal West and of the Legislative Council of Lower Canada, 1814-1825. He died in 1825 in London, England. Franchère crossed the pass in 1814. Further research has revealed that it was probably William Henry not J. Henry who gave this name and who crossed the pass in 1812. (From *Gabriel Franchère's Narrative* edited by W. T. Lamb, 1970).

McGREGOR. lake (M-6)
After J. D. McGregor of Brandon, who initiated the irrigation scheme in which Lake McGregor is a reservoir. He was formerly managing director of the Southern Alberta Land Company.

McGUFFIN, lake (H-7)
After Squadron Leader W. C. McGuffin, D.F.C., Calgary, killed in World War II. (1951)

McHARG, mount (9,476 feet) (M-4)
After Lieutenant Colonel W. Hart McHarg. 1st B.C. Regiment; killed in action during the First World War. (1918)

McIVOR, river (C-6)—(D-6)
After one Dan McIvor, a member of a survey party, (prior to 1928).

McKAY, creek (N-8)
After Edward McKay, an Indian trader who settled on the creek in 1895

McKEAN, mount (9,000 feet) (J-2)
After Captain G. B. McKean, V.C., M.C., M.M., Edmonton, 14th Battalion. C.E.F. He died in 1926. (1951)

McLAREN, mount (7,500 feet) (M-5)
After Brigadier-General Charles H. McLaren, D.S.O., Ottawa, who commanded a brigade of Canadian artillery during World War I. (1918)

McLAREN, mount (9,300 feet) (O-5)
After Senator Peter McLaren (1833-1919) who had extensive lumbering interests in the North-West Territories. (1962)

McLAUGHLIN, hamlet (J-8)
After Thomas and John McLaughlin, early settlers. (1908)

McLENNAN, town (G-3)
After Dr. J. K. McLennan, who at the time of founding, was secretary of the Edmonton, Dunvegan and British Columbia Railway. (1915)

McLEOD, lake (C-7)
After Captain G. McLeod, D.L.S. (1916)

McLEOD, river (J-3)-(I-4)
McLeod's on David Thompson's map, 1814. Probably after Archibald Norman McLeod, North West Company fur trader.

McMILLAN, lake (F-5)
After Stanley Ransome McMillan, Edmonton, former bush pilot. (1954)

McMULLEN, lake (F-5)
After Archie McMullen, Edmonton, former bush pilot, who flew the first airmail out of Fort McMurray on December 10, 1929. (1954)

McMURTRY, ridge (L-5)
For D. J. McMurtry of Beaverlodge who hunted on this ridge for many years.

McNAB, locality (O-6)
After one McNabb, master mechanic of the Alberta Railway and Irrigation Company at Lethbridge; erroneous spelling. This branch of the railway opened in 1890, and ran from Lethbridge to Great Falls, Montana. (1912)

McNEILL, lake (G-2)
After Wing Commander J. G. McNeill, D.F.C., Calgary, killed in World War II. (1947)

McNEILL, locality (M-8)
After the late A. K. McNeill of Empress, Alberta. (1963)

McPHAIL, mount (9,500 feet), and creek (M-5)
After N. R. McPhail, of the Surveyor General's staff; killed in action, November, 1917. (1918).

McPHERSON, coulee (L-5)
In Blackfoot *namahkanes*, meaning "rifle bed", (Nelson). The connection is not clear.

McPHERSON, creek (J-3)
The McPherson and Quigley Lumber Company operated on this creek. (1925)

McQUEEN, mount (7,500 feet) (I-2)
After Dr. David George McQueen (1854-1930), Minister of First Presbyterian Church, Edmonton, (1887-1930). Dr. McQueen was a native

of Ontario and came to Edmonton as a young man. His ministry spanned
forty-three years and he was noted for his part in the community and
for his ecumenical outlook. (1953)

McRAE, locality (H-7)
After W. M. McRae, first postmaster. (1924)

MEADOWBROOK, locality (H-6)
Descriptive of the countryside.

MEADOWVIEW, locality (I-5)
The name is descriptive and was given by a resident, Colin Campbell.

MEANDER, river and hamlet (D-3)-(D-4)
Named by Hulbert Footner and mentioned in his book *New Rivers of
the North* (1912). Footner writes: (he is en route overland by foot from
Fort Vermillion to Hay River to visit Alexandra Falls) "On the third day
(from Fort Vermilion) we crossed the imperceptible divide and thereafter the streams flowed westward. The ground was stonier and less
fertile on the side. We passed two pretty lakes drained by a smoothly flowing river that wound its crooked way through meadows of grass waist
height. We christened it the Meander."

MEANOOK, locality (H-6)
Cree Indian for "good camping place." Meanook is at the geographical
centre of Alberta. (1912)

MEDA, mount (9,527 feet) (J-3)
After the Indian heroine of Earl of Southesk's poem, *The Meda Maiden*.
(1925)

MEDALLION, lakes (I-1)
Descriptive.

MEDICINE, lake (J-2)-(J-3)
Maligne River. The name was reported, 1875, by H. A. F. MacLeod,
Canadian Pacific Railway engineer.

MEDICINE, lake and river (K-5)
Red Deer River; it appears on Arrowsmith's map, 1859; in Cree, *muskiki*
and *nipagwasimow sipi* or Sundance River; in Stoney, *to-go-wap-ta*,
"mussel river", (Tyrrell).

MEDICINE HAT, city (N-8)
The site of Medicine Hat ("the town with all Hell for a basement",
Kipling) is so called in the report of the North-West Mounted Police
for 1882 and it was about this year that the first house was erected.
Medicine Hat is a translation of the Blackfoot Indian name *saamis*
meaning "head dress of a medicine man."
  There are several explanations of the name. One associates it with a
fight between the Cree and Blackfoot when the Cree medicine man lost
his war bonnet in the river. A second refers to the slaughter of a party
of white settlers and the appropriation of a fancy hat worn by one of
the victims. A third is that the name was applied originally to a hill east
of the city, from a fancied resemblance to the hat of an Indian medicine
man. This hill appears as Medicine Hat on a map of the Department of

the Interior dated 1883. Still another explanation mentions the rescue
of an Indian woman from the South Saskatchewan by an Indian brave,
upon whose head a well-known medicine man placed his own hat as
a token of admiration of the act of the rescue. A final tale is that the
name was given to the locality because an Indian chief saw in a vision
an Indian rising out of the South Saskatchewan River wearing a plumed
hat of a medicine man.

MEDICINE LODGE, hills   (K-5)
The Medicine hills are on the Arrowsmith map, 1859. These hills were
a favourite place for Indian spring festivals.

MEDICINE TENT, river   (J-3)
East fork of Rocky River. It appears on the Southesk map of 1875 and
is a translation of an Indian name indicating magic and mystery.

MEDLEY, river   (G-8)-(H-8)
After one C. Medley, Calgary.

MEETING, creek and MEETING CREEK, hamlet   (J-6)
In Cree, *nukh-kwa-ta-to* (Tyrrell). The Crees of the north and the Blackfoot of the south frequently met here when on their buffalo hunts. The
hamlet was formerly known as Edensville. (1905).

MEKASTOE, locality   (N-6)
After Mekastoe or Red Crow, head chief of the Southern Bloods who
signed the treaty of September 22, 1877, at Blackfoot Crossing. Mekastoe
was loyal throughout the 1885 rebellion and was next in rank in the
Blackfoot Confederacy to the famous Chief Crowfoot. His grave is near
Stand Off on the Fort Macleod-Cardston road. (1915)

MELLOWDALE, locality   (H-5)
Melrose was the name requested, but was modified by the Post Office
Department to its present form. (1909)

MELLSTROM, lake   (H-7)
After Flight Lieutenant M. L. Mellstrom, D.F.C., Calgary, killed in World
War II. (1951)

MENAIK, locality   (J-6)
Cree for "tamarac" (larch); Lacombe gives *minahik*-pine. (1908)

MERCER, mount (9,700 feet)   (L-4)
After Major-General M. S. Mercer, C.B., C.E.F.; killed in action near
Zillebeke, Flanders, June 2, 1916. (1918)

MERCOAL, locality and creek   (J-3)
A compound of portions of the name of the McLeod River Hard Coal
Company Limited. (1913)

MERE, lake   (I-5)
Most likely named by the surveyors who were surveying the district.
Mere is an old word for "lake." (1950)

MERLIN, lake and MERLIN CASTLE, mountain   (L-4)
After the magician, named in 1911. It is at the foot of a mountain, "a
picturesque cluster of tower-like rocks", which bears a fancied
resemblance to Merlin's castle. (Mountain, 1960)

MERLIN, mount (8,400 feet) and pass (J-2)
After the famous bard of Arthweian romance.

MERRYWEATHER, lake (B-6)
South of Conibear Lake; after Coder Hugh Merryweather, M.I.D., Fallis, Alberta, killed in World War II. (1949)

MESEKUM, locality (M-7)
Indian for the "land is rich"; descriptive. (1912)

MESSINES, mountain (10,290 feet) (K-3)
After Messines in West Flanders, about five and a half miles south of Ypres; in commemoration of the fighting there of Canadian troops, June, 1917 and April, 1918. (1920)

MEWASSIN, locality (I-5)
Indian for "good"; a descriptive name. (1903)

MICHEL, Indian Reserve (I-5)
After Chief Michael (Michel) Calahoo, who was supposed to have migrated to the West in the early days from eastern Canada; an Iroquois Indian Reserve. (1880)

MICHICHI, hamlet and creek (L-6)
The name *michichi* is Cree for hand. It takes its name from the Hand Hills (q.v.), *michichi ispatinan* (Tyrrell) from their resemblance to an outstretched hand. The name is variously spelled *macheche* or *mitchitchiy* (Lacombe).

MIDDLE, creek (I-8)
Arrowsmith map, 1859; descriptive.

MIDDLE KOOTENAY, pass (O-5)
See North Kootenay, pass.

MIDLANDVALE, hamlet (L-6)
Midlandville prior to 1918; after the Midland coal mine.

MIDWAY, peak (9,570 feet) (K-3)
Descriptive. (1918)

MIETTE, ROCHE, mountain (7,599 feet), and river (J-2)
This prominent feature, known to thousands of motorists who drive Highway 16 to and from Jasper, takes its name from a hunter named Miette who climbed it from its south side. Franchère, Kane and Hector mention this and Kane adds that when Miette reached the top he sat dangling his feet over the fearful precipice, smoking his pipe and as he (Miette) himself put it "having a good talk with St. Peter at the gate."

MIKKWA, river (D-4)-(D-5)-(D-6)
Cree for "red".

MILK, river (O-7)
The river is shown on the Palliser map, 1863. The name comes from the milky, murky colour of the river water as it flows through readily erodable light coloured soil. The river was known as *kenushsisuht* meaning "little river" to the Bloods. In the *Journals of Lewis and Clark*

dateline May 8, 1805 is this statement: "the waters of the river possess a peculiar whiteness being about the color of a cup of tea with the admixture of a tablespoon of milk. From the color of its waters we called it Milk River. The river appears to have been known to certain of the Missouri tribes as "the river that scolds all the others." (*Canadian Cattlemen*, October, 1957)

MILK RIVER, town   (O-7)
See Milk. river.

MILL, creek   (N-5)
Oldman River; after a mill near the mouth of the creek.

MILLARVILLE, locality   (M-5)
After Malcolm Millar, first settler and postmaster, 1885.

MILLERFIELD. locality   (L-6)
After John M. Miller, first postmaster. (1913)

MILLET, village   (J-6)
It has been commonly thought for many years that Millet received its name from the famous French painter François Millet. Recent research has revealed that it was in fact named after a fur buyer August Millet. He was an independent fur trader; sometimes he was engaged by the Hudson's Bay Company and at times he was under contract to the North-West Mounted Police at Fort Saskatchewan. His agreement with the police was to provide horses. Millet also on occasion worked for Father Lacombe as canoeman on long river trips.

At the time of the naming of the railway sidings in 1891 Sir William Van Horne. president of the Canadian Pacific. asked Father Lacombe to name stations from Lacombe north on the Calgary-Edmonton line. In responding to this request. Father Lacombe did not overlook his friend and travelling companion August Millet and accordingly the siding was given this name.

August Millet was drowned when attempting to cross the flooded Red Deer River and is believed to have been buried in the vicinity; the location of the grave has been lost.
(*Frontier Days in Leduc and District*. 1956)

MILLICENT, locality   (M-7)
Christian name of the fourth Duchess of Sutherland, also of her daughter, Rosemary Millicent. The Duke of Sutherland had an extensive farm at Brooks.

MILO, village   (M-6)
After Milo Munroe, first postmaster. (1908)

MINARET, locality   (L-5)
It is at the highest point of the railway between Calgary and Edmonton. (1902)

MINBURN, village and county.   (J-7)
After Miss Mina Burns. Ottawa, who described the Canadian West in magazine articles. (1905)

MINISTIK, lake   (J-6)
Cree for "island"; descriptive.

MINNEWANKA, lake (L-4)
Applied as a name to the lake in 1888 by the Department of the Interior, replacing the existing name Devil's or Devil's Head Lake. *Minnewanka* means "lake of the water spirit." Formerly called "Devil's Lake", *m'ne-sto*, or "Cannibal Lake", in Stoney; *ki'noo-ki'mow*, or "Long Lake", in Cree. Sir George Simpson named it "Peechee Lake" after his guide, but, as this name had not appeared on any map or obtained any recognition, Dr. G. M. Dawson transferred it to a mountain south of the lake.

MINTLAW, locality (K-5)
After a village in Aberdeenshire, Scotland. (1914)

MIQUELON, lakes, provincial park (J-6)
After P. A. Miquelon, former postmaster, Wetaskiwin. (1893)

MIRROR, lake (L-4)
From the reflection in the lake when seen from a great height above.

MIRROR, village (K-6)
After the London newspaper *Daily Mirror*. An article from the paper (August 10. 1911) paints a glowing picture of the rising town as a divisional point on the Edmonton-Calgary line of the Grand Trunk Pacific and centre of a farming area. (1911)

MISSAWAWI, lake (H-6)
Indian name meaning "big egg."

MISSION BEACH, locality (J-5)
Pigeon Lake; from its proximity to the Rundle Mission, established in 1847.

MIST, mountain (10,030 feet) and creek (M-5)
From the mists swirling around the mountain when named by Dr. G. M. Dawson in 1884.

MISTAYA, mountain (10,100 feet), lake and river (K-3)
The Indian name, meaning "grizzly bear", was first applied to the river in 1901; the river was formerly known as "Bear river", also as "Little Fork." The name was changed to avoid duplication.

MISTEHAE, lake (F-5)
From the Cree Indian for "big"; descriptive.

MISTY, range (M-5)
Named by Dr. G. M. Dawson in 1884 from mists that covered the summits.

MITFORD, locality (L-5)
T. B. H. Cochrane, son of Admiral Sir Thomas Cochrane, held ranching leases in the vicinity and the name was suggested by his wife, Lady Adela Cochrane, daughter of the Earl of Stradbroke, after Mrs. Percy Mitford, sister of the first Earl of Egerton, who was a great friend of hers, and who was also interested financially in the ranch. (1889)

MITRE, THE, mountain (9,470 feet) (L-4)
Named about 1893 by S. E. S. Allen, from its resemblance to a bishop's mitre.

MITSUE, lake, creek and locality (G-5)
Cree name meaning "eating'," so-called on account of the abundance of game in the district.

MOBERLY, hill, creek and flats (J-2)
Named by Hector in 1859, after Henry J. Moberly, who was in charge of Jasper House, 1858-1861, later, Factor, Hudson's Bay Company, living at Duck Lake, Saskatchewan.

MOKOWAN, butte (N-6)
This landmark with lofty escarpments of clay facing the Belly River appears on Arrowsmith's map of 1810. The Belly River (q.v.) is called Mokowans River; *mokowanis* being Blackfoot for "belly." The Belly River is named after the Atsina Indians, commonly known as the "Gros Ventres" or "Big Belly Indians."

MOLAR, mountain (9,914 feet), creek and glacier (L-4)
Hector says "it so much resembles a large tooth that we named it mount Molar."

MONARCH, mountain (9,500 feet) (J-2)
Descriptive.

MONCHY, mountain (10,530 feet) (K-3)
After the village in France which the British attacked and took on August 26, 1918, during World War I. (1920)

MONKHEAD, mountain (10,535 feet) (J-3)
From a fancied resemblance to a monk's head.

MONS, peak (10,114 feet), glacier and icefield (K-3)
After the Belgian town which saw the first British fighting in the First World War, on August 23, 1914, and which was recaptured and entered by the Canadians immediately before the Armistice, November 11, 1918. (1920)

MONTANA, Indian Reserve (J-6)
After *Keeskayo* alias "Bobtail", of the Montana band, a famous Cree Chieftain. (1885)

MOON LAKE, locality (I-5)
Translation of Indian name applied to an adjacent small lake. (1926)

MOONSHINE, lake (H-8)
Named by a Metis Marcel Cardinal who had manufactured "home brew" there, until the R.C.M.P. put an end to his activities in 1920. (1950)

MOONSHINE LAKE, provincial park (F-2)
Probably named for a similar reason to the above.

MOOSE, hills (I-8)
In Cree, *mooswachi* (Tyrrell). (1859)

MOOSE, lake (H-7)
Appears as Moon Lake (misprint?) on Harmon's map, 1820; this is Lac d'Orignal where Angus Shaw built a trading post for the North West Company in 1789. The lake was reached from the Beaver River up Moose-

lake River; although only fifteen miles long it took nine days to transport the goods on it, there being thirty-six rapids with swamps on either side. The post was called Fort Lac d'Orignal or "Shaw's House."

MORAINE, lake and creek   (L-4)
This now famous attraction was discovered by Wilcox in 1899, and so named because of a large terminal moraine at its outlet. Wilcox notes that while exploring this area he and a companion were delayed by adverse weather in the Moraine Creek valley and he set out for a walk up the valley. "I walked about a mile and half and came to a ravine where a roaring cascade, encumbered with logs and great boulders comes out of the valley to the south-east. I got across on a slippery log and after another mile, came to a massive pile of stones, where the water gurgles as it rushes along in subterranean channels. Ascending a ridge about fifty feet high, there lay before me one of the most beautiful lakes that I have ever seen. This lake, which I called 'Moraine Lake' from the ridge of glacial formation at its lower end is about a mile and half long."

MORDEN LONG, mount (9,500 feet)   (K-3)
After Morden Heaton Long (1886-1965). A native of Ontario he came to Edmonton where, after a short interval of teaching history in a high school, he joined the Department of History at the University of Alberta. Ultimately, he became Head of the Department. When the Geographic Board of Alberta was formed in 1946 he was its first Chairman, and continued in that capacity until his death.

MORECAMBE, hamlet   (I-7)
After Morecambe Bay, Lancashire, England, which was so called because of its identification with Ptolemy's *Morikombe* suggested in 1771 by Whitaker. (Ekwall). It means "curve of the sea".

MOREN, mount (8.405 feet)   (J-2)
After Arthur Moren, M.D., member of the Sandford Fleming party of 1872, in its journey across the Rockies.(1923)

MORINVILLE, town   (I-6)
Founded in the spring of 1891 by Abbé Jean-Baptiste Morin (1852-1911). Abbé Morin was born at St. Paul-de-Joliette, Quebec, and studied at Rigaud and Montreal, where he was ordained, 1884. In 1894, he published a pamphlet, *Le Nord-ouest Canadien et ses Ressources Agricoles*.

MORKILL, pass (5,434 feet) and mount (7,500 feet)   (I-2)
After D. B. Morkill, a British Columbia land surveyor. (1925)

MORLEY, station and Indian Reserve   (L-5)
In 1873, John McDougall established a mission at Morleyville among the Stoneys and Blackfeet. It soon included the mission, his brother's (David) trading post and the Bow River trading post of the Hudson's Bay Company. The name Morley is said to be after Reverend Dr. Morley Punshon a well-known Methodist minister from whom McDougall had secured endorsation to establish the mission. In 1875, a frame church was built; it still stands and is preserved by the United Church of Canada as a summer museum.

MORNINGSIDE, hamlet   (K-6)
After a suburb of Edinburgh, Scotland. (1892)

MORRIN, village   (L-6)
"Formerly known as Blooming Prairie. And a blooming prairie was not
the bald-headed prairie beloved by present day writers! Lush green
prairie, purpled with the early blooming crocus, the nodding bluebell
and the bright beard's tongue greeted the pioneers . . . No wonder the
early settlement and post office became known as Blooming Prairie.
With the arrival of the railroad and the establishment of a more permanent post office, the hamlet was called Morrin. Postal authorities preferred
shorter names. Although folklore has it that the descriptive label was
changed to the prosaic name of Morrin to appease the bloomin' English,
the accepted version is that Morrin was so named in honour of the
engineer who brought in the first train over the newly laid steel. No
official confirmation of the name Morrin has been received in spite of
considerable research on the subject. May we concede then, that the
person responsible for naming this station was so optimistic about the
area's future than an unknown benefactor's surname (which implied that
there is 'more in' here than elsewhere) was chosen to designate this
favourite spot. In this year, of 1970, the prairie still blooms throughout the
Morrin countryside—a multi-colored collage of purple alfalfa, blue flax,
off-white safflower, and sulphur yellow mustard amidst the varied greens
of wheat, oats, barley and rye. A Blooming Prairie Indeed!" (From
Blooming Prairie a history of Morrin and district supplied by D. M.
Concannon. Secretary-Treasurer, August, 1970). See also supplement.

MORRISON, mount (9,500 feet)   (M-4)
After the late Major-General Sir E. W. B. Morrison, D.S.O., officer
commanding 1st Artillery Brigade, Canadian Expeditionary Force, 1914-
1915; General Officer commanding Canadian Corps Artillery, 1916-1919.
(1918)

MORRO, peak (5,504 feet) and creek   (J-2)
Spanish for "castle" which it is said to resemble. (1916)

MORSE, lake and river   (H-4)
After C. H. Morse, former Inspector of Forest Reserves, (prior to 1928).

MOSQUITO, creek   (M-5)
In Blackfoot, *pahmahsois* or "foul-water" creek, the water being fouled
by the buffalo, which were very numerous here in the early days (Steele).
In Blackfoot, it is *pak-si-may-so-yiskway,* meaning "white willow place",
(Nelson).

MOSSIDE, locality   (I-5)
After Mosside, Manchester, England. (1908)

MOUND, locality   (K-5)
The name was given in 1896 to the cabin of H. A. Muntz, early settler,
who died in 1902. The name was suggested by a nearby hillock. (1905)

MOUNTAIN VIEW, hamlet and county   (O-6)
Descriptive of the view of the Rocky Mountains. (hamlet, 1894)

MUHIGAN, mountain (8,559 feet) and creek   (J-2)
Indian for "wolf." (1916)

MUIR, mount (9,000 feet) and creek   (M-4)
After Alexander Muir (1830-1906), author and composer of *The Maple Leaf Forever* written in 1867. (1918)

MUIRHEAD, locality   (M-5)
After Peter Muirhead, original owner of the townsite. (1912)

MULESHOE, lake   (L-4)
Descriptive of the outline of the lake.

MULHURST, hamlet   (J-5)
After G. Mulligan, first postmaster and early resident of the district. Hyrst" is Old English for "hill wood," (Ekwall). (1912)

MULLIGAN, creek and lake   (F-2)
Named after the first owner of land adjoining the lake.

MUMM, peak (9,740 feet)   (J-2)
After A. L. Mumm, F.R.G.S., who made the first ascent. (1912)

MUNDARE, town   (I-6)
Possibly after the first station agent, William Mundare. (1906)

MUNRO, lake   (H-7)
After Lieutenant Campbell Stuart Munro, M.I.D., Calgary, killed in World War II. (1951)

MUNSON, village   (L-6)
Local information states that it was named for a railroad engineer. Another version is that it was for one J. A. Munson, K.C., of a Winnipeg law firm, possibly retained by the C.N.R. (1911)

MURCHISON, mount (10,936 feet), creek, icefield (K-3) and lake   (A-7)
Named by Hector, 1858, after Sir Roderick Impey Murchison (1792-1871), Director-General of the Geological Survey of Great Britain, who recommended Hector for the post of surgeon and geologist to the Palliser Expedition. Hector was thanked by Murchison in a letter of February 16, 1859, "for attaching my name in this culminating point." Murchison's name is also perpetuated in Murchison Falls on the upper reaches of the Nile in Uganda. The lake was named in 1958.

MURRAY, island   (H-8)
This island located in Cold Lake is named after Bert Murray, member of a survey party.

MURRAY, mount (9,920 feet)   (M-4)
After General Sir A. J. Murray, Chief of the Imperial General Staff, 1915, and General Officer commanding in Egypt, 1916-1917. (1918)

MUSKRAT, creek   (J-5)
Translation of Cree Indian name, *wachask*; in Stoney, *hthumptodab wapta*, (Tyrrell)

MUSKWA, river   (F-5)
Indian for "bear."

128

MYOSOTIS, lake (L-4)
Named for the forget-me-nots which its blue colour suggests. (1960)

MYRNAM, village (I-7)
Ukrainian for "peace to us." It is a Ukrainian settlement. (1908)

— N —

NACMINE, hamlet (L-6)
A combination of the initial letters of "North American Collieries,
Limited" operating at this point, and the word "mine." (1919)

NACO, locality (L-8)
After Naco, Arizona. (1926)

NADEAU, lake (H-7)
After an old Canadian hunter near the lake, who gave Gabriel Franchère
half a buffalo in 1814. Franchère noted: "We descended the Beaver
River, dragging our canoes and walking along the banks on swampy
ground where the mosquitoes began to bother us. Our hunter scoured the
neighbouring hills without success. We soon came to a lodge where we
found an old Canadian hunter, a freeman of the name of Nadeau, who was
in a sad state as he had been without food for two days. A young Indian
who was married to one of his daughters, arrived towards evening with
the good news that he had just killed a buffalo; this made us decide
to come there and we sent our men to fetch the meat. Nadeau made us
a present of half of it."

NAKAMUN, lake (I-5)
Cree word for "song of praise."

NAKAMUN PARK, summer village (I-5)
See Nakamun, lake. (1966)

NAMAKA, locality (M-6)
From the Blackfoot *nama*, "bow", and *nietakhtai*, "river", pronounced by
the Indians *namokhtai*, but corrupted by those who did not know the language to Namaka. Archdeacon J. W. Tims, an early Anglican missionary
in southern Alberta, says: "I think the late General Strange was responsible for the name and probably the spelling of it. I remember him telling
me that the Canadian Pacific Railway had suggested that the station
should be called 'Strange', but he asked the Company to call it Namaka,
as that was the name he had chosen for his ranch on Bow River and
friends would know where to leave the train."

NAMAO, locality (I-6)
Cree for "sturgeon."

NAMEPI, creek (I-6)
Cree word for "carp." It is Carp Brook on David Thompson's map, 1814

NAMPA, village (F-3)
After Nampa, Idaho. "The first settler in this area opened a general store
near the N.A.R. water tank and named the settlement Tank. There was
apparently some confusion between Tank and the town of Frank, there-

fore he was requested to change the name of the settlement. This man, being originally from Idaho in the U.S. thought of a town called Nampa in Idaho and apparently the interpretation of Nampa (an Indian word) means 'the place' so he named the settlement Nampa." (J. S. Krall, Municipal Secretary, Nampa, letter, September, 1970).

NANGA PARBAT, mountain (10,780 feet)   (K-3)
   After the mountain of the same name in the Himalayas on which A. F. Mummery, the noted British climber, perished. (1920)

NANTON, town   (M-5)
   Named after Sir Augustus Nanton (1860-1925). The settlement was originally known as Mosquito Creek, but received its present name in 1902. Nanton was an associate of the Galts and of the Winnipeg firm of Osler, Hammond and Nanton. He was also a managing director of the Alberta Railway and Irrigation Company. He spent the greater part of his life in Winnipeg and his firm there handled townsite properties on the Calgary and Edmonton Railway. He was also associated with D. B. Hanna after whom the town of Hanna (q.v.) is named.

NAPLES, locality   (I-5)
   Italian settlers were numerous here. (1924)

NARRAWAY, river   (H-1)
   This river, crossing the 120th Meridian from British Columbia and flowing into the Wapiti River was named after A. M. Narraway, D.L.S., Controller of Surveys, Ottawa, whose duties took him to the river in 1922.

NASH, lake   (B-6)
   After Sub-Lieutenant R. A. Nash, M.I.D., Killam, killed in World War II. (1948)

NASSWALD, peak (9,985 feet)   (L-4)
   After Nasswald, birthplace in Austria of Conrad Kain, who climbed the peak in 1913 while with a survey party. (1913)

NAVARRE, locality   (J-6)
   After the Spanish province. (1914)

NAYLOR, hills   (D-3)
   After the manager of Revillon Frères Trading Company at Keg River Post. (1916)

NEEDLE, peak (9,668 feet)   (J-2)
   Descriptive of its summit. (1922)

NEERLANDIA, hamlet   (H-5)
   The first settlers came from the Netherlands (Neerlandia). (1913)

NELSON, lake   (J-6)
   After V. D. Nelson, who owned land in the vicinity for more than fifty years. (1955)

NEPTUAK, mountain (10,607 feet)   (L-4)
   Named by S. E. S. Allen; Stoney Indian word for "nine", it is the ninth of the "Ten Peaks" (q.v.) by Moraine Lake.

130

NESTOW, locality (H-6)
Cree for "brother-in-law." (1908)

NETOOK, locality (K-5)
The name is taken from the Blackfoot Indian word *nee-tuck-kis* meaning one lone pine tree. Peter Fidler, in his journal (1792) mentions that they were some twelve or thirteen miles away from a point of woods containing a large single pine tree called *nee-tuck-kis*. According to David Thompson, the Indians made offerings there.

NEUTRAL, hills and locality (K-7)
The area was frequented by various tribes of Indians and buffalo hunters in the summertime and the necessities of that period of the year suggested the cessation of the usual hostilities for the time being. The feature appears on the Palliser map, 1860.

NEVIS, locality (K-6)
After the Ben Nevis coal mine which was located here; possibly after Ben Nevis, Scotland. (1905)

NEW BRIGDEN, hamlet (L-8)
Name suggested by settlers from Brigden, Ontario. (1912)

NEW DAYTON, hamlet (N-7)
Named by settlers from Dayton, Ohio. (1908)

NEW LINDSAY, locality (J-8)
The first postmaster was one John Lindsay. The name New Lindsay was chosen to distinguish it from Lindsay, Ontario. (1911)

NEW LUNNON, locality (I-6)
After London, England.

NEW NORWAY, village (J-6)
The area was mainly settled by Norwegians. (1903)

NEW SAREPTA, village (J-6)
After the city of Sidon (St. Luke IV, 20); formerly Little Hay Lakes. A second account written by Mrs. Bertha McLean notes that many of the early settlers in the area had been born in Wohlynia, Russia and that they had come to make their homes in this part of Canada at the suggestion of Bishop Clement Hoyler of the Moravian Church. At the time of the immigration to Canada and the search for new homes in a strange land the leases on their farms in Wohlynia held by the Czarina of Russia were about to expire and they feared for the terms that would have to be signed for renewal. The name is also regarded by those in the district to be in remembrance of a Russian settlement Sarepta, and selected by Bishop Clement Hoyler. The word "New" was added to designate the Alberta hamlet from a settlement in Ontario named Sarepta. The name New Sarepta was also decided upon because of the ease of pronunciation by the peoples of different nationalities who were making their homes in and about the district. (*Frontier Days in Leduc and District*, 1956). (1905)

NEWBROOK, hamlet (H-6)
The first post office was in a building by a creek, which was discovered when a trail was cut to the settlement in 1914, hence the name "New Brook." (1917)

NEWMAN, peak (8,500 feet)   (O-5)
Named by Blakiston in 1858, after Edward Newman (1810-1875), English naturalist.

NEZ PERCÉ, creek   (N-5)
After the Nez Percés, a name applied by the French to all Indian tribes which pierced the nose for the insertion of a piece of dentalium (shell) ornament. The term is now applied only to the main tribe of the Shahaptian family, now found in northern Idaho and Oregon.

NIBLOCK, mount (9,764 feet)   (L-4)
After one Superintendent Niblock, Canadian Pacific Railway. (1904)

NIGEL, peak (10,535 feet), creek and pass   (K-3)
Named by Stutfield and Collie, 1898, after Nigel Vavasour, their guide in 1897. The peak was named during a hunt for Bighorn sheep and Collie writes: "We gave them another hour, and then followed them up an open valley, towards a lake that lay at the foot of a high snow-clad peak of which Nigel is now the eponymous hero."

NIGGLI, lake   (A-7)
The name is after a prominent German petrologist, P. Niggli, famous for his work on igneous rocks and ore deposits. (1958)

NIGHTINGALE, locality   (L-6)
After Florence Nightingale (1820-1910), the English nurse, celebrated for her devotion to the wounded in the Crimean War, 1854-1855. (1911)

NIHAHI, ridge and creek   (M-5)
Stoney Indian word signifying "rocky." The name is descriptive. (1922)

NIKANASSIN, range   (J-3)
From the Cree Indian *nikan* "in front", "first", and *assin*, "rocks"; the name was suggested by the fact that it is the first or front range when approaching the Rockies from the east. (1909)

NILREM, locality   (J-7)
Merlin reversed, after the half-legendary magician of the sixth century.

NINASTOKO, locality   (O-6)
Located in the Blood Indian Reserve and the name translated means "Chief Mountain."

NIPISI, lake and river   (F-5)
Abbreviation of Indian *nipisikopau*, "the place of many willows."

NISBET, locality   (K-5)
After the oldest settler. (1912)

NISKU, hamlet   (J-6)
Cree for "wild goose." Edmonton International airport is located here.

NIVERVILLE, mount (9,720 feet) and glacier   (K-3)
After Joseph Boucher, Chevalier de Niverville, who, in 1751 sent a party up the Saskatchewan River to build a post. It is, however, not known whether they went up the North or South Branch. Whether they built their post, Fort La Jonquiere at the foot of the Rockies, is

open to question. It may even have been below the forks of the river. In any event, Fort La Jonquière was destroyed in 1752 and Louis Chapt, Chevalier de la Corne, built another, possibly on the site of Fort la Jonquière just below the forks. A tradition that Fort La Jonquière was built on the site of the present city of Calgary is based on a casual inference of a North-West Mounted Police officer concerning the remains of an American Fur Company post of 1833 found when the police built Fort Calgary in 1875.

NOBLEFORD, village   (N-6)
Charles Sherwood Noble, M.B.E., LL.D. (1873-19?) was a native of Iowa and homesteaded near Claresholm in 1902 but later bought 5,000 acres of land near Lethbridge and commenced large scale farming there. He ultimately formed a company, the Noble Foundation and eventually some 33,000 acres were put under cultivation. The settlement was first known as Noble but in 1918 was incorporated into a village and named Nobleford in honor of the founder. The Noble Farms are still operated by members of the family.

NOIRE, ROCHE, peak (9,504 feet)   (J-2)
Noire is French for "black"; the summit of the peak is black.

NOLAN locality   (N-6)
After P. J. Nolan, K.C., (1864-1913). Patrick James (Paddy) Nolan was a native of Ireland (he was born on March 17!). He arrived in Calgary in 1889 to practise law and he soon became famous not only as a barrister, but for his good humour as well, whether in or out of Court and stories about him are legion. He was appointed King's Counsel in 1907. He was a member of the first Senate of the University of Alberta until his death. (1911)

NONNE, LAC LA, lake   (I-5)
Lac la Nane in Edward Ermatinger's journal, May 18, 1827; in Cree, *mi-ka-sioo*, or "eagle" (Tyrrell). As related by one A. D. Henderson, of Belvedere, Alberta, the lake owes its name to a duck, the white-winged scoter (*melanitta deglandi*). The species is very common on the lake. The birds are black with white wing bars and a white spot on the head and suggest a black-robed nun. This explanation is doubtful.

NORBUCK, locality   (J-5)
On the trail to the north end of Buck Lake. (1926)

NORDEGG, hamlet (K-4) and river (J-4)
After Martin Nordegg (1868-1948), a native of Silesia, Germany. Nordegg arrived in Canada in 1906 and within ten years, aided by German capital he had been instrumental in establishing a railway, the Canadian Northern Western, a coal mine (Brazeau Collieries) and the townsite that bears his name. He was the director, vice-president and general manager of Brazeau Collieries. During World War I his fortunes declined as he was considered an enemy alien but later his holdings were returned to him. He wrote his memoirs under the title *The Possibilities of Canada are Truly Great* which were published in 1971 under the editorship of T. D. Regehr.

NORGLENWOLD, summer village (K-5)
Before the village was incorporated it was part of the County of Red Deer and comprised the subdivisions of *Nor*they Point, *Glen* Innes and White*wold* Beach. The group of ratepayers who met to incorporate a summer village picked syllables from these names and came up with Norglenwold. (W. F. Gordon, Secretary-Treasurer, letter, August, 1970). (1965)

NORMA, locality (I-7)
A prize was offered for the best name of not more than five letters. The name Norma was selected; after Mrs. Norma V. Richardson. (1918)

NORMANDEAU, locality and lake (H-7)
After Abbé Joseph-Aldrie Normandeau. (1915)

NORMANDIN, lake (J-8)
After a homesteader who lived on its shores.

NORQUAY, mount (8,275 feet) (L-4)
After Hon. John Norquay (1841-1889), Premier of Manitoba, 1878-1887; he climbed the mountain in 1887 or 1888. (1904)

NORTH FORK, locality (N-5)
Known as Olin Creek until 1912. It is near north fork of the Oldman River.

NORTH FORK, pass (6,537 feet) (N-5)
West of Gould Dome mountain, at head of what was, formerly, designated as North Fork of Oldman River.

NORTH KANANASKIS, pass (M-4)
See Kananaskis, range, lake, etc.

NORTH KOOTENAY, pass (6,700 feet) (N-5)
After the Kootenay Indians who formerly crossed the Rockies every spring and autumn to kill buffalo, returning with the dried meat which they traded for blankets, etc., with the Hudson's Bay Company at Kootenay post. This pass was crossed by Blakiston of the Palliser Expedition in 1858.

NORTH SASKATCHEWAN, river (K-3)-(I-8)
Saskatchewan is from the Cree Indian word *kis-is-ska-tche-wan,* meaning "swift current". the Blackfoot name is *omaka-ty,* or "big" river (Nelson). See also, South Saskatchewan, river.

NORTHLEIGH, locality (I-5)
After Northleigh, Devonshire, England. The name was suggested by H. G. Foye, postmaster who was killed in First World War. (1915)

NORTHOVER, mount (10,000 feet) (M-4)
After Lieutenant A. W. Northover, V.C., 28th Battalion, C.E.F. (1917)

NORTON, locality (N-8)
After one H. A. Norton, first postmaster. (1907)

NORWAY VALLEY, locality (I-8)
After the school district. It was a Norwegian settlement. (1923)

NOSE, creek (L-5)
From the Cree Indian *os-kewun*; in Stoney, *tap-o-oi wapta* (Tyrrell).

NOSE, hill (K-7)
From the Cree *os-ke-wun-à-Chio* (Tyrrell).

NOSE, mountain (5,000 feet) (H-1)
Probably descriptive.

NOSE, THE (4,853 feet), mountain (H-1)
Prominent point at western extremity of the plateau of Nose mountain, (q.v.).

NOYES, mount (10,040 feet) (K-3)
Named by Stutfield and Collie, after one Reverend C. L. Noyes.

NOYES CROSSING, locality (I-5)
After Daniel E. Noyes, first postmaster. (1906)

NUGENT, locality (J-5)
After the maiden name of the wife of M. Donovan, onetime postmaster. (1911)

— O —

OATES, mount (10,220 feet) (K-3)
After Captain L. E. G. Oates (1880-1912), a member of the British Antarctic Expedition under Captain R. F. Scott. On the fatal march from the South Pole Oates, whose strength had diminished as the result of frostbite and hunger walked from the tent to his death in a blizzard thereby hoping to save his companions, Scott, Wilson and Bowers. (1914)

OBED, locality and lake (I-3)
After Lieutenant-Colonel John Obed Smith (1864-1937). Smith was a native of England but came to Canada as a young man. He was called to the Manitoba Bar in 1891 and served the Manitoba Government until he was appointed Commissioner of Immigration at Winnipeg in 1901. In 1908 he became Assistant Commissioner of Emigration in England and afterwards Commissioner for European Emigration. He was later a delegate to the League of Nations. (1915 and 1967)

O'BEIRNE, mount (8,400 feet) (J-2)
After "O'B" (Eugene Francis O'Beirne), who attached himself to Milton and Cheadle at Edmonton, and accompanied them through the Yellowhead Pass to Kamloops in 1863, adding greatly to the difficulties of their journey. Cheadle spells the name O'Byrne. It appears that O'Byrne was a "drifter" who had travelled around doing various jobs and living off the good will of others. He was a liability not only to Milton and Cheadle but to the other members of their party. They parted with him at Kamloops. (1918)

OBERLIN, locality (K-6)
Probably after Oberlin, Ohio, U.S.A. (1914)

OBSERVATION, peak (10,214 feet)   (L-3)
Noyes says that it was so named because, when climbed, it was "the most satisfactory view-point, we agreed, that we had reached in the Rockies." (1898).

OCHRE, peaks   (N-5,)
Oldman River; after beds of red shale on the shoulder of this mountain.

ODLUM, mount (8,966 feet) and creek   (M-4)
After Brigadier General V. W. Odlum (1880-19?), C.M.G., Canadian Expeditionary Force. (1917)

O'HAGAN, mount (8,021 feet) and creek   (J-2)
After Dr. Thomas O'Hagan who was medical officer at Jasper Park for 28 years. (1960)

OHATON, hamlet   (J-6)
A combination of names of Osler, Hammond and Nanton, a prominent Winnipeg financial firm. (1906)

OKOTOKS, town   (M-5)
For many years it was thought that the name Okotoks was derived from a Cree word meaning "stony crossing." This derivation is mentioned in *Place-names of Alberta* (1928) and has consequently been perpetuated elsewhere.

According to W. D. Helten, of Okotoks (1970), recent investigations have revealed that "Okotoks" is not Cree at all since the Cree word for "stone" is *asinee* and that for "crossing" or "ford" is *asoowuhum* and it is impossible for "Okotoks" to be derived from either; nor is there any word in the Cree language resembling it nor one from which it could possibly be derived. Finally it should be pointed out that the Crees did not live in the area although they may have ventured there on war parties.

The Blackfeet, Stoney and Sarcees did, however frequent the area. The Sarcees called the place *chachosika* or "valley of the Big Rock", referring to a glacial boulder or erratic some five miles west of the present town. The Stoney name is *ipabitunga-ingay* or "where the Big Rock is", again referring to the same large boulder.

It is the Blackfoot name which gives us the derivation. It is simply *okatok* which means "rock" and again refers to the large erratic mentioned earlier. It is from this word that the name "Okotoks" is derived.

OLD FORT, creek   (L-5)
After ruins of Old Bow Fort, a Hudson's Bay Company fort near its mouth.

OLD FORT, river, bay and point   (C-7)
After old Fort Chipewyan, situated at the mouth of the Athabasca River until 1799 when it was moved to its present site.

OLDMAN, river   (N-5)-(N-7)
Appears as Oldman or Arrow on Palliser map, 1865. Dawson says that near the point at which the Livingstone (Oldman) River issues from the mountains, "are three cairns; the first, a wide mount, about eight feet high, composed of stones and small boulders, and evidently very old, the two others smaller. As these are of no use as landmarks, they

have probably been formed in the course of years by the addition of a stone, by each Indian entering the mountains by this route, 'for luck'. On a narrow piece of flat, open ground, a short distance further on, are the obscure remains of a couple of rectangles formed of larger stones. This place is well known to all the Indians, and named by them the 'Old Man's playing ground.' It is from this spot that the Old Man River derives its name, many superstitions attaching to the neighbourhood. The 'Old Man,' *wi-suk-i-tshak* of the Crees, is a mythical character, with supernatural attributes, familar under one name or other, to all students of American folklore." The name of the river in Cree is *is-e-enoo-met-ewe-win-si-pi*, Blackfoot name is *apistoki* and in Stoney, *is-sa-goo-win-ih-ska-da-wap-ta*. The cave out of which the river issues is called Oldman cave. *Is-e-enoo* signifies aged man and is not connected with *wi-suk-i-ushak*, the imp (Tyrrell).

OLDS, town and creek (L-5)
Long known as the "Lone Pine" district because of the Lone Pine stopping place on the Edmonton Trail just northeast of the present town. There was some controversy when it came to choosing an official name. During the railway construction period the siding was known as the "Sixth Siding." It fell to a committee of C.P.R. officials to designate names for the various sidings. Some favoured the name "Lone Pine", others felt the siding should be called "Shannon" because of David Shannon's association with the construction but when asked to consent to the use of his name, the modest Shannon declined, though he was certainly the first resident of Olds, having filed on the N.E. ¼ of 32-32-2-5, relinquishing his rights to the C.P.R. so they could use the land as a townsite.

The name Olds was finally chosen in honour of George Olds, C.P.R. traffic manager. (1893) (*See Olds First*, Olds Old Timers Association, 1968).

OLIVE, mount (10,270 feet) (L-3)
Named by H. B. Dixon, of the English Alpine Club, after his wife. (1899)

OLIVER, creek (N-5)
Oldman River; after W. Oliver, one of the early settlers in the area.

OLIVER, mount (9,400 feet) and locality (J-2) (I-6)
After the Hon. Frank Oliver (1853-1933), founder of the *Edmonton Bulletin* in 1880. He was elected to the North-West Council in 1883 and to the Legislative Assembly of the N.W.T. He represented first Alberta and then Edmonton in the House of Commons from 1896 to 1917, and was Minister of the Interior for Canada from 1905-1911. From 1923 to 1928 he was a member of the Board of Railway Commissioners for Canada. (1954)

OLSON, creek (I-2)
Berland River; after Ben Olson who trapped for many years and lived off the land along this creek. (1947)

OMAKTAI, locality (O-6)
Located in the Blood Indian Reserve and translated means "Big Bend."

ONEFOUR, locality (O-8)
So named from its location in township one, range four, west of the Fourth Meridian. (1913)

ONOWAY, village (I-5)
Error for Onaway; after the character in Longfellow's poem *Hiawatha*. "One story is that the name Onoway was taken from the poem *Hiawatha* in which the Indian singer began the lines of the 11th canto with the exclamation 'Onaway' which in English means 'awake'. The original spelling was changed to Onoway probably by error. At any rate in 1904 Onoway it became. Another explanation is that the local settlers wanted it to be Beaupré to honour an early pioneer. However, the postal people found the name had already been used and so could not accept it. The word Beaupré by translation can be "good, rich or sweet meadow" and by translation to the Chippewa Indian tongue it becomes Onoway. So the words Onoway and Beaupré are the same." (Betty Ripski, Secretary-Treasurer, letter, August, 1970). In the 11th canto of *The Song of Hiawatha* Chibiabos is asked to sing at the wedding feast of Hiawatha and Minnehaha and in the course of his song:

> "Onaway! Awake beloved!
> Thou the wild flower of the forest
> Thou the wild bird of the prairie! . . ."
> and again
> "O awake, awake, beloved!
> Onaway awake, beloved! . . ."

According to Longfellow the word "Chibiabos" means a musician, friend of Hiawatha, ruler of the Land of Spirits. (1904)

OPABIN, creek (J-3)
Brazeau River; Stoney Indian word signifying "rocky", replacing the names Boulder and Rocky.

OPAL, range (M-4)
Named by G. M. Dawson after small cavities found here, lined with quartz crystals, coated with films of opal.

OPPY, mountain (10,940 feet) (K-3)
After the village about six miles southeast of Lens, France, in commemoration of the fighting that took place there during the First World War. (1920)

ORION, locality (N-8)
Probably for the constellation; changed from Needmore, 1916.

O'ROURKE, mount (M-5)
After Private M. J. O'Rourke, V.C., 1st B.C. Battalion, Canadian Expeditionary Force. For three days and nights in August, 1917, Private O'Rourke who was a stretcher bearer worked unceasingly in bringing the wounded into safety, dressing them and getting them food and water. (1917).

ORTON, locality (N-8)
After Josiah Orr, postmaster (1907).

OTWAY, locality (K-5)
Named after Thomas Otway (1652-1685), English dramatist. (1961)

138

OUTPOST, peak (9,100 feet)   (J-2)
Descriptive. (1916)

OUTRAM, mount (10,670 feet), and lake   (K-3)
After Sir James Outram, Bart., (1864-1925), noted mountain climber
who in 1900 and succeeding years made first ascents of many of the
highest peaks in the Rockies including Mount Assiniboine. He was the
author of *In The Heart of the Canadian Rockies*, 1903. See also
Sir James, glacier. (1920; lake, 1961)

OVERTURN, mountain (8,400 feet)   (I-1)
Named after overturned rock strata and structures in this mountain
and along the ridges leading towards it. (1960).

OWLSEYE, lake and locality   (I-7)
The name is said to commemorate a hunter so nicknamed who was
killed by Indians here.

OXLEY, creek   (N-5)
After the Oxley Ranch, which in turn was named after Oxley Manor,
Wolverhampton, England.

OXVILLE, locality   (J-8)
The settlers drove oxen in 1907. (1907).

OYEN, town   (L-8)
The settlement of the community started in 1910 and received its
name from a Norwegian settler, Andrew Oyen who sold his homestead for a townsite. It obtained town status September 1, 1965. (1912)

OYSTER, peak (9,110 feet) and lake   (K-4)
Named by Dr. G. M. Dawson in 1884, after "certain curious formations
of limestone resembling oysters that were found in the shale around its
base," probably *ostrea fossils*. The lake southeast of Oyster Peak was
named in 1960.

OZADA, locality   (L-4)
From a Stoney Indian word meaning "the forks of the river" signifying
its location at the junction of the Bow and Kananaskis Rivers. (1909)

— P —

PACKENHAM, mount (9,250 feet)   (M-5)
After Rear Admiral W. C. Packenham, in command of the Second
Battle Cruiser Squadron at the Battle of Jutland, 1916. (1922)

PACKRAT, creek   (I-2)
Named as a cabin on this creek was known as 'Packrat' cabin. (1947)

PADDLE, river   (I-4)-(I-5)
The river is mentioned by this name in E. Ermatinger's *York Factory
Express Journal*, 1827, when the author was on his way from Edmonton
to Jasper. It is a translation of the Cree name *aby sipi*, given possibly
because a canoe could be propelled on it upstream by use of the
paddle alone, while on the swifter Pembina River the voyageurs had to

resort to the pole and track line. Hector under date of January 16, 1859 notes that his party "crossed the Paddle River, a tributary of the Pembina River. . . ."

PADSTOW, locality (I-4)
After Padstow, Cornwall, England. The name of Padstow appears first as *Petroces stow* in 981 and as *Petrokestowe* in 1297, *Padristowe* in 1351 and *Padestou* in 1361. The name means "St. Petroc's Church", (Ekwall). (1911)

PAINTEARTH, creek and county (K-7)
This creek, a tributary of the Battle River takes its name from the red ochre found there and used by the Indians to paint their faces. It is referred to as Vermilion Creek by Hector while a Paintearth Creek also mentioned by him is to-day known as Castor Creek (q.v.). The county takes its name from the creek.

PAKAN, locality (I-6)
It is the name of a former Cree Indian chief at Whitefish Lake Reservation 50 miles north. His Indian name Pakan, means "the nut" in English. Earlier known as Victoria it was named after Queen Victoria by Rev. George McDougall, who chose the place as the site for a Methodist mission in 1862. Hudson's Bay Company post under this name was established two years later. The name was changed to Pakan to avoid confusion with other places in Canada named Victoria. Pakan Post Office was opened in 1887.

PAKASHAN, Indian Reserve (G-4)
After one John Pakashan and family.

PAKKWAW, lake (K-5)
Indian for "shoal lake"; descriptive.

PAKOWKI, lake and locality (O-8)
The lake appears as *Peekopee* on Palliser map, 1865; Blackfoot for "badwater" lake; descriptive.

PALLISER, range and pass (6,500 feet) (L-4)
Named after Captain John Palliser (1817-1887), and on his map, 1859. Palliser headed an exploring expedition for the period of 1857-1860 exploring the country between the 49th parallel and the North Saskatchewan River and between the Red River and the Rockies. He was also under instructions to determine if a suitable pass for a railway existed through the Rockies south of the Yellowhead Pass. In 1863 his report of his explorations was published and it is remarkable, for its clarity. The background for the expedition stemmed from a controversy over the renewal of the Hudson's Bay Company Charter (which was up for renewal in 1870). The Company opposed settlement and at a hearing held in London the only people who knew anything about the area in question were Company servants. In any event the Imperial Government was concerned enough about the area to send out an expedition to report upon it. The result was the Palliser Expedition.

PALU, mountain (9,610 feet) (J-2)
Similar in structure to a mountain of this name in Switzerland. (1923)

PANGMAN, peak (10,420 feet) and glacier   (K-3)
After Peter Pangman (1744-1819), fur trader, who, in 1790, carved his name on a pine tree. "Pangman's tree" was three miles above Rocky Mountain House, North Saskatchewan River. (1920)

PANTHER, mountain (9,655 feet) and river   (L-4)
Dr. G. M. Dawson says "Panther river is probably a sufficiently near approach to the Indian name of the stream which signifies 'The river where the mountain lion was killed';" in Stoney, this is rendered *it-mos-tungá-moos-ta-ga-te-wap-ta*; in Cree, *mis-si-sioo-ka-nipa-hiht-si-pi.*

PARADISE, valley   (L-4)
Discovered in 1894 by Wilcox and named by him. Wilcox and his companions had crossed a snow pass from Mount Lefroy and when they reached the summit they saw (as Wilcox wrote) "a new group of mountains in the distance while a most beautiful valley lay far below us. Throughout a broad expanse of meadows and open country many streams were to be seen winding through this valley, clearly traceable to their various sources in glaciers, springs, and melting snowdrifts. With all its diversity of features spread like a map before our eyes, this attractive place was seen to be closely invested on the south by a semi-circle of high and rugged mountains, rising steeply from a crescent-shaped glacier at their united bases." Later he writes: "This beautiful place which had been discovered in such a delightful way we called Paradise Valley."

PARADISE VALLEY, village   (J-8)
"The topography of this area of the province has several ranges of low hills. The Paradise Valley district as seen from these hills from almost any direction presents a valley of bowl-like appearance. Since this is in the parkland area with numerous bluffs of trees and sloughs the view from any of the hills is very pleasing. therefore early settlers named it Paradise Valley." (Mrs. Anna M. Miller, Municipal Secretary, letter, September, 1970) (1910)

PARAGON, peak (9,800 feet)   (J-2)
Descriptive. (1921)

PARK COURT, locality   (I-5)
The appearance of the country reminded an old lady (Mrs. Bigland) of an English park. (*West of the Fifth*, Lac Ste. Anne Historical Society, 1959). (1910)

PARKER, creek   (K-4)
After a former forest ranger.

PARKLAND, county   (I-5)
Descriptive of landscape.

PARKLAND, hamlet   (M-6)
After an old resident, Park Hill. (1907)

PARLBY, creek and lake   (K-6)
Named after Honourable Irene Parlby (1868-1965). She was the first woman cabinet minister in Alberta serving as Minister Without Portfolio in the government of the United Farmers of Alberta from 1921-1935.

She was a Canadian delegate to the League of Nations at Geneva in 1930. She and her husband had established the Dartmoor Ranch at Alix where Mrs. Parlby lived following her retirement from public life.

PARRISH, mount (8,300 feet)   (N-5)
After Sherman Parrish who pioneered in the district and resided a few miles north of the mountain. (1962)

PASHLEY, locality   (N-8)
Maiden name of the wife of David McNicoll (1852-1916), then general manager of the Canadian Pacific Railway; later, first vice-president. (1900)

PASQUE, mountain (8,337 feet)   (M-5)
So named from the abundance of pasque flowers found near the summit. The pasque flower here is likely the western anemone (*anemone occidentalis*).

PASTURE, creek   (I-2)
Named for good pasture land near the creek. (1947)

PATENAUDE, lake   (B-6)
After Private George Patenaude, M.M., Ponoka, killed in World War II. (1949)

PATIENCE, locality   (J-6)
It is said that when the area was settled it required "patience" to travel over the roads in the vicinity. (1902)

PATRICIA, hamlet   (M-7)
After Princess Patricia (1886-   ), daughter of H.R.H. the Duke of Connaught, Governor General of Canada, 1911-1916. The adjoining locality is Princess. (1914)

PATTERSON, mount (10,490 feet)   (L-3)
After J. D. Patterson, one time president, Alpine Club of Canada. (1918)

PATTISON, mount (7,600 feet)   (J-2)
After Private J. G. Pattison, V.C. (posthumous), Calgary, killed in World War I. (1951)

PAUL, mount (9,200 feet)   (J-3)
Named by Mrs. Mary Schäffer in 1911, after Paul Sharples, the first white child to go into the Maligne Lake country. He made all the climbs, although only nine years old.

PAULINE, mount (8,704 feet) and creek   (I-1)
After F. A. Pauline, once Agent General for British Columbia in London, England. (1925)

PAXSON, locality   (H-6)
After a former employee of G. Schaffer, postmaster. (1913)

PAXTON, lake   (C-7)
After one F. R. Paxton. (1917)

PEACE, hills (J-6)
Translation of Cree Indian name *wi-ta-ski-oo-cha-ka-tin-ow* (Tyrrell). The Crees and Blackfeet made peace here in 1867 and the occasion is commemorated by a monument erected near Wetaskiwin in 1927. See Also, Wetaskiwin.

PEACE, river (F-1)-(B-6), and point (B-6)
The name "Peace River" has been known to the white man from earliest exploring days. It actually takes its name from Peace Point near Lake Athabasca which was where the Knisteneaux (Crees) and Beaver Indians settled a dispute. Alexander Mackenzie notes: "On the 13th at noon we came to the Peace Point from which according to the report of my interpreter, the river derives its name. It was the spot where the Knisteneaux (Crees) and Beaver Indians settled their dispute. The real name of the river and point being that of the land which was the object of contention. When this country was formerly invaded by the Knisteneaux, they found the Beaver Indians inhabiting the land about Portage la Loche; and the adjoining tribe were those whom they called slaves. They drove both these tribes before them; when the latter proceeded down the river from the Lake of the Hills (Lake Athabasca) in consequence of which that part of it obtained the name of the Slave River. The former proceeded up the river; and when the Knisteneaux made peace with them, this place was settled to be the boundary." The Peace River was known by the Beaver Indians as *unijigah* of which the name "Peace" is a translation. The Sekani who dwelt further up the river knew it as *isetaieka*, "the river which runs by the rocks", a reference to its passage through the Rockies.

PEACE RIVER, town (F-3)
See Peace, river

PEACE RIVER CROSSING, Indian Reserve (F-3)
See Peace, river

PEARCE, locality (N-6)
After William Pearce (1848-1930), D.L.S. In charge of surveys in Manitoba and North-West Territories (1873-1881). Later he was with the Department of Natural Resources of the Canadian Pacific Railway. He wrote a rather rambling history of the prairies. (1910)

PEAT, locality (I-7)
The name is spelled in error for Peet as it was named after John Peet, first postmaster. (1915)

PEAVINE, locality (I-4)
Peavines grow abundantly in the vicinity. (1908)

PECTEN, locality (O-5)
The station is on a C.P.R. spur line to a Shell Oil Company plant. Pecten is the name of the genus of mollusc or shell fish of which the scallop is a member and which is the familiar symbol of the company. (1961)

PEECHEE, mount (9,585 feet) (L-4)
Named by G. M. Dawson, in 1884, after Sir George Simpson's Metis guide during his trip across the continent, 1841.

PEERLESS, lake (E-5)
So called from the "peerless" beauty of its blue water. (1912)

PEERLESS LAKE, hamlet (E-5)
See Peerless, lake. (1958)

PEERS, hamlet (I-4)
After the family name of the mother of Sir Charles Peers Davidson, Montreal; Chief Justice, Superior Court, Quebec, 1912-1915. (1911)

PEIGAN, locality and Indian Reserve (N-5)
After the Peigan tribe of the Blackfoot Confederacy, whose reservation is nearby. It is a corruption of *pikuni,* referring to people having badly made robes. (1901)

PEKISKO, locality and creek (M-5)
Highwood River. Derived from the Blackfoot Indian word for "foothills" or "rolling hills." The name was suggested for the creek in 1896 by Fred Stimson. See Stimson, creek.

PELTIER, creek (B-7)
After Sergeant Joseph M. E. Peltier of Lac la Biche killed in World War II. (1963)

PEMBINA, river (J-3)-(H-5)
It appears on David Thompson's map, 1814. Thompson notes for November 2, 1810: "We went ten miles, in this distance we crossed the Pembinaw (Pembina) River of forty yards in width and shoal; this name is a corruption of *Neepinmenan* (summer berry)."

PEMBINA HEIGHTS, locality (H-5)
See Pembina, river. (1961)

PEMBURTON HILL, locality (J-5)
After C. Burton, postmaster; "Pem" was added to distinguish it from Burtonville. (1913)

PEMUKAN, locality (K-8)
A Cree word for "across the water," (William Pearce). (1914)

PENGELLY, mount (8,512 feet) (N-5)
Named by A. O. Wheeler in 1917. A. J. Campbell, D.L.S., his assistant on the British Columbia-Alberta Boundary survey, married a Miss Pengelly of Cornwall, England.

PENHOLD, village (K-5)
"When the railway were putting the line through (The Calgary-Edmonton Railway, C.P.R.) they had a little conference trying to determine a name for what is now Penhold but could not come to any agreement. One of the men accidentally dropped his pen and the nib stuck in the map they were looking at. This gentleman said (you guessed it) 'Let's call it Penhold'." (Mrs. Florence Long, Secretary-Treasurer, letter, September, (1970). (1893)

PENNINGTON, lake (K-5)
After an owner of land in vicinity. (1919)

144

PENTLAND, lake (F-4)
After Squadron Leader W. H. Pentland, D.F.C, Calgary, killed in World War II. (1947)

PEORIA, locality (G-2)
South of Birch Hills; after Peoria, Illinois, because some of the early settlers had lived there or worked there, also because some were admirers of machinery manufactured there.

PERBECK, locality (K-6)
After the Isle of Purbeck, Dorset, England. The spelling was changed by the Post Office Department. The name in its original form appears about 948 as *Purbicinga* possibly derived from *becca* meaning "bill" (beak) and Old English *pur* (bittern); the bill (beak) of the bittern, (Ekwall). The Isle of Purbeck is in reality a headland, sometimes called a 'bill'. (1908)

PERDRIX, ROCHE À, peak (7,002 feet) (J-2)
From the French *perdrix* meaning "partridge." So called from a fancied resemblance of the foliations of its rock to the tail of a partridge. The peak is mentioned in Grant's *Ocean to Ocean*, 1873.

PERRY, creek (A-2)
After Pilot Officer Woodrow J. Perry, Grimshaw, Alberta, killed in World War II. (1964)

PESKETT, mount (10,200 feet) (K-4)
After the Reverend Louis Peskett who was very active in the Youth for Christ Movement and who died in 1966, the result of an accident in the mountains. (1968)

PETERS, mount (9,000 feet) and creek. (L-4)
After Frederick Hathaway Peters, D.L.S., Surveyor General of Canada from 1945-1948.

PETITOT, river (A-2)
After Father Émile Petitot, O.M.I., (1838-1917). A native of France, Petitot came to Canada in 1862 and from that year until 1868 was a missionary in the Mackenzie district serving at Fort Providence, Great Bear Lake and the Mackenzie Delta. In 1879, he built a mission at Cold Lake. Shortly after this he became insane and returned to France where he recovered but when he returned to Canada signs of this again appeared and he tried to commit suicide. He was then sent to France and to a mental hospital there. It appears that at about this time he left the Order. Father Petitot left behind an amazing set of diaries and publications on explorations of Great Bear Lake, the Eskimos and Indian traditions as well as a dictionary of the Dené languages and a grammar. He also wrote a monograph on the theory of the origin of the Dené. He was also a keen artist and left a number of paintings and sketches. One of these a painting of Fort Edmonton, (ca. 1867) now hangs in the Alberta Provincial Library.

PEYTO, lake, peak (9,805 feet), and glacier (L-3)
Named by Wilcox after Bill Peyto (pronounced pee-toe) (1868-1943), a well-known figure in the Banff area. Peyto was born in England, coming to Canada at the age of 18 and worked for a time for Tom Wilson,

a well-known guide at Banff. He subsequently served in the Boer War and the First World War. After that war he established his stables and packing business in Banff but this was not successful. Later he was a park warden in the vicinity of Banff.

Wilcox and Outram considered Peyto one of the best guides in the Canadian Rockies. He educated himself highly in geology.

PHILIPS, locality (J-7)
After Henry Philips, secretary, Grand Trunk Pacific Railway. Lake Thomas Post Office until 1910. (1909)

PHILLIPS, mount (10,660 feet) (J-2)
After Donald Phillips, a well-known guide at Jasper, Alberta.

PHILLIPPS, peak (9,364 feet) and pass (N-5)
After Michael (Michel) Phillipps of Elko, B.C.; Hudson's Bay Company clerk in charge of a post at the mouth of the Wild Horse River, B.C., in 1864. He died in 1916. The mountain overlooks Michel Creek, B.C. The peak was named in 1960.

PHILOMENA, hamlet (G-7)
From the Greek word for nightingale. (1917)

PIBROCH, hamlet (H-5)
Pibroch was a Scottish settlement. The word refers to the music of the bagpipe. The name is said to have been chosen by a settler whose cat was named Pibroch. The station name was formerly Debney after Philip Debney, Edmonton, Dunvegan and British Columbia Railway engineer. (1910)

PICHÉ, lake and river (G-7)
After a Chipewyan Indian who lived on the Heart Lake Indian Reserve nearby.

PICKARDVILLE, hamlet (I-5)
After William Pickard, first postmaster. (1907)

PICTURE, butte (N-6)
Near Piyami coulee. Known in Blackfoot as a-natskimikway, "the beautiful hill", (Nelson). The name is descriptive.

PICTURE BUTTE, town (N-6)
See Picture, butte.

PIERRE, river (E-7)
After one Pierre Shetler, a well-known Indian trapper who once lived in the area. (1950)

PIGEON, lake and hills (J-5)
Formerly known as Woodpecker Lake; in Cree hmi-hmoo; in Stoney ka-ka-gamna (Tyrrell). Hector in his Journal of November 27, 1858 uses the modern name of Pigeon Lake: "We were travelling through a wide shallow valley that lies between the Beaver Hills and the Woodpecker Hills that overhang Pigeon Lake."

PIGEON LAKE, creek (J-5)
Known formerly as Woodpecker Creek; in Cree hmi-hmoo sakha'-higan si-pi-sis; in Stoney ke-gemni-wapta, (Tyrrell). See also Pigeon, lake.

PIGEON LAKE, Indian Reserve (J-5)
See Pigeon, lake.

PIGEON, mountain (7,855 feet) (L-4)
Named by Bourgeau of the Palliser Expedition in 1858; probably after the wild pigeons seen in the vicinity.

PIKA, peak (10,015 feet) (L-4)
So named because a rock formation at the top is said to resemble the pika, a small rodent dwelling at high altitudes.

PILKINGTON, mount (10,830 feet) (K-3)
After Charles Pilkington, president, Alpine Club, England; it is on the Collie map of 1899.

PILOT, mountain (9,650 feet) (L-4)
Named by G. M. Dawson in 1884 because it is visible for a long distance down the valley.

PINCHER, creek (N-5)
Oldman River. The name used in surveyors' reports dated 1880. Dawson gives the name as *in-oks-spitz* or "little Highwood river." "A pair of pincers (pinchers as it is sometimes spelt) were lost by a party of prospectors around 1868 and tools being precious in those days, this was a natural calamity and as such was commemorated in the name given to this stream." (Terry Lyon, Secretary-Treasurer, Town of Pincher Creek, letter, August, 1970)

PINCHER, hamlet (N-5)
See Pincher, creek (1960)

PINCHER CREEK, town (N-5)
After Pincher, creek, (q.v.).

PINE LAKE, locality (K-6)
Situated on Ghostpine Lake, (q.v.). (1895)

PINGLE, locality (F-7)
After Charles Stewart Pingle (1880-1928). He was Mayor of Medicine Hat from 1910-1912 and was elected to the Alberta Legislature in 1913 as Member for Redcliffe and again in 1917. In 1920 he was elected Speaker of the Legislature on the death of the former Speaker, C. W. Fisher. He was defeated in 1921 when the United Farmers of Alberta assumed office. He was again elected in a by-election as Member for Medicine Hat and again at the general election of 1926. (1925)

PINHORN, locality (O-8)
Formerly a quarantine station; it was named after Dr. G. C. Pinhorn, first Veterinary Inspector appointed to represent the Department of Agriculture. (1914)

PINNACLE, mountain (10,062 feet) (L-4)
Upper Bow River; a descriptive name given by Wilcox.

PINTO, lake (K-4)
A. P. Coleman (1852-1939), says that though Pinto "was more trouble as a packhorse than all the others put together, we immortalised him by giving his name to an exquisite lake."

PIPESTONE, pass (8,033 feet) and river (L-4)
The Pipestone Pass was first crossed by the Earl of Southesk and shortly thereafter by Hector in one of his side explorations from the main Palliser Expedition. It is said to have been named by Hector from the occurrence along the river of soft-fine-grained grey-blue argilite, a soft easily workable rock which the Indians used in the manufacture of pipes. In Stoney it is known as *pa-hooh-to-hi-agoo-pi-wap-ta* and in Cree *mono-spaw-gun-na-nis-si-pki* signifying "blue pipestone river."

PIRMEZ CREEK, locality (L-5)
After one Count Raoul Pirmez, one time owner of the Belgian Horse Ranch. (1910)

PITLOCHRIE, locality (H-7)
After Pitlochry, Perthshire, Scotland. (1916)

PIVOT, locality (M-8)
A turning point of the railway. (1924)

PLAIN, lake and PLAIN LAKE, locality (I-7)
From the position of the lake between two plains (Steele).

PLAMONDON, village (H-6)
After settlers from Michigan who first settled at Morinville, then at Plamondon. (1909)

PLANTE, creek (I-3)
After one Tommy Plante a trapper in the district. (1947)

PLATEAU, mountain (8,000 feet), and creek (N-5)
Head of Livingstone River; a descriptive name

PLEASANT VIEW, locality (G-6)
A descriptive name. It was known as Windy Ridge until 1915.

PLUVIUS, lake (E-3)
Latin for "rainy."

POBOKTAN, pass (7,400 feet), mountain (10,902 feet), and creek (K-3)
The Stoney word for "owl." The creek and pass were named by A. P. Coleman in 1892. Coleman notes: "Crossing the barren pass next morning, we followed a creek flowing north-west toward a wide river valley which we had looked at longingly from a mountain top some days before. We named the pass and creek Poboktan from the big owls that blinked at us from the spruce trees . . ."

POCATERRA, creek (M-5)
After George Pocaterra (1882-1972), pioneer rancher. The son of an aristocratic Italian family, Pocaterra came to Canada as a young man and after a short time in Winnipeg, came to Calgary and got a job on the Bar D Ranch near High River. After working for a time as a cowhand he established one of Canada's first dude ranches, the Buffalo Head on the Highwood River. In 1906 he penetrated into the area southwest of his ranch and from the summit of the Rockies saw the Kananaskis Lakes, the first white man to do so from the south. Subsequently he made a number of trips into the area, exploring and faithfully noting

what he had observed. In 1933 he returned to Italy and while there married, but in 1940 he returned to Calgary and settled on the Ghost River in 1941 and in 1955 established a home and school in Calgary for singers as his wife was an opera singer. Elpoca Mountain (q.v.), was also named for him. (*The Albertan*, March 14, 1972)

POE, locality (J-6)
After Edgar Allan Poe (1809-1849), American novelist and poet. (1909)

POLLOCKVILLE, hamlet (L-7)
After R. Pollock, one time postmaster. (1910)

PONITA, lake (G-1)
Cree word for "end"; as the surveyors finished their work near the lake.

PONOKA, town and county (J-6)
Blackfoot Indian for "elk." Prior to receiving its present name the town was known as Siding 14. (1904)

POPES, peak (10,376 feet) (L-4)
After John Henry Pope (1824-1889). He was a Member of the Legislative Assembly for the old Province of Canada from 1857-1863. He became a Member of the House of Commons from 1867-1871 and was Minister of Agriculture from 1871-1873 and from 1878-1885. From 1885-1889 he was Minister of Railways and Canals. The feature was formerly known as Boundary Peak but the name was changed by Order-in-Council of 1887.

POPLAR RIDGE, hamlet (F-2)
It is situated on a ridge where there is a heavy poplar growth. (1951)

PORCUPINE, hills (N-5)
On Palliser map, 1865; from resemblance of one of the hills, in outline, to a porcupine; the Blackfoot name, *ky-es-kaghp-ogh-suy-iss*, means porcupine tail. Palliser refers to them as "Montagne de Porquepique" which would infer that they had been named by Canadian hunters at an earlier date.

PORTAL, peak (9,552 feet) (L-3)
West of Bow lake; named by Thompson in 1916, being descriptive of its position at the entrance to the valley.

PORTAL, THE, pass (6,100 feet) (J-2)
A descriptive name.

POTHOLE, creek (N-6)
St. Mary River; from the appearance of a hole in the side of a hill.

POUCE COUPÉ, river (F-1)
This river, which flows from British Columbia into Alberta where it joins the Peace, is named for a Sikani trapper who was given the nickname of "Pouce Coupé" by the French Canadian voyageurs as he had lost a thumb as a result of an accident with his gun. He is mentioned in Simon Fraser's journal in 1806.

POWELL, lake (G-1)
After Flying Officer L. W. Powell, D.F.C., of Edmonton, who was killed in World War II. (1947)

PRAIRIE, creek (M-5)
Clearwater River; it appears as Prairie River on Arrowsmith map, 1859.
In Cree it is *mas-kioo-te-oo*; in Stoney, *tin-dow-wap-ta* (Tyrrell).

PRAIRIE BLOOD, coulee (N-6)
So named because it is in the Blood Indian Reserve. The Indian name
means "many ghosts river", (Steele). (1960)

PRETTY, hill (J-6)
Translation of Cree *ka-mi-wa-sitis-pa-tin-ow*. (Tyrrell).

PRIDDIS, locality (M-5)
After Charles Priddis who homesteaded in the area in 1886. He was
actually the second settler; the first was Jim Ockley who arrived in
1883. (1894)

PRIME, creek (J-3)
After W. Prime, who located coal on the creek.

PRIMROSE, locality (I-8)
Formerly known as Primula Post Office; probably after the primula or
primrose. (1913)

PRINCE, lake (J-5)
Origin of name unknown but lake visited by Hector, 1858; on Palliser
maps, 1859. Possibly named after a prince of royal blood.

PRINCESS, locality (M-7)
After Princess Patricia (Lady Patricia Ramsey, 1886); the adjoining
community is Patricia (q.v.). (1914)

PRINCESS MARGARET, mountain (L-4)
East of Banff, Fairholme Range; in honour of Her Royal Highness
Princess Margaret (1930-   ), who visited Alberta in 1958.

PROSPECT, mountain (9,000 feet) and creek (J-3)
McLeod River; the mountain was named in 1922 after the creek,
which was the local name, describing a pleasing prospect.

PROSPECT VALLEY, locality (J-8)
A descriptive name. (1910)

PROTECTION, mountain (9,140 feet) (L-4)
East of Baker Creek; it shuts off an unusually beautiful valley from
Baker Creek valley. (1911)

PROVOST, town and municipal district (K-8)
"Provost" is the title applied to the chief magistrate of a Scottish
town and is the equivalent of mayor in Canada.
"Having lived in the area between Macklin, Saskatchewan and
Amisk, Alberta since 1926 and having known many of the original
settlers throughout those districts I have come to the conclusion that
most of the railroad town names were chosen haphazardly by some
official in the Canadian Pacific Railway Company office in Eastern
Canada prior to settlement. Perhaps only Metiskow and Amisk do not
fall into this category. They may be of Cree Indian Origin.

'Provost' is probably in memory of the chief magistrate (mayor) of a Scottish city (cathedral town). In support of this theory it may be pointed out that the streets (north-south) are named after urban centres in Scotland", (J. S. Stewart, Municipal Secretary, letter, 1970).

PROW, mountain (9,535 feet)   (K-4)
So called because it resembles the prow of a ship.

PTARMIGAN, peak (10,060 feet), and lake   (L-4)
From the large numbers of ptarmigan that frequent the area.

PTOLEMY, mount (9,234 feet) and creek   (N-5)
Crowsnest River; J. N. Wallace says that the peak and shoulders of the mountain resemble a man lying on his back and that the peak was named "Mummy" in 1900. Later it was changed to Ptolemy after the dynasty that ruled Egypt as having "a similar meaning and being more dignified."

PUFFER, locality   (K-7)
After W. F. Puffer (1861-?), Lacombe, member of the Alberta Legislative Assembly, 1905-1917. (1908)

PULLAR, lake   (H-7)
After Flight Lieutenant W. S. Pullar, D.F.C., Delia, killed in World War II. (1951)

PULPIT, peak (8,940 feet)   (L-3)
Named by Thompson, 1898; descriptive.

PULSATILLA, mountain (10,060 feet) and pass   (L-4)
Pulsatilla is a sub-generic name for one section of the genus *anemone* and many of these were probably seen in the vicinity. (1911)

PURPLE SPRINGS, locality   (N-7)
After a spring in a coulee where purple flowers grow. (1893)

PUSKIAKIWENIN, Indian Reserve   (I-8)
Name of a chief who was a noted gambler.

PUSKWASKAU, lake and river   (G-2)-(G-3)
A Cree name meaning "dry grass."

PYRAMID, mountain (9,076 feet), lake and creek   (J-2)
Descriptive; this well-known landmark near Jasper was named by Hector in 1859.

— Q —

QUADRA, mountain (10,410 feet)   (L-4)
It has four pinnacles.

QUARREL, locality   (J-7)
After a lake, now dry, known in Cree as *kekatomokichewonepekehsakigan* or "quarrel spring lake", an old Indion camping place where there were many quarrels between hunting parties, (Steele).

QUEEN ELIZABETH, mount (9,349 feet) (M-4)
After the former Queen of Belgium, Consort of King Albert I (1875-1934). (1918)

QUEEN ELIZABETH, ranges (J-3)
Named after Her Majesty Queen Elizabeth II (1926-   ) to commemorate her coronation, June 2, 1953. This range almost encircles Maligne Lake, (q.v.). (1953)

QUIGLEY, creek (J-3)
After the McPherson and Quigley Lumber Company, who operated a sawmill on the creek. (1925)

QUINCY, mount (10,400 feet) and creek (K-3)
Named by A. P. Coleman in 1892, after his brother, Lucius Quincy Coleman, a rancher at Morley, Alberta. Their mother (née Adams), was a relative of John Quincy Adams, sixth President of the United States.

QUIRK, mount (6,200 feet) and creek (M-5)
After J. Quirk, early settler.

— R —

RACEHORSE, creek (N-5)
Flows into Oldman River; probably descriptive as it has a swift current.

RADIANT, creek (K-4)
Flows into Idlewild Creek; probably descriptive.

RADNOR, locality (L-5)
After Wilma, daughter of the 5th Earl of Radnor and wife of the 2nd Earl of Lathom. (1884)

RADWAY, village (I-6)
Named after Orland S. Radway, first postmaster and storekeeper in the district.

RAE, mount (10,150 feet) and creek (M-5)
This mountain was named by Hector after Dr. John Rae (1813-1893) who was appointed surgeon in 1833 to the Hudson's Bay Company's ship. Two years later he became resident surgeon at Moose Fort. In 1846 he made his first journey of exploration surveying some 100 miles of the Arctic coast on Committee Bay. In 1848-1849 he took part in the search for the Franklin Expedition. After his appointment to the Mackenzie River district he took charge of searching expeditions for Franklin in 1850 and again in 1853-1854 and it was on this latter expedition that he at last obtained some information about the ill-fated Franklin Expedition. Later he toured the United States and conducted a survey for a telegraph from Red River to the Pacific Coast.

RAFT, lake (F-8)
Surveyors used a raft to cross it.

RAINIER, hamlet (M-7)
It was founded about 1906 by Americans and named after Rainier, Washington which in turn was after Mount Rainier which was named by Captain George Vancouver in 1792 after Rear Admiral Peter Rainier, (1741-1808).

RAJAH, peak (9,903 feet) (J-2)
East Indian for "king"—descriptive; see also Ranee, peak.

RALEY, locality (O-6)
After one C. Raley, Lethbridge. (1902)

RALSTON, hamlet (M-7)
Northwest of Medicine Hat. After Colonel J. L. Ralston (1881-1948), Minister of National Defence from 1940-1944. He was an able minister and administrator but found himself at odds with the Prime Minister (W. L. Mackenzie King) and resigned in 1944 over the conscription issue. (1949)

RAM, river (K-4)
North Saskatchewan River. It appears as Ram rivulet on David Thompson's map, 1814; probably after the male of the Rocky Mountain sheep.

RAM RIVER, glacier (K-4)
At head of Ram River (q.v.). (1965)

RAMPARTS, THE, range (J-2)
West of the Amethyst Lakes. Resembles a series of fortresses. (1916)

RANCHING, locality (K-6)
Descriptive of its location in a ranching area. (1911)

RANCHVILLE, locality (N-8)
So named because it is in the centre of a ranching area. It was known as Peighan Post Office until 1913.

RANDALL, lake (F-4)
Northeast of Utikuma Lake. After Captain Robert Cheethan Randall former bush pilot of Edmonton and later associated with Canadian Pacific Airlines. (1954)

RANEE, peak (9,641 feet) (J-2)
East Indian for "queen"—descriptive; see also Rajah, peak.

RANFURLY, hamlet (I-7)
After Sir Uchter John Mark Knox (1856-1933), the 5th Earl of Ranfurly, Renfrew, Scotland; Governor of New Zealand, 1897-1904. (1905)

RAVEN, river and locality (K-5)
Translation of the Cree name, ka-ka-koo; in Stoney, kai-him-bu-wap-ta, (Tyrrell).

RAVINE, locality (I-4)
So called because the original site of the post office was in a ravine. (1911)

RAYMOND, town (N-6)
After the elder son of Jesse W. Knight, prominent Mormon citizen. "Ray" Knight as he was known, became a rancher and owned two large ranches, the K2 and the Kircaldy. (1902)

RECO, locality (J-3)
A compound name of the initial letters of *Reliance Coal* Company. (1926)

RED DEER, city and county (K-5)
The City of Red Deer takes its name from the Red Deer River (q.v.) which flows through it. For a number of years the Calgary-Edmonton trail crossed the river at a point known as Red Deer Crossing and with the coming of the Canadian Pacific Railway to Calgary traffic over the trail increased and a trading post and stopping place were established.

The present city owes its location to a combination of circumstances whereby Dr. Leonard Gaetz (1841-1907) gave some 1,240 acres of land to the Calgary and Edmonton Railway for a townsite. With the coming of the railway the former Red Deer Crossing came to an end.

Leonard Gaetz was a native of Nova Scotia. He originally was destined to be a minister of the Methodist Church and actually had churches in Montreal and Ontario. However, his health began to fail and he came west, stopping first at Calgary and then going north to Edmonton. He decided to homestead on the west half of a section on the Red Deer River and one of his sons, Halley Gaetz took up the other half section and parts of three other sections were purchased from the Saskatchewan Colonization Company and by the time that the survey of the Calgary and Edmonton Railway reached the Red Deer River, the Gaetz holdings covered some 1,200 acres at the junction of the Red Deer River and Waskasoo Creek. At this time Gaetz bought out the trading post at Red Deer Crossing, putting one of his sons in charge. He sold produce from his farm to the North-West Mounted Police posts at Calgary and Fort Saskatchewan, operated a sawmill, and drew attention to the possibilities of the area for farming.

At a meeting in Dr. Gaetz's house the location of the railway station for Red Deer was determined and the townsite was set up on the land he gave the railway and Red Deer came into existence.

In 1895 Dr. Gaetz returned to the ministry and went to a charge in Manitoba later transferring to a large church in Winnipeg. Once again this proved detrimental to his health and he returned to Red Deer in 1901 where he resided for the remainder of his life. (*Edmonton Journal*, January 22, 1955)

RED DEER, river (L-4) - (M-8) and lake (J-6)
Translation of the Indian name *was-ka-sioo si-pi* in Cree meaning "the Elk River"; *pa-chi-ci* in Stoney (Tyrrell); from the numerous elk in the area in the early days and mistaken by the Scottish factors for the "red deer" of their homeland. (K. Wood, *The Albertan*, January 13, 1973.)

RED MAN, mount (9,493 feet) (M-4)
From the red colour of the rock, and in contrast to Mount White Man, (see also White Man, mount). (1918)

REDAN, mountain (8,400 feet) (J-2)
Descriptive. A redan is a military field work with two faces forming a salient angle. (1916)

REDCAP, mountain (7,852 feet) (J-3)
Head of Pembina River; a descriptive name.

REDCLIFF, town (N-8)
The word Redcliff had become a commonplace name long before the town was thought of, and it was appropriate that the town be called Redcliff after the outcropping of the red shale overlooking the river just south and east of the present town site.

REDEARTH, creek (L-5)
So named from the red ochre found in places on its banks. It was formerly called "Vermilion", but the name was changed at the suggestion of G. M. Dawson to avoid duplication.

REDOUBT, lake and mountain (9,510 feet) (L-4)
Named by Wheeler in 1908, as the rock formation resembled a huge redoubt or a military outwork or fieldwork without flanking defences.

REDWATER, river (I-6)
It was Vermilion River on David Thompson's map, 1814, and was changed to avoid duplication. The name is from the beds of red ochre which give the water at times a distinctive red colour.

REDWATER, town (I-6)
The town of Redwater is named after the Redwater River. The original name of the river was Vermilion, given to it by David Thompson, the great explorer, when he journeyed through this district map making for the North West Company. Because of the fact that it was confused with another river of the same name, it was changed to Redwater River (q.v.) by one of the pioneer women settlers. It is located one and one half miles north of the townsite and joins the North Saskatchewan River at a point eight miles east of the town.

REEF, icefield (J-2)
East of Mount Robson; so called because the icefield is traversed by rock reefs.

RELIANCE, locality (N-7)
After a coal mine of the Reliance Coal Company.

RENO, hamlet (F-3)
Presumably after Reno, Nevada, U.S.A., though there are other places of the name in the United States. The U.S. name is that of one General J. L. Reno, killed at South Mountain in 1862. (1915)

REPLICA, peak (9,167 feet) (J-3)
Presumably it closely resembles another peak. (1923)

RESTLESS, river (J-2)
Tributary to Rocky River. The river frequently changes its course.

RETLAW, locality (N-7)
The name of the original post office was changed from Barney, September 1, 1913; "Walter" reversed; after Walter R. Baker, private secretary, 1874-1878 to the Earl of Dufferin, then Governor General of Canada; afterwards assistant to the general manager, Canadian Pacific Railway and ultimately secretary.

RHONDDA, mount (10,025 feet) (K-4)
After David Alfred Thomas, 1st Viscount Rhondda (1856-1918). A native of the Rhondda Valley of Wales (from which he took his title), he was manager of the Rhondda Valley Coalfields and for 22 years sat as a Member of Parliament for Merthyr Tydfil. In 1915 he visited Canada on a war purchasing mission. Prior to that he had headed a syndicate to develop the Peace River area; this involved agriculture, the building of a railway from the B.C. coast to Prince Albert, Saskatchewan and the development of river transportation but World War I halted this. In 1916 he was head of the Board of Local Government and in 1917 Minister of Food. (1918)

RIBSTONE, lake and creek (J-8)
Battle River on Palliser map, 1865; in Cree *as-sin-i-kos-pike-gan-it;* a large stone bears marks resembling a man's ribs, (Tyrrell).

RICHARDS, mount (7,800 feet) (O-5)
After Captain (later Admiral) G. R. Richards, R.N., second Commissioner, British Boundary Commission, Pacific to the Rockies and who made hydrographic surveys of the British Columbia coast, 1856-1863. He was Captain of H.M.S. *Plumper,* a ship engaged extensively in surveys of the British Columbia coast. (1917)

RICHARDSON, mount (10,125 feet) (L-4)
Named by Hector after Sir John Richardson (1787-1865) who was surgeon and naturalist on the Arctic expeditions of Franklin, 1819 and 1825. In 1848-1849, he accompanied Rae on the Franklin search expedition. See also Rae, mount and creek.

RICHARDSON, river and lake (C-7)
After a member of a survey party.

RICHDALE, locality (L-7)
A descriptive name. (1910)

RICINUS, locality (K-5)
Latin name of the castor oil plant. (1913)

RIDGECLOUGH, locality (J-8)
After the farm, in Ontario, of W. B. Gordon, former postmaster. (1912)

RIMBEY, town (J-5)
After Samuel Newton Rimbey (1868-1952). Samuel Rimbey was a native of Illinois and, as a young man moved first to Kansas with his two brothers. In 1901 he led a trek of some two hundred pioneers to Alberta where they homesteaded in the Blindman River valley. The homestead of the Rimbey brothers was on the site of the present town.

RINGROSE, peak (10,755 feet) (L-4)
Named by S. E. S. Allen, 1894, after one A. E. L. Ringrose, London, England, an extensive traveller in the Rockies.

RIO GRANDE, locality (G-1)
Named "Grande", because it is in the Grande Prairie country; "rio" because of the Red Willow River, half a mile distant. (1919)

RIVERBEND, locality   (I-6)
Named for its location at a bend of the North Saskatchewan River.

RIVERBOW, locality   (M-7)
Descriptive of its situation on the Bow River. (1909)

RIVERCOURSE, locality   (J-8)
So named because it is near Blackfoot Coulee. (1907)

RIVIÈRE-QUI-BARRE, hamlet   (I-5)
See Barre, Rivière-qui, river. (1895)

ROBB, hamlet   (J-3)
Named after P. A. Robb; it was formerly Minehead. The mine was sold to the Balkan Coal Company and the hamlet was re-named Robb.

ROBERTSON, locality and lake   (L-5) (B-6)
After Private James Peter Robertson. V.C., 27th Battalion, Canadian Infantry, former locomotive engineer; killed in World War I in November, 1917. When his platoon was held up by a machine gun and uncut wire, he reached the machine gun, killed four of the crew and turned the gun on the remainder. (1919)

ROBERTSON, mount (10,400 feet)   (N-5)
After General Sir William Robertson, Chief of Imperial General Staff at Headquarters, until February, 1918. (1918)

ROBSON, pass (5,147 feet)   (J-2)
This pass, on the Alberta-British Columbia boundary takes its name from nearby Mount Robson (12,972 feet) the highest mountain in the Canadian Rockies.

    The origin of the name is obscure. It was known as "Robson's Peak" and is so mentioned by Milton and Cheadle in their book *North West Passage by Land* (London, 1865) for they passed it on their famous overland journey.

    The most probable explanation for the origin of the name is that the mountain and pass take their name from Colin Robertson (1783-1842) who served with both the North West Company and the Hudson's Bay Company in the Athabasca Department and who after his retirement from the fur trade became a Member of Parliament of the United Provinces of Upper and Lower Canada. Robertson in 1820 sent a company of Iroquois fur hunters into the area (possibly including François Decoigne or "Tête Jaune", the fair haired trader). They must have passed near the mountain, sighted it and Decoigne may then, or on a previous occasion, (for he was familiar with the area) named the peak in honour of his superior officer. As it would be easy to slur the name "Robertson" to Robson, the mountain, and later the pass, may well have received their common name in this manner.

ROCHE, mount (8,100 feet)   (O-5)
Named after Lieutenant Richard Roche, R.N., a member of the British Boundary Commission party which surveyed and marked the International Boundary from the Pacific to the Rockies. Roche entered the Royal Navy in 1845 and served on the Pacific Coast and later in the Arctic during the search for Sir John Franklin. In 1857 he was

posted as third lieutenant to H.M.S. *Satellite* and served with the Boundary Commission. He retired in 1879 with the rank of Captain. (1917)

ROCHESTER, hamlet (M-6)

After Herbert Rochester, secretary to M. H. MacLeod, who was at one time general manager of western lines of the Canadian Northern Railway from 1909 to 1915. In 1912 the Canadian Northern built a railway to Athabasca Landing from Edmonton. A townsite was laid out and given the name of Ideal Flat. This did not please the residents and at a public meeting the name was changed to Rochester.

ROCHFORT BRIDGE, hamlet (I-4)

The post office name was changed from Wanekville, 1921, although it was formerly known as Rockfort; after the first storekeeper Mr. Rochfort. The bridge located one half mile east of the hamlet was at one time the largest wooden railroad trestle in Canada and spans the Paddle River. (1920)

ROCKY, buttes (M-7)

Translation of Blackfoot name, *okotokskway* (Nelson). It is a descriptive name.

ROCKY, mountains (I-1) (O-5)

The Rocky Mountains were known to the Cree as *as-sin-wati;* to the Stoneys as *ni-a-ha* (Tyrrell) and to the Blackfoot as *mis-tokis* (Nelson). Viewed from the plains they resemble a great wall of rock. The name "montagnes de Roche" first appeared in the journal of Legardeue de St. Pierre in 1752 although it is doubtful if he saw the main range.

For years the fur traders had been told by the Indians of a great range of mountains far to the west of the plains, the "Shining Mountains". James Knight (d. 1719) Governor of Fort Churchill wrote in 1716 that the "Mountain Indians" dwelt at a great distance in a land where the mountains rose almost to the skies. This is perhaps the earliest description of the Rockies.

The Rocky Mountains remained an enigma until 1754 when Anthony Henday who was exploring the western prairies for the Hudson's Bay Company viewed them from a hill near the present site of Innisfail and was thus the first European to see them.

ROCKY, river (J-2)

A descriptive name.

ROCKY LANE, locality (C-4)

The name is derived from a formation of a narrow strip of rocks which runs through the district.

ROCKY MOUNTAIN HOUSE, town (K-5)

Rocky Mountain House was established in 1799 by the North West Company and was for seventy years the most westerly and southerly fort in the Blackfeet country. In 1802 David Thompson made his first attempt to cross the Rocky Mountains from here. In 1807 he set out on the expedition which succeeded in crossing the mountains to the headwaters of the Columbia.

In 1799 James Bird of the Hudson's Bay Company built Acton House nearby. It was closed in 1807, re-opened in 1813 but was finally aban-

oned in 1821 in favour of Rocky Mountain House after the union of
the two companies in that year. From 1828 to 1861 Rocky Mountain
House was open only in the winter months for trade. It was abandoned
in 1861 but rebuilt in 1864. It was finally closed permanently in 1875
in favour of a post at Calgary. The post was known in Blackfoot as
a-pastan (Nelson), in Stoney as *ti-shi-a* and in Cree as *kai-as as-wati
was-ka-higan* (Tyrrell).

ROCKY RAPIDS, hamlet   (J-5)
After rapids in the North Saskatchewan River, nearby.

ROCKY VIEW, locality and municipal district   (L-6)
It is on a spur line of Canadian Pacific Railway in Rocky View
Municipal District and the Rocky Mountains can be viewed from here.
(1962)

ROCKYFORD, village   (L-6)
Descriptive. (1914)

RODNEY, creek   (I-3)
After a member of Grand Trunk Pacific Railway survey party. (1910)

ROMA, locality   (F-3)
After Stanley Roma Lamb, former resident engineer of the Canadian
Pacific Railway. (1922)

ROMEO, lake and creek   (I-5)
After J. R. Romeo, early settler.

RONALANE, locality   (N-7)
After one Major-General Sir Ronald B. Lane. He served in the Zulu
War, 1879, the Egyptian Campaign of 1882 and the South African War,
1899-1901. He was later Lieutenant Governor and Secretary of the
Chelsea Royal Hospital. (1914)

RONAN, post office   (I-4)
After Ronan, Montana. (1912)

RONDE, ROCHE, mountain (7,014 feet) and creek   (J-2)
French for "round", descriptive; mentioned by Grant in *Ocean to
Ocean,* 1873.

ROROS, locality   (J-8)
After Roros copper mine, Norway. It is a Norwegian settlement. (1914)

ROSALIND, village   (J-6)
Name combination of Montrose and East Lynn. (1905)

ROSE LYNN, locality   (L-7)
The ridge on which the former post office was situated was covered
with rose bushes. (1910)

ROSEBUD, river and hamlet   (L-5) (L-6)
Known in Cree as *mis-sas-ka-too-mina* or Serviceberry Creek; in Stoney
as *mi-thaga-waptan* (Tyrrell); and in Blackfoot as *akokiniskway,*
meaning "many rosebuds," Grierson was the post office name until 1896.

ROSEDALE, hamlet (L-6)
After Rosedale Colliery, an adjoining mine. It is believed that Peter Fidler in 1793 saw coal at the mouth of Rosebud Creek near Rosedale but there is some doubt as to this. Frank Moody opened the Rosedale Mine in 1912 and ferried both coal and supplies across the Red Deer River until a pile bridge was placed across the river in 1914.

ROSEGLEN, locality (M-8)
There are said to be no more than the usual amount of roses here. (1913)

ROSELAND, lake (H-7)
Approximately 11 miles east of Lac la Biche; after Flight Lieutenant A. W. Roseland, Black Diamond, Alberta, killed in World War II. (1951)

ROSELEA, locality (I-5)
Harry Howard, postmaster, gave the name of his mother's cottage in England for this place. (1913)

ROSEMARY, village (M-7)
After Rosemary Millicent, daughter of the 4th Duke of Sutherland, who acquired an extensive farm at Brooks. (1914)

ROSENHEIM, locality (K-8)
After a town in Bavaria, the former home of early settlers. (1909)

ROSEVEAR, locality (I-4)
After one J. M. Rosevear, chief clerk, Audit Department, Grand Trunk Pacific Railway. (1911)

ROSS, creek (N-8)
After one Roderick Ross, Indian trader, who resided on the creek in 1875.

ROSS COX, mount (9,840 feet) and creek (J-2)
After Ross Cox (1793-1853) traveller and author. Cox was a native of Dublin and emigrated to America in 1811 entering the service of J. J. Astor's Pacific Fur Company. He was at Astoria at the time of its surrender to the North West Company in 1812 and took service with that company as a clerk but retired in 1817 after which he returned to Ireland. On his return he travelled from the Columbia to Montreal via the Athabasca Pass and recounted his adventures in a book *Adventures on the Columbia River*, 1831.

ROSYTH, locality (J-7)
After Rosyth, Scotland, a famous naval base in World War I. (1909)

ROULEAU, lake (O-5)
This name was supplied by field topographer J. A. Macdonald, and is said to be named after a former member of the Royal Canadian Mounted Police, who owned a farm there. (1942)

ROUND HILL, hamlet (J-6)
From a round hill two miles west. (1904)

ROWAND, mount (8,800 feet) (J-2)
After John Rowand (1787-1854) fur trader who became Chief Factor at Edmonton in 1826 and continued in that capacity until his sudden

death in 1854 at Fort Pitt. He was a colourful figure, a man of quick temper and was extremely adept at dealing with the Indians.

Rowand was a great friend of Sir George Simpson and accompanied him on his journey around the world as far as Hawaii. Shortly before his death he expressed to Simpson his wish to be buried in Montreal. After he died, his remains were exhumed on Simpson's orders and conveyed in a rum keg down river but as the voyageurs came to realize what the keg contained, Simpson deemed it wise not to send it directly to Montreal as it might be surreptitiously disposed of enroute. Accordingly the remains went by ship to England and then back to Montreal where they were ultimately interred.

ROWE, mount (8,043 feet) and creek (O-5)
After Lieutenant Rowe, R.E., surveying officer, British Boundary Commission, Lake of the Woods to the Rockies, 1872-1876. (1917)

ROWLEY, hamlet (L-6)
After C. W. Rowley, one time assistant general manager, Canadian Bank of Commerce, Toronto. He was formerly stationed in Calgary. (1911)

ROYAL PARK, locality (I-7)
A descriptive name alluding to parkland. (1921)

RUBY, mountain (9,500 feet) and creek (J-3)
Cardinal River; after the red colour of the strata in it.

RUBY, ridge (O-5)
After the beds of bright red shale near its summit. (1915)

RUMSEY, village (K-6)
This village takes its name from a banker — Reginald Arthur Rumsey (1875-19?) who was chief inspector and subsequently assistant general manager of the Canadian Bank of Commerce. This bank provided financial backing for the construction of the Canadian Northern Railway. (1911)

RUNDLE, mount (9,338 feet) (L-4)
This well-known landmark at Banff takes its name from Reverend Robert Terrill Rundle (1811-1896), the most famous Methodist missionary to the Indians of the Northwest. He travelled among them from 1840-1848, ministering to their needs. In 1849 he returned to England, broken in health as a result of the strain of his travels and privations in all seasons.

RUSSELL, lake and creek (E-4)
After John Russell, D.L.S. (1915)

RUSSELL, mount (9,000 feet) (J-3)
After one Thomas Russell, pioneer prospector. (1925)

RUSYLVIA, locality (I-7)
A combination of Latin words to represent "wooded country." (1912)

RUTHERFORD, mount (9,342 feet) (J-2)
After Alexander Cameron Rutherford (1857-1941). Rutherford was a native of Ontario and a graduate of McGill University in Arts and Law. He came west in 1895 to set up a law firm in Strathcona (now South

Edmonton). In 1902 he was elected to the Assembly of the North-West Territories and served for three years as Deputy Speaker. In 1905 when Alberta became a province he headed the first Liberal administration. In 1910 he was forced to resign over dissensions within his party due to the Alberta and Great Waterways Railway troubles. He became Chancellor of the University of Alberta in 1928 and held that post until his death.

RUTLEDGE, lake (A-7)
After a distinguished English geologist, Harold Rutledge, killed in the early stages of a promising career in igneous-metamorphic geology. (1958)

RUTTAN, lake (H-5)
After Private Wilmot Ruttan, Flatbush, killed in World War II, whose homestead adjoined the section in which the lake is situated. (1948)

RYCROFT, village (F-2)
Until 1920 Rycroft was known as Spirit River. In that year the post office (Rycroft) was moved to the crossroads while Spirit River was moved two miles to the west.

Mr. N. E. Persson, Municipal Secretary of Rycroft writes: "This is to advise that the Village of Rycroft was named after an early settler named 'Roycroft' who arrived in this area in the early twenties. The name was later shortened and changed to 'Rycroft'," (letter, August, 1970).

RYLEY, village (J-6)
The original hamlet known as Equity was established in 1908 when a few stores were established under squatters' rights about half a mile east of the present townsite. When the main line of the Grand Trunk Pacific Railway arrived about half a mile west of Equity in 1908 the present townsite was surveyed and named Ryley in honour of G. U. Ryley, then land commissioner at Winnipeg. (1909)

— S —

SADDLE, lake and Indian Reserve (H-7)
In Cree, *unechekeskwapewin*, or "dark objects sitting on the ice." Once upon a time the Indians could find no buffalo and were forced to cut holes in the ice and angle for fish and so could be seen all over the lake, (Erasmus).

SADDLE, mountain (7,983 feet) (L-4)
South of Lake Louise; it is on the S. E. S. Allen map of 1894. The name is from its shape, having a resemblance to a saddle.

SAGE, creek (O-8)
Probably after the sage bush.

SAGE, mountain (7,769 feet) and pass (O-5)
Castle River; probably after the sagebrush found in sub-arid districts.

ST. ALBERT, town (I-6)
After Father Albert Lacombe, O.M.I., well-known pioneer missionary in Alberta. According to Father Tardif, former Archivist of the Oblates, Bishop Taché of St. Boniface visited the mission at Lac Ste. Anne in January, 1861 and it was on this occasion that Father Lacombe mentioned his plan of moving the mission to the Sturgeon Valley. Bishop Taché was much impressed by the beautiful scenery and stuck his cane into a snow bank and said: "This will be the site of your new mission and I will name it after your patron St. Albert."

ST. ANNE, LAC, lake (I-5)
This is the Manito Lake of David Thompson but it appears as St. Ann on the Palliser map. The present name dates from 1844 when Reverend Jean Baptiste Thibault founded a mission here and named it and the lake after Ste. Anne de Beaupré, Quebec.

ST. BRIDE, mount (10,875 feet) (L-4)
South of Mount Douglas at the headwaters of the Red Deer River; after the patron saint of the Douglas family. (1916)

ST. EDOUARD, locality (I-7)
Edouard Coté and Edouard Labrie were the first two settlers in the area. St. Edouard was the name of the local church prior to the opening of the first post office. (1909)

ST. ELOI, mountain (8,216 feet) (O-5)
After the village south of Ypres, Belgium, where the Canadian troops fought in 1916. (1917)

ST. JULIEN, mountain (10,140 feet) (K-4)
After the village about three miles northeast of Ypres, where the Canadian troops fought from April 24-May 4, 1915. (1920)

ST. KILDA, locality (O-7)
Named by Donald MacDougall originally from St. Kilda, Outer Hebrides. (1911)

ST. LINA, hamlet (H-7)
Said to have been named for a relative of L. Mageau, one time postmaster. (1912)

ST. MARY, river (N-6)
It was formerly known as *pa-toxiapis-kun* "banks damming the river" (Blackfoot). It takes its present name from the two St. Mary Lakes which form its source in Glacier National Park, Montana. These lakes were named by Father Pierre-Jean De Smet (1801-1873) when on his way to a conference with the Blackfoot. He and his party camped at the foot of the lower lake, erected a large wooden cross and named the lakes St. Mary's Lakes. In 1841 Father De Smet established St. Mary's Mission on the Bitteroot River, Montana, some 150 miles south of the St. Mary River. He also called this river St. Mary's at one time but the name Bitteroot prevailed. (*Montana* Vol. 7, no. 3, July, 1957).

ST. MICHAEL, hamlet (J-6)
The name was taken from that of the local church. (1923)

ST. NICHOLAS, peak (9,616 feet) (L-3)
Southwest of Bow Lake; from a striking rock formation on the side of the peak which is said to resemble Santa Claus. (1908)

ST. PAUL, town (I-7)
St. Paul got its name when Father Lacombe established a mission on the banks of the Saskatchewan in 1866 at Brousseau which was called St. Paul des Cris. Later on Father Thérien established a mission in St. Paul in 1909 and being a Metis settlement the place was then called St. Paul des Metis. In 1912 the village of St. Paul des Metis was incorporated and in 1936 it was incorporated into a town named St. Paul. (Laurent Richard, Secretary-Treasurer, letter, August, 1970).

ST. PIRAN, mount (8,691 feet) (L-4)
West of Lake Louise railway station; it is on the S. E. S. Allen map, 1894 and was named by Wilcox after St. Piran's, Liggan Bay, Cornwall, England, the birthplace of W. J. Astley, sometime manager of the Lake Louise chalet.

SAKAYO, lake (H-6)
Indian for "blackbird".

SALIENT, mountain (9,220 feet) (J-1)
A descriptive name from a fancied resemblance to a projecting fortification. (1923)

SALINE, creek and lake (E-7)
From the saline characteristics of its water.

SALTER, creek (M-5)
Named by G. M. Dawson in 1884 after his packer who lived on the Stoney Reserve at Morley.

SAMSON, lake and Indian Reserve (J-6)
The reserve is named after Chief Samson, while the name of the lake was changed from Battle River Lake to avoid duplication with Battle Lake some fifty miles distant.

SAMSON, peak (10,108 feet) (J-3)
Named by Mrs. Schäffer after a Stoney Indian, Sampson Beaver, who drew a map that guided her to find Maligne Lake. Mrs. Schäffer spells the name "Sampson." (1911)

SAND, river (H-7)
A descriptive name.

SANDSTONE, locality (M-5)
From the sandstone quarries there. (1907)

SANDY, lake (I-5)
A descriptive name. The lake appears on the Palliser map, 1865 and Hector, 1859, refers to "the Sandy Lakes" as forming part of the route from Fort Edmonton to Fort Assiniboine. Edward Ermatinger in his *York Factory Express Journal* notes under date of May 19, 1827 that when en route from Fort Assiniboine to Edmonton "3 men set off to make a wear (weir) at Berland's Lake to supply fish on our arrival." He may have been referring to Sandy Lake as the trader Berland was active in the area at the time.

SANDY BEACH, summer village (I-5)
The name is from Sandy, lake (q.v.) and is descriptive.

SANG, lake   (I-4)
After Tom Sang, pioneer settler whose original homestead was located
near the shore of the lake. (1951)

SANGUDO, village   (I-5)
Deep Creek was the name first suggested for the original settlement here
because most of the settlers lived in the vicinity of Deep Creek. The
Post Office, however, would not accept that name as there was
already a Deep Creek Post Office. So, to get an original name the
settlers decided to make one from the names of some of their number:

   S for Sutton or Sides
   A for Albers
   N for Nanton where Mrs. Albers originally lived
   G for Gaskell
   U they were united in that name
   D for Deep Creek
   O for Orangeville, their school district which was organized before
     there was a post office. (*West of the Fifth*. Lac Ste. Anne
     Historical Society, 1959)

SANSON, peak (7,495 feet)   (L-4)
A peak of Sulphur Mountain where the Dominion Observatory is
situated was named Sanson Peak after Norman Sanson, for many
years the official meteorologist at Banff. His duties required him to
make a trip each day over the trail leading to the summit of the
northern peak of Sulphur Mountain where the observatory is located
in order to take observations. (1948)

SARBACH, mount (10,700 feet)   (K-3)
Named by J. N. Collie, 1897, after Peter Sarbach, first Swiss guide in
Canada. With G. P. Baker and J. N. Collie, he made a first ascent in
August, 1897. Collie notes: "On the 25th we climbed a peak 10,700
feet high, which we named after our guide, Sarbach."

SARCEE, butte and Indian Reserve   (L-5)
After the Sarcee or Sarsi, an Indian tribe of the Athapascan family.
(1882)

SARRAIL, locality (H-6) and mount (10,400 feet)   (M-5)
Both were named after General M. Sarrail, noted French officer in the
First World War. (1916, 1918)

SASKATCHEWAN, mount (10,964 feet) and glacier   (K-3)
After the Saskatchewan River which in turn is from the Cree *kis-is-ska-
tche-wan* meaning "swift current." The North Saskatchewan River
rises at the base of this mountain. See also North Saskatchewan, river
and South Saskatchewan, river.

SASKATOON, hill and lake   (G-2)
After the saskatoon berry.

SAULTEAUX, locality and river   (G-5) (H-5)
After the Ojibwa or Saulteaux Indians of the Lake Superior region.
They were called Saulteaux from their meeting place at the Sault
(Sault St. Marie).

SAUNDERS, locality and creek (K-4)
It was named after B. J. Saunders, D.L.S., O.L.S., Commissioner for Ontario on the Manitoba-Ontario Boundary Survey, 1897, and who surveyed the 11th base line, 1908.

SAURIAN, mountain (9,896 feet) (I-1)
So called because the summit resembles the back of a prehistoric monster. (1925)

SAWBACK, range and locality (L-4)
The range was named by Hector from the vertical beds of grey limestone that form the serrated peaks of the range. The jagged appearance of mountains reminded him of a saw.

SAWDY, locality (H-6)
It was named after W. E. Sawdy, the first postmaster. (1913)

SAWLE, lake (F-4)
It was named after North Sawle, formerly of Edmonton, a one time bush pilot. He was killed in 1953 in India while delivering a jet airliner to Canada for Canadian Pacific Airlines. (1954)

SAWTOOTH, mountain (9,624 feet) (J-3)
Probably descriptive.

SCANDIA, hamlet (M-7)
It was founded as a Scandinavian settlement. (1924)

SCAPA, locality (K-7)
After Scapa Flow, Orkney Islands, Scotland, British naval base during both World Wars.

SCARP, mountain (9,900 feet) (J-2)
Descriptive of its "steepness." (1922)

SCARPE, mountain (8,500 feet) and creek (O-5)
After the river flowing through Arras, France. The Canadian troops fought on the Scarpe in 1917 and 1918. (1917)

SCHELTENS, lake (G-8)
After Pilot Officer Gordon J. Scheltens of Lac la Biche, Alberta. Killed in World War II. (1963)

SCHULER, hamlet (M-8)
After N. B. Schuler, sometime postmaster. (1910)

SCOLLARD, locality (K-6)
Maybe after Bishop D. J. Scollard (1862-1934) of Sault 6te. Marie, Ont. (1911)

SCOTT, mount (10,826 feet), glacier and creek (K-2)
The name was suggested by one G. E. Howard after Captain Robert Falcon Scott, Commander of the British Antarctic Expedition who, with four companions perished on their return journey from the South Pole in 1912.

SCOVIL, creek (J-2)
After a prospector who discovered coal here.

SCRIMGER, mount (9,000 feet) (N-5)
After Captain F. A. C. Scrimger, V.C., M.D., 14th Battalion, C.E.F. On April 25, 1915, when in charge of an advanced dressing station near Ypres, he directed, under heavy fire, the removal of the wounded and personally carried a wounded officer to safety during very heavy fighting. For three days he displayed, day and night, the greatest devotion among the wounded. (1918)

SCULLY, creek (C-3)
After Pilot Officer John J. Scully of Grande Prairie, killed in World War II. (1964)

SEABOLT, creek and ridge (J-2)
After F. Seabolt (1877-1970), rancher, originally from Atlanta, Ga.

SEBA BEACH, summer village (I-5)
The name is said to have been chosen by the postal authorities and may have been taken from the Bible after Seba, one of the sons of Cush, (Genesis 10: 7).

SEDALIA, locality (L-8)
After Sedalia, Missouri, U.S.A. former home of early settlers. (1911)

SEDERHOLM, lake (A-7)
After Jakob Johannes Sederholm (1863-1934), Finnish geologist, famous for his petrologic studies of precambrian rocks in Finland.

SEDGEWICK, town (J-7)
After the Honourable Robert Sedgewick (1848-1906), Puisne Judge, Supreme Court, Ottawa. (1906)

SEEBE, hamlet (L-4)
From the Cree Indian for "river", *si-pi*. It is near the Bow River.

SEENUM, lake (I-7)
After James Seenum, a Cree Indian chief. See also Pakan.

SEIBERT, lake (H-7)
After F. V. Seibert, D.L.S., who explored a very large area in the north and who subdivided this particular township. (1918)

SENTINEL, mountain (9,400 feet) (K-3)
The name of this mountain, above the junction of the Cline and the North Saskatchewan Rivers is descriptive of its isolated position.

SENTINEL, peak (7,785 feet) and pass (M-5)
Descriptive of its lone position. The pass, which takes its name from the peak, served as a route for moving cattle from the Pekisko area to the Highwood area.

SENTRY, mountain (7,988 feet) (N-5)
South of Crowsnest Lake; descriptive of its conspicuous position.

SERENITY, mountain (10,573 feet) (J-2)
A descriptive name. (1921)

SERVICEBERRY, creek (L-6)
After the serviceberry of the plains.

SEVEN PERSONS, hamlet, creek, coulee, and lake   (N-8)
A translation of the Blackfoot name of the river, *ki-tsuki-a-tapi* (Dawson). The name comes from an incident in 1872 when Calf Shirt, a leader of a band of Blood Indians, was travelling with a small war party when they encountered a band of Crees near a creek in southeastern Alberta. In the battle that followed seven Crees were killed and their medicine pipe was captured by Calf Shirt. In commemoration of this battle the creek became known as *ki-tsuki-a-tapi* or "seven persons."

SEXSMITH, village   (G-2)
The original post office was located some three and one half miles south of the present village and was named Bennville after John Bernard Foster, who was known as "Benny" by all oldtimers, having arrived in 1911. The surrounding area had been surveyed for homesteads in 1907 and the townsite was surveyed in 1915. When the Edmonton, Dunvegan and British Columbia Railroad arrived in 1916 the post office and townsite were named Sexsmith after David Sexsmith who was the first settler ever to visit the district. A native of Lennox County, Ontario, he came west to Manitoba in 1890. In 1898 he travelled west as far as Spirit River with a group of men who were heading for the Klondike and he was the first to drive a wagon from Spirit River to the site of Grande Prairie; this he did in 1898. He spent the next three years trapping in the Grande Prairie district but then went to Edmonton where he lived until he returned to Bennville and commenced farming in 1912.

SHADOW, lake   (L-5)
A descriptive name.

SHALKA, locality, lake   (I-7)
After Matt Shalka, the first postmaster. (1911)

SHANDRO, locality   (I-6)
After Andrew Shandro, the first postmaster. He was the first Ukrainian to be elected to any Legislative Assembly in Canada. (1905)

SHANKS, lake and creek   (O-6)
After Thomas Shanks, D.L.S., sometime Assistant Director General of Surveys.

SHARK, mount (9,100 feet)   (M-5)
After a destroyer which was sunk in the Battle of Jutland, 1916. (1922)

SHARPLES, locality   (L-6)
After John Sharples, railway fireman, Saskatoon, who won the D.C.M. during the First World War. (1923)

SHARROW, locality   (M-8)
A title of a novel written in 1912 by Baroness von Hutten. She was born in the United States but lived in London, England, for the greater part of her life, (*Who's Who*, 1938).

SHAUGHNESSY, hamlet   (N-6)
Named Thomas George, 1st Baron Shaughnessy (1853-1923), who was a shareholder in the Canadian Pacific Railway.

SHAVER, river (G-8)

After P. A. Shaver (1869-1960) D.L.S. He was engaged in railway construction and irrigation projects near Calgary and Red River and surveying in the Peace River country. (1909)

SHAW, locality (J-3)

After one R. L. Shaw, a former member of the Alberta Legislative Assembly, formerly of Stettler.

SHEEP, river (M-5)

It appears as *itou-kai-you* on David Thompson's map, 1814; *itukaiup* or Sheep on Arrowsmith map, 1859. It is so named because it is a favourite haunt of the Rocky Mountain sheep or bighorn.

SHEERNESS, hamlet (L-7)

Probably after Sheerness, Kent, England. The name means "bright headland", (Ekwall).

SHEOL, mountain (9,108 feet) (L-4)

Named by S. E. S. Allen, 1894, from the gloomy appearance of the valley at the base. Previously called Devil's Thumb; the name was changed to avoid confusion with Devil's Head and similar names.

SHEPARD, hamlet (M-5)

After one Shepard, a partner in Langdon and Shepard, railway contractors who built part of the Canadian Pacific Railway in the vicinity. Shepard and Langdon are neighbouring hamlets. See also Langdon, hamlet. (1884)

SHERBURNE, lake (N-7)

After Charles Sherburne early settler in the Grassy Lake district. This is a recently created irrigation reservoir about six miles south of Grassy Lake. (1955)

SHERWOOD PARK, hamlet (I-6)

The actual origin of the name is not known but it was likely a promotional idea to induce people to live in what was in effect a planned subdivision in a rural surrounding with associations of Sherwood Forest, England. The original name was to be Campbelltown. Sherwood Park, although a hamlet, has a population of 16,000. (1957)

SHINING BANK, locality (I-4)

See Shiningbank, lake.

SHININGBANK, lake (I-4)

The name refers to the yellow clay bank of the hills around from which dirt and stones keep falling; they shine like gold in the sun and are visible for miles.

SHONTS, locality (J-6)

After T. P. Shonts (1856-1919). He was a director of many railway companies and was the chairman of the Isthmian Canal Commission which studied the possibilities of the Panama Canal in 1905-1907. (1909)

SHORNCLIFFE, lake and creek (K-8)

After the Canadian military camp at Shorncliffe, Kent, England in World War I.

SHOULDICE, hamlet (M-6)
Named for James Shouldice (d.1925), the original owner of the townsite.

SHOVEL, pass (7,500 feet) (J-3)
The name is said to have been suggested by Mrs. M. Schäffer who found snow shovels in the pass.

SHUNDA, creek (K-4)
The Stoney Indian for "mire." It appears as Mire Creek on Palliser map, 1859 and is descriptive of the ford where the trail crosses it. (1912)

SIBBALD, creek and lake (L-5)
After Frank Sibbald, nearby rancher, son of Andrew Sibbald who settled near Morley in 1875.

SIDCUP, locality (J-8)
Probably after Sidcup, Kent, England. The name is said to mean "set camp" (Ekwall).

SIDNEY, creek (G-4)
After Sidney Parnall of Edmonton, a member of a survey party.

SIFFLEUR, mountain (10,266 feet) and river (K-4)
Named by Hector after the whistler or hoary marmot which was often referred to as the siffleur by the fur traders. The word is from the French *siffler* to whistle.

SIGNAL, mountain (7,397 feet) (J-2)
There was a telephone near the summit. (1916)

SILVER HEIGHTS, locality (K-7)
After Lord Strathcona's residence near Winnipeg. (1923)

SILVERHORN, mountain (9,550 feet) (K-3)
The name is descriptive of its snow covered summit.

SIMON, peak (10,899 feet), glacier and creek (K-2)
A peak of Mount Fraser; after Simon Fraser. See Fraser, mount.

SIMONS VALLEY, locality (L-5)
Named after W. E. Simons, the first postmaster.

SIMPSON, pass (6,954 feet) (L-4)
After Sir George Simpson (1792-1860), for over forty years Governor of Rupert's Land and head of the Hudson's Bay Company in Canada. Simpson was a dynamic little man who was made Governor shortly before the Union of the Hudson's Bay Company and the North West Company in 1821. He was an untiring administrator and an inveterate traveller and travelled widely over the area entrusted to him which extended from the Lakehead to the Pacific Coast. Under his guidance the chaotic conditions which had prevailed prior to the Union, were eliminated and the Hudson's Bay Company enjoyed unprecedented prosperity. He journeyed around the world in 1841-45 and crossed the mountains by this pass which was named for him.

SINCLAIR, lake (H-8)
Named after Wing Commander F. Willard Sinclair, D.F.C., Croix de Guerre, Calgary who served in World War II and who died in 1946. (1951)

SINCLAIR, lake and creek (G-1)
Named after Tom Sinclair, Grande Prairie, member of a survey party.

SIR DOUGLAS, mount (11,174 feet) (M-4)
Named after Field Marshal Sir Douglas Haig (1861-1928), K.T., G.C.B., Commander-in-Chief of the British Armies in France during World War I; later Earl Haig of Bemersyde. This may have been the mountain which Palliser named "Robinson" but it is not certain. (1918)

SIR JAMES, glacier (K-3)
After Sir James Outram; see Outram, mount.

SIRDAR, mountain (9,198 feet) (J-2)
A sirdar is a term for a person in command or a commander-in-chief. Sirdar mountain is said to have been named because of its prominence but it may have been named for Field Marshal Lord Kitchener (1850-1916) who was made 'sirdar' of the Egyptian Army. The mountain was named in 1916. See also Kitchener, mount.

SKARO, locality (I-6)
After K. H. Skaro, a Norwegian by birth, who was the first postmaster.

SKENE, mount (10,100 feet) (K-3)
After Peter Skene Ogden, fur trader (1794-1854). He entered the service of the North West Company in 1809 or 1810 and for some seven years was at Ile à la Crosse following which he served in the Columbia district. In 1820 he was made a partner. After the union of the North West Company and Hudson's Bay Company in 1821 he was made chief trader in 1823. For the next six years he led fur trading expeditions to the Snake River country and in 1834 was made Chief Factor and in 1846 a member of the Company's board of management at Fort Vancouver.

SKIFF, locality (N-7)
The townsite streets were named after parts of a small boat or skiff. Thus, Bow avenue, Stern avenue, Rudder street, Tiller street.

SKOKI, mountain (8,750 feet) (L-4)
Said to be the Indian name signifying "marsh" or "swamp" as reported by one Porter. (1911)

SLATE, range (L-4)
Bow River; from the slate rock composing the range.

SLAVE, river (A-7)-(B-7)
After the Etchareottine Indians, named *awokanak* or "slaves" by the Crees from their timid disposition. *Etchareottine* means "people dwelling in the shelter." This name, under the form *lotchyniny*, is applied to the river on the Peter Pond map, 1790.

SLAVE LAKE, town (G-5)
Known as Sawridge until 1922; it is near Lesser Slave Lake.

SLAWA, locality and creek (I-7)
From the Russian for "praise." (1912)

SLIDE, mountain (7,800 feet) and creek (J-2)
After an extensive rock slide which fell from the western slopes of the mountain and now blocks Slide Creek and parts of the Fiddle River at the northwest end of the Nikanassin Range, (1960)

SMITH, creek   (H-1)
Flows east into the Wapiti River; named after a homesteader, Frank
Smith. (1962)

SMITH, creek   (J-3)
Blackstone River; after one of the men employed when staking coal
claims in the vicinity.

SMITH, hamlet   (G-5)
After W. Rathbone Smith, former engineer and later general manager of
the Edmonton, Dunvegan and British Columbia Railway. The post office
name was formerly Mirror Landing. (1914)

SMITH-DORRIEN, mount (10,300 feet) and creek   (M-5)
After General Sir H. L. Smith-Dorrien, in command of 2nd Army
British Expeditionary Force, 1915-16.

SMOKY, lake and creek   (I-6)
A translation of the Cree name, *kas-ka-pi-te sakigan*. According to legend,
Smoky Lake was named by the Indians for a smoke like vapour which
rose from the lake, obscuring the opposite shore.

SMOKY, river   (H-1)-(H-2)-(G-2)
A translation of the Indian name; from smouldering beds of coal in
the river banks. In Cree, *kas-ka-pi-tesi-pi*; in Stony, *swo-da* (Tyrrell).

SMOKY LAKE, town (I-6)
See Smoky, lake (1918)

SMUTS, mount (9,600 feet) and creek   (M-4)
After General J. C. Smuts (1870-1950), in command of British troops
in Africa, 1916-17; later Prime Minister of South Africa. (1918)

SNAKE, hills   (I-7)
On Arrowsmith map, 1859; in Cree *kinapikuchachltenau*, referring to an
Indian tradition about the hills.

SNAKE, lake   (L-6)
Translation of Cree name *kinapik;* in Stony, *mnohemna* (Tyrrell).

SNAKE-INDIAN, river, mountain (9,608 feet), pass and falls   (J-2)
After a tribe of Indians who were murdered by the Assiniboines. Hector
notes in his journal: "There was once a little tribe of Indians known as
the Snakes that lived in the country to the north of Jasper House but
which during the time of the North West Fur Company was treacher-
ously exterminated by the Assineboines. They were invited to a peace
feast by the latter Indians, when they were to settle all their disputes, and
neither party was to bring any weapons. It was held about three miles
below the present site of Jasper House but the Assineboines being all
secretly armed fell on the poor Snakes in the midst of the revelry and
killed them all."

SNAKES HEAD, THE, hill   (K-5)
From a fancied resemblance to a snake's head.

SNARING, river, mountain (9,615 feet) and locality (J-2)
After a tribe of Indians which, as Hector says, lived there "dwelling in holes dug in the ground and subsisting on animals which they captured with snares of green hide." Hector further notes that these Indians were adept at catching large animals in this way such as bighorn sheep and moose.

SNEDDON, creek (F-1)
After Flying Officer J. A. Sneddon formerly of Edmonton. (1949)

SNIATYN, locality (I-6)
After Snyatyn, U.S.S.R., from which settlers came. It was formerly known as Hunka which was the name given in 1902.

SNOWBIRD, glacier (L-3)
This glacier lies on cliffs at two levels and is joined down the centre thus giving the effect of a large white bird, "Snowbird." (1960)

SNOW DOME, mountain (11,340 feet) (K-3)
This well-known feature was discovered and named in 1899 by Stutfield and Collie. They noted when exploring the immediate area that: "To the eastward of where we stood . . . rose a great white dome and we determined to ascend it. After a hot and very tiring climb through snow that broke under our feet at every step, we finally reached the summit at 8:15 p.m. We have named this peak The Dome." The name "Snow Dome" was later given and Cautley mentions it. Snow Dome is at the centre as it were of the Columbia Icefield for from it waters descend to the Arctic, Pacific, and Atlantic. It is visible from the highway and its thick layer of glacial ice resembles a frosting on a giant cake. (1899)

SOCIAL PLAINS, locality (M-8)
Originally it was a school district but when the post office was opened it was given this name to convey the idea of a sociable community. (1915)

SOFA, mountain (8,268 feet) and creek (O-5)
Descriptive of the outline of the mountain.

SOLDAN, lake (I-5)
After the family who owned the land on which the lake is situated. (1950)

SOLITAIRE, mountain (10,800 feet) (K-3)
Descriptive of its isolated position at the centre of Conway Glacier. See also Conway, mount. (1920)

SOUNDING, lake and creek (K-8)
Known in Blackfoot as *oghta-kway* (Nelson); in Cree as *ni-pi-kap-hit-i-kwek*, "sounding water" (Tyrrell). The Indian legend is that an eagle with a snake in its claws flew out of the lake making a rumbling noise like thunder.

SOUTH FERRIBY, locality (I-8)
After South Ferriby, Lincolnshire, England, the former home of the postmaster's wife. In England North Ferriby (Yorkshire) and South

Ferriby are on opposite sides of the Humber and the name means literally, "by" (habitation) at the ferry. The name appears as *Ferebi* in Domesday Book, 1190, (Ekwall).

SOUTH KANANASKIS, pass   (M-4)
See Kananaskis, pass

SOUTH KOOTENAY, pass (7,950 feet)   (O-5)
For derivation see North Kootenay, pass.

SOUTH SASKATCHEWAN, river   (N-7)-(N-8)-(M-8)
"Bow River", on David Thompson's map, 1814; see North Saskatchewan, river.

SOUTHESK, mount (10,277 feet), lake, river, pass (J-3) and locality (M-7)
After Sir James Carnegie, Bart., 9th Earl of Southesk (1827-1905). A native of Scotland he succeeded his father in the baronetcy in 1849 and became the Earl of Southesk but to do this he had to obtain a special Act of Parliament to reverse the attainder of his great grandfather the 5th Earl who had been implicated in the Jacobite uprising of 1715. He was made a Knight of the Thistle in 1869 and created Baron Balinhard in the peerage of the United Kingdom. In 1859-1860 he travelled in the Canadian Northwest and in 1875 published an account of this exploration entitled *Saskatchewan and the Rocky Mountains.* His travels in Alberta took him to Fort Edmonton, Jasper House, the headwaters of the North Saskatchewan, the Red Deer River and Old Bow Fort. He was the first to cross the Pipestone Pass. See also Balinhard, mount.

SOUTHESK CAIRN, mountain (8,330 feet)   (J-3)
Head of Medicine Tent River; "Southesk's Cairn" on map, 1875; climbed by Southesk (q.v.) in 1859.

SPANKIE, lake   (H-7)
East of Beaver Lake; after Flight Lieutenant E. Spankie, D.F.C., Bowden, who was killed in World War II.

SPARROWHAWK, mount (10,200 feet)   (L-4)
After a destroyer engaged in the Battle of Jutland, 1916. (1922)

SPEARS, creek   (N-5)
After one "Barbwire" Johnny Spears who had a cabin on the creek for a number of years.

SPHINX, mountain (8,200 feet) and creek   (J-3)
It has the appearance of a sphinx when viewed from the north and east. (1960)

SPIONKOP, ridge (8,020 feet) and creek   (O-5)
After a battle in the South African War, 1899-1901.

SPIRIT, river   (F-2)
This stream some two and a half miles from the town of the same name flows into the Burnt River which in turn empties into the Peace River some twenty miles downstream from Dunvegan. Spirit River is a translation of the Cree Indian name *chepe-sepe* meaning "Ghost River" and

this latter name appears on old maps. The original settlement along the banks of this stream grew up around two trading posts, one of the Hudson's Bay Company and the other belonging to Revillon Frères.

SPIRIT RIVER, town   (F-2)
    Named after Spirit, river (q.v.). The original settlement was along the banks of the river.

SPOTTED, lake and creek   (K-6)
    Known in Cree as *mahsenasou sakigan,* from the "spots" of open water and rushes.

SPRAY, mountains and river   (M-4)
    The name of this range was originally applied to the river, after the spray from the falls in the Bow River, near the mouth of the Spray.

SPRAY LAKES, reservoir   (M-4)
    See Spray, river.

SPRING, lake   (I-5)
    So named because it is fed by several springs and also has outlets that appear to run like springs.

SPRING COULEE, hamlet   (O-6)
    A coulee with numerous springs. (1902)

SPRING LAKE, locality   (J-7)
    From a small lake formerly known as Never-go-dry Lake. (1904)

SPRING-RICE, mount (10,745 feet)   (K-3)
    After Sir Cecil Spring-Rice, one time British Ambassador to the United States; died February 14, 1918; Mount Bryce, commemorating an earlier ambassador rises on the opposite side of the valley. (1920)

SPRINGDALE, locality   (J-5)
    From springs in the vicinity when named. (1906)

SPRINGPARK, locality   (I-7)
    A spring ran through the original settlement. (1913)

SPRINGRIDGE, locality   (N-5)
    It was on a ridge with many springs.

SPRUCEFIELD, locality   (H-6)
    Named from spruce trees that grew in the vicinity. (1913)

SPRUCE GROVE, town   (I-5)
    When the Spruce Grove Post Office was first established it was kept at the farm of Mr. John A. McPherson whose house was near a fine grove of spruce trees and so far as is known this determined the name. (1894)

SQUARE, lake   (H-8)
    Said to be descriptive of its shape.

STAIRWAY, peak (9,840 feet)   (K-3)
    Descriptive of shape.

STAND OFF, hamlet (N-6)

After Fort Standoff the second most important fort built by the American whisky traders in Canadian territory. It was built in 1871 at the junction of the Belly and Waterton Rivers. The party of men that built this post had left Fort Benton, Montana, with a load of stolen goods including whisky. The U.S. marshal learned of the supply of liquor and pursued the party, catching up with them at the Milk River. When he ordered them back to Fort Benton, they refused on the pretext that they were now on Canadian territory and beyond the marshal's jurisdiction. They then proceeded to the Belly River, built their fort and named it Standoff as they had managed to "stand off" the marshal.

STANDARD, village (L-6)

Probably refers to the flag, the Royal Standard. (1911)

STANDISH, lake (H-7)

After Sapper William H. Francis Standish, M.I.D., Calgary, killed in World War II. (1951)

STANGER, locality (I-5)

Named for a village or dorp in South Africa by the first settlers who were Boer War veterans. (1911)

STANMORE, locality (L-7)

Probably after Stanmore, Middlesex, England, meaning stony mere or lake. (Ekwall). (1913)

STAPLEHURST, locality (I-8)

After Staplehurst, Kent, England, the former home of H. C. Rawle, postmaster. The name, dating back to 1242 means "grove and hurst (wooded hill) where the posts were got." (Ekwall). (1910)

STAUFFER, locality and creek (K-5)

After one C. H. Stauffer from Idaho, who opened a store on the post office site in 1906. (1907)

STAVELY, town (N-6)

When the English-owned Oxley Ranching Company became lease holders on a vast tract of land surrounding what is now Staveley about 1880, its first chairman was the financier the Rt. Hon. Alexander Staveley Hill, M.P., from Oxley Manor, Staffordshire. It was in his honour that the town was named. Alexander Staveley Hill visited the area in 1881, and the three following years. He recounted his visits in *From Home to Home* (London, 1885). At first the name of the town contained two "e"s but the last one has been dropped. It is not known when but it is likely that it was in 1912 when the village became a town as the present spelling appears in plans and minutes after that date. Hill died in 1905.

STEELE, lake (H-6)

After Ira John Steele, D.L.S., 1906.

STEEPBANK, river (E-7)

A descriptive name.

STELFOX, mount (8,600 feet)   (K-4)
After Henry Stelfox pioneer resident of Rocky Mountain House. He
came to Alberta in 1906 settling first near Wetaskiwin and then Rocky
Mountain House. He devoted much of his life to conservation on the
eastern slope of the Rocky Mountains. (1956)

STERCO, locality   (J-3)
A compound of the words Sterling Collieries. It was formerly known as
Basing.

STERNE, creek   (I-2)
After Flight Lieutenant J. R. Sterne, D.F.C., Edmonton, killed in World
War II.

STETTIN, locality   (I-5)
After Stettin formerly in Germany but since World War II in Poland.
It was the former home of H. Libke, first postmaster. (1913)

STETTLER, town   (K-6)
Stettler takes its name from Carl Stettler (1861-1919), a native of Berne,
Switzerland. He arrived in Alberta in 1903 and homesteaded two miles
west of the site of the town that was later to be named for him. His
homestead became the centre of a German-Swiss colony and a post
office was opened on his land in 1905 and was known as Blumenau and
Carl Stettler was the first postmaster. The hamlet of Stettler itself came
into being in 1905 with the coming of the C.P.R. at which time the post
office was moved to the site of the present town and the hamlet named
in honour of Carl Stettler. He himself became the first postmaster and
C.P.R. Land Agent and when the hamlet became a village in 1906 he was
one of the first councillors. Stettler became a town in November, 1906.
Carl Stettler built the National Hotel on the site of the present Stettler
Hotel but when it was destroyed by fire in 1908 he sold the site and moved
to Castor the following year. He remained there until 1919 when he
returned to Stettler. He died that same year while on a visit to Memphis,
Tennessee but his remains were brought back to Stettler for burial.

STEVEVILLE, locality   (M-7)
Named for Stephen Hall, one time postmaster. (1910)

STEWART, canyon   (L-4)
After George A. Stewart, D.L.S., former Superintendent of Rocky
Mountains Park (now Banff National Park).

STEWART, mount (10,869 feet)   (K-3)
After Louis B. Stewart (1861-1937), D.L.S., D.T.S., Professor of
Surveying and Geodesy, University of Toronto. He surveyed Banff
National Park with his father, George A. Stewart, C.E.

STEWARTFIELD, locality   (H-5)
After the birthplace of Earl Haig's mother, who was a daughter of Hugh
Veitch of Stewartfield, Aberdeenshire, Scotland. (1919)

STIMSON, creek   (M-5)
After Major Fred Stimson, for many years resident manager of the
Bar-U Ranch (North West Cattle Company). (1896)

STIRLING, village and lake (N-6)
After J. A. Stirling, managing director of the Trusts, Executors and Securities Corporation, of London, England. This corporation had large holdings in the Alberta Railway and Coal Company. (1899)

STOBART, locality and lake (M-6)
After F. W. Stobart and Company, traders. (1906)

STOLBERG, locality (K-4)
Probably after Stollberg, Saxony, Germany.

STONELAW, locality (K-7)
Named by one John Watts after his former home, Stonelaw, Scotland. (1913)

STONEY, Indian Reserve (L-5)
After the Stoney or Assiniboine Indians.

STONEY-SQUAW, mountain (6,130 feet) (L-4)
According to the *Canadian Guide Book,* Part II, by Ernest Ingersoll (1892) this feature takes its name "from the traditional story that some years ago a brave old Assiniboine woman sustained her husband, who lay sick for several months in their lodge at its base, by hunting upon its top and sides, where there are open glades which still form favourite spring feeding-places for the big-horn or mountain sheep."

STONY, creek (I-8)
A translation of the Cree name *ka-as-sin-is-kak* (Tyrrell).

STONY PLAIN, town and Indian Reserve (I-5)
The origin of the name is generally attributed to the region having been the former camping place of the Stoney Indians, but Hector under the date, January 10, 1858, says that the plain "well deserves the name from being covered with boulders which are rather rare in general in this district or country."

STOPPINGTON, locality (L-7)
After Louisa E. Stopp one time postmistress. (1910).

STORM, creek (M-5)
There was a very heavy rainfall while Dr. G. M. Dawson was camped by the stream in 1884.

STORM, mountain (10,332 feet) (M-5)
West of Twin lakes; named by G. M. Dawson in 1884, after the numerous storm clouds seen on its summit.

STORNHAM, locality (N-8)
After Stornham Castle, England.

STOVEL, lake (C-6)
After Flying Officer C. C. Stovel, D.F.C., Craigmyle, killed in World War II.

STOWE, locality (N-6)
After Harriet Beecher Stowe, author of *Uncle Tom's Cabin,* (1851-52).

STRACHAN, locally (K-4)
Formerly called Vetchland because of an abundance of wild vetch, but later renamed after David Gordon Strachan killed in the First World War.

STRACHAN, mount (8,800 feet) (M-5)
After Lieutenant Henry Strachan, V.C., Fort Garry Horse. In November, 1917, during World War I, he led a squadron through the enemy line of machine guns. He then led the charge on the enemy battery, killing seven gunners with his sword.

STRAHAN, mount (9,960 feet) (L-4)
After Dr. Aubrey Strahan, one time director, Geological Survey of Great Britain. (1920)

STRANGE, mount (9,471 feet) (J-2)
After General T. Bland Strange (1831-1925) who commanded the Alberta Field Force in the second North-West Rebellion in 1885. (1954)

STRANGMUIR, locality (M-6)
After the residence of General T. Bland Strange, of the Military Colonization Ranch. General Strange commanded the Alberta column in the Rebellion of 1885. He died in England, 1925. (1914)

STRATHCONA, county (I-6)
Named after Sir Donald Smith, Lord Strathcona (1820-1914) prominent in the building and completion of the Canadian Pacific. Later Canadian High Commissioner in London and Governor of the Hudson's Bay Company. Strathcona was the name of South Edmonton and was a separate town until it amalgamated with Edmonton in 1912.

STRATHMORE, town (L-6)
After Claude Bowes-Lyon, 13th Earl of Strathmore (1824-1904). He was the grandfather of Queen Elizabeth, the present Queen Mother, (1902-   ).

STRAWBERRY, creek (J-5)
A translation of the Cree name, *a-te-min* (Tyrrell).

STREAMSTOWN, hamlet (I-8)
Named by Reverend R. Smith after Streamstown, Westmeath, Ireland. (1906)

STRETTON, creek (I-8)
The earliest settler in the area came from Stretton, Cheshire, England.

STROME, village (J-7)
Strome derived its name from a pioneer Swedish family of that name who settled in the district. The first post office in the district, it was named Knollton but was changed in 1906.

STRY, locality (I-7)
After Stry (Stryj), which prior to World War II was in Poland but is now in Ukrainian S.S.R. It was the former home of the settlers who first came to this area. (1910)

STUBNO, locality (I-7)
After Dubno, Ukrainian S.S.R. It was in Poland prior to World War II.
It was the former home of M. Stepanick, the first postmaster. (1921)

STURGEON, river and municipal district (I-5)-(I-6)
The river appears as Sturgeon rivulet on David Thompson's map of 1814,
as Red Willow or Sturgeon River on Arrowsmith's map of 1859. It is
known in Cree as *mi-koo-oo-pow* or "Red Willow" creek (Tyrrell). It
gets its name from the abundance of sturgeon formerly caught in the
river.

STUTFIELD, peak (11,320 feet) (K-3)
Sunwapta River (1899); after Hugh E. M. Stutfield, member of the
English Alpine Club and joint author, with J. N. Collie, of *Climbs and
Explorations in the Canadian Rockies*, (London, 1903).

STYAL, locality (I-4)
Imrie P.O. until 1919. The present name is probably after Styal, Cheshire,
England; Ekwall mentions it appearing as "Styhale" around 1200.

SUFFIELD, hamlet (M-7)
After Charles Harbord, 5th Baron Suffield (1830-1914). In 1854 he
married Cecilia Annetta, sister of Edward, 1st Lord Revelstoke who was
head of the British banking house of Baring Brothers. This firm had
bought $15,000,000 of a C.P.R. bond issue and in so doing had averted
the last financial crisis in the building of the line.

SUGDEN, locality (H-7)
After D. S. Sugden, the first postmaster. (1916)

SULLIVAN, creek (M-5)
After a settler on it; "the Indian name is *makkoye* or Wolf creek",
(Stimson). (1896)

SULLIVAN, mount (9,915 feet) and lake (K-3) (K-7)
Both features, although some distance apart are named for John W.
Sullivan, secretary of the Palliser Expedition from 1857-1859. The Cree
name of the lake was *ka-ki-na-ka-mak*, (Tyrrell).

SUNDANCE, creek and pass (L-4)
This creek near Banff is so named because it was near the scene of
numerous Indian sun dances. The pass takes its name from the creek.

SUNDANCE, locality (I-5)
The name was changed in 1923 from Little Volga. The name Sundance
appears to have no particular meaning other than being descriptive but
was thought to be in keeping with Indian names (such as Wabamun)
in the vicinity. A new thermal power plant, recently opened here is
called the Sundance Thermal Plant.

SUNDAY, creek (G-7)
The name was given by a survey party which camped at this creek on
a Sunday, (1955)

SUNDIAL, butte (N-6)
Known in Blackfoot as *onoka-katzi* (Nelson); there is a cairn here
with concentric circles and radiating lines of stones.

SUNDIAL, mountain (10,438 feet)   (K-3)
The crest resembles the index arm of a sundial. (1921)

SUNDRE, town   (L-5)
In a letter to Mr. A. Ogden, Secretary of the Town of Sundre, Muriel
Eskrick a resident of the area writes "The name Sundre was chosen
by Mr. N. T. Hagen when a post office was being placed on the west
side of the Red Deer River. Mr. Hagen had purchased this land from
Dave McDougall, brother of Reverend John McDougall of Morley.
Dave had moved here from the Morley area in 1895. Sundre was the
home town in Norway where Mr. Hagen had been born and raised. As
a young man he emigrated to the United States. He made his home here
in Sundre until a few years prior to his death when he moved to
California where his daughter still resides. Mr. Hagen established a store
on the McDougall land around 1906 and the post office came into
being (as closely as we can ascertain) in 1908", (letter, September,
1970).

SUNNYBROOK, hamlet   (J-5)
A descriptive name. (1911)

SUNNYDALE, locality   (L-8)
A descriptive name. (1911)

SUNNYNOOK, hamlet   (L-7)
New settlers in the area submitted this name. (1911)

SUNNYSLOPE, hamlet   (L-6)
The post office, when opened, was on the western slope of a hill towards
Kneehill creek.

SUNWAPTA, peak (10,883 feet) river, falls, lake and pass (6,675 feet) (K-3)
The river, (after which the other features are named) was named by
A. P. Coleman and is a Stoney Indian word meaning turbulent river.
Coleman and his party, when they were exploring the area were not sure
which stream this was and as Coleman notes "we decided to keep the
Stoney name Sunwapta, at least for the present."

SURPRISE POINT, peak (7,873 feet)   (J-2)
It took longer to reach the top than was expected. (1916)

SURVEY, peak (8,700 feet)   (K-3)
Named by J. N. Collie and climbed by him and Stutfield, August 11,
1898, to enable him to begin his plane table survey.

SUTHERLAND, creek   (G-4)
South of Lesser Slave Lake; after Robert Sutherland, a member of the
survey party.

SUTTON, creek   (E-8)
After Gordon Sutton, a member of a survey party.

SUTTON, lake   (G-4)
After Flight Lieutenant H. R. Sutton, D.F.C, Edmonton, killed in World
War II. (1947)

SWALWELL, hamlet (L-6)
After one Swalwell, a local auditor, for the Grand Trunk Pacific Railway. Prior to 1911 it was known as Rawdonville.

SWENSEN, mount (7,700 feet) (I-2)
After Flying Officer Stanley Powell Swensen, Roll of Honour, Battle of Britain, Calgary, killed in World War II. (1949)

SWINNERTON, lake (A-7)
Named for the prominent British paleontologist, H. H. Swinnerton, researcher and teacher. (1958)

SWODA, mountain (9,400 feet) and creek (I-2)
The Stoney Indian name swo-da (Tyrrell) for Smoky River. (1923)

SYLVAN, lake (K-5)
It appears as Methy Lake on David Thompson's map of 1814 and as Swan Lake on the Palliser map of 1859. In Cree it is known as wa-pi-sioo; in Stoney as ko-gamna (Tyrrell).

SYLVAN LAKE, town (K-5)
After Sylvan, lake (q.v.).

SYLVESTER, locality and creek (G-1)
Named after the first settler in the area, Sylvester Belcourt. (1962)

SYNCLINE, mountain (8,008 feet) (O-5)
Descriptive of synclinal folds in the rocks composing the mountain.

SYNCLINE, ridge (J-2)
After a prominent synclinal fold in the Devonian rocks on the ridge. (1960)

— T —

TABER, town, lake, provincial park and municipal district (N-7)
It is the first part of the word "tabernacle" and was named out of consideration for Mormon settlers in the vicinity. The adjoining locality is Elcan — last part of the word reversed. Original spelling on the townsite plan was "Tabor" after Mount Tabor. (1,843 feet) near the Sea of Galilee, Israel. (1904)

TABLE, mountain (7,324 feet) (O-5)
Castle River; a descriptive name.

TAERUM, lake (C-6)
After Flight Lieutenant T. H. Taerum, D.F.C., of Calgary, killed in World War II. (1949)

TAIL, creek (K-6)
It drains Buffalo lake and resembles the tail of a stretched skin. It is known in Cree as o-sooi; in Stoney as sin-doo (Tyrrell) and in French as La Queue.

TAIT, lake (K-6)
After one Thomas Tait, a Metis settler. (1894)

TALBOT, mount (7,787 feet) and locality (K-7)
Named in 1925 after Honourable Peter Talbot (1854-1919), Lacombe; Member of the Senate of Canada, 1906-1919. (1907)

TALLON, peak (6,000 feet) (N-5)
Crowsnest River; after L. Tallon, an assistant to W. S. Drewry in surveys of the Rockies in 1888 and 1892.

TANGENT, hamlet (F-3)
At the commencement of a 35 mile tangent or straight stretch of railway track. (1916)

TANGLE, ridge (9,859 feet) and creek (K-3)
The creek was so named by Mrs. M. Schäffer, 1907, because the valley was difficult to travel through. The party was descending from Wilcox Pass to the Sunwapta River and Mrs. Schäffer notes "A good size morning's work on the right side of that stream next day inspired us to christen it 'Tangle Creek'."

TAPLOW, locality (L-7)
Probably after Taplow, Bucks, England. The name appears as *Tappelawe* in 1196 although the origin is uncertain, (Ekwall). (1920)

TASSOSAU, lake (I-5)
An Indian name, meaning "trapped", "caught by a falling tree"; an Indian woman was killed in this way.

TASTING, lake (N-6)
Translation of Blackfoot *matapokway* (Nelson).

TATEI, ridge (J-1)
East of Robson Pass. The Stoney Indian word for "wind". (1912)

TAWAKWATO, lake (H-7)
Indian for "toothless", said to refer to a legend.

TAWATINAW, river, lake and hamlet (H-6)
Athabasca River; Indian name meaning "river which divides the hills" or "valley river."

TAWAYIK, lake (I-6)
Cree Indian name meaning "in the middle of", literally "Middle Lake."

TAYLORVILLE, locality (N-6)
After James H. Taylor, first postmaster. (1900)

TEES, hamlet (K-6)
After W. S. Tees, original owner of the townsite. Brook P.O. until 1906.

TEITGE, creek (I-2)
After a onetime district forest ranger.

TEKARRA, mount (8,818 feet) and creek (J-2)
Named by Hector, 1859, after Tekarra, an Iroquois hunter who accompanied him during his trip up the Athabasca River.

TELFORD, lake (J-6)
After R. T. Telford of Leduc, first settler on the lake. He served in the North-West Mounted Police from 1885-1889 and was a member of the first Legislature of Alberta, 1905.

TELFORDVILLE, hamlet (J-5)
See Telford, lake.

TEMPLE, mount (11,636 feet) (L-4)
The mountain was named by Dr. G. M. Dawson, 1884, after Sir Richard
Temple, president, Economic Science and Statistics section, British
Association, 1884. He was elected leader of the British Association
excursion party to the Rockies in that year.

TEN PEAKS, valley (L-4)
The mountains surround the valley which was formerly called Desolation Valley; the summits are numbered from east to west and most
are now named. The peaks form a back drop for Moraine Lake, (q.v.).

TENNESSEE, creek and coulee (N-5)
From a man so nicknamed who built a house here in 1876 (Steele).

TENT, mountain (7,209 feet) and pass (N-5)
Descriptive of the outline of the mountain. (1915)

TERMINAL, mountain (9,300 feet) (J-2)
A descriptive name; it is at the end of a group. (1916)

TERRACE, mountain (9,570 feet) (K-3)
Named by Hector; the name was suggested by the appearance of the
strata. (1920)

TERRAPIN, mount (9,600 feet) and lake (M-4)
From a fancied resemblance to a turtle. (1918)

TERSHISHNER, creek (K-3)
The Stoney Indian name meaning "burnt timbers"; Stoney Indians
lived near the stream for years.

TÊTE, ROCHE, mountain (7,932 feet) (J-2)
Suggested by Tête Jaune, French for "Yellowhead", nickname of a
trapper who used to store his furs near present Tête Jaune Cache Station,
B.C. According to Malcolm McLeod, the trapper was François Decoigne, who is listed as a North West Company servant in 1799 and who
was in charge of Jasper House, Brûlé Lake, in 1814. (1918) See also
Yellowhead, mountain and pass.

THERIEN, hamlet (H-7)
After Rev. J. A. Therien, O.M.I., first director of the colony of St.
Paul des Metis. The colony was not a success and it was closed in
1909. (1910)

THICKWOOD, hills (E-7)
West of Fort McMurray; descriptive of thickly wooded hills.

THIGH, hills (M-6)
Known in Blackfoot as *motuksina,* meaning "thigh flesh" (Nelson); in
Blackfoot, *ohsokinascu* or "man's thigh", from the shape (Steele).

THISTLE, mountain (8,500 feet) and creek (J-3)
Brazeau River; mountain named after creek. Probably because of the
abundance of thistles.

THOMPSON, mount (10,119 feet)   (L-3)
    North Saskatchewan River. After C. S. Thompson, Appalachian Club,
    Boston, one of the most enthusiastic of the pioneers of mountaineering
    among the ranges of both the Selkirks and Rockies.

THORHILD, village   (H-6)
    The name "Thorhild" is said to be Norwegian in origin. Mr. John
    Jardy was the first postmaster and gave the name to the post office
    four miles east of the present village. According to Mr. D. Yachimec,
    Secretary-Treasurer of the village in a letter dated May 11, 1972, the
    original site of the post office was on a hill and during thunderstorms
    there were frequent lightning strikes. Local tradition has it that Mr.
    Jardy named the hill "Thor's Hill" after the Norse god of thunder and
    thence "Thorhild" to give it a Scandinavian ring. This is, however,
    uncertain since "hilde" in Norwegian is part of a girl's name but the
    name does sound Scandinavian. (1914)

THORNTON, mount (9,028 feet)   (J-2)
    North of Victoria Cross Ranges, after Sir Henry Thornton (1871-
    1933), president of the Canadian National Railway from 1922-1932.

THORSBY, village   (J-5)
    After a community in Sweden. Literally village (BY) of Thor.

THREE, hills   (L-6)
    After three small hills running from northwest to southeast. The old
    buffalo trail crosses the creek and is one of the oldest trails in Alberta,
    having been in use long before the Edmonton and Calgary trail; in Cree,
    nis-to; in Stoney, *pa-ha-amni*, (Tyrrell).

THREE HILLS, creek and town   (L-6)
    See Three, hills. (1904)

THREE SISTERS, THE, mountains (average height 9,280 feet)   (L-4)
    There are three peaks in the same ridge and they resemble each other.
    This well-known feature is south of Canmore. (Dawson, 1886).

THREEPOINT, mountain (8,513 feet) and creek   (M-5)
    A three-pointed mountain. The creek takes its name from the mountain.

THRONE, mountain (10,144 feet)   (J-2)
    Descriptive; the summit resembles a throne. (1916)

THUNDERBOLT, peak (8,745 feet)   (J-2)
    The summit was shattered by lightning. (1916)

TILLEY, village   (M-7)
    After Sir Samuel Leonard Tilley (1818-1896), one of the Fathers of
    Confederation. He first entered politics in 1850 when he was elected
    to the New Brunswick Legislature. He resigned the following year but
    was elected again in 1854 and became Provincial Secretary. After some
    political vicissitudes he became a delegate to the Charlottetown and
    Quebec conferences in 1864. Although at this time he suffered setbacks
    because of anti-confederation sentiment he ultimately became Provincial
    Secretary again when a pro-confederation group came to power. In

1867 he left provincial politics and served as Minister of Customs and as Minister of Finance. Later he was Lieutenant Governor of New Brunswick.

TILTED, mountain (8,500 feet) (L-3)
East of Baker Creek. Descriptive of the strata composing it. (1911)

TINCHEBRAY, locality (K-7)
After Tinchebrai, France, where the Roman Catholic Pères de Ste. Marie-de-Tinchebrai had a college. Five or six members of the order settled here in 1904. (1907)

TINDASTOLL, creek (K-5)
After a mountain in Iceland. The area was settled by Icelanders.

TITKANA, peak (9,200 feet) (J-1)
East of Robson Pass. A Stoney Indian word meaning "bird." (1912)

TODD, creek (O-5)
After William Todd, who settled here about 1886.

TOFIELD, town (I-6)
After Dr. J. H. Tofield (d. 1918), who first settled in the district. An interesting origin of the name is as follows. In 1950 the unsuccessful separation of the Tofield Siamese twins attracted worldwide attention. Mr. F. H. Hewitt of Stewkley, (Bucks), England, wrote in response to inquiries by Mr. Stinson, the Town Secretary: "Although Dr. J. H. Tofield was presumably born in Yorkshire, it is quite possible that his ancestors originate from Stewkley in Buckinghamshire which was and still is looked upon as 'the home of the Tofields'; in fact one area of Stewkley still goes under the name of Tofield and we would suggest that your town is the only other place in the world to bear the name." Stewkley goes back at least to 1066 and is mentioned in the Domesday Book. It has a very fine Norman Church built ca. 1150. Mr. Hewitt continues: "It is understood that many of the old tombstones, most of which were in a state of decay were removed from the churchyard over a hundred years ago but among the old ones which still remain are a number belonging to the Tofield family. It is possible that the Tocquefields or Tofields as they are now known were of Saxon origin and were living in the forest settlement of Steuclai at the time of the Norman Conquest of England." (*Tales of Tofield*, 1969. Tofield Historical Society)

TOMA, mount (9,100 feet) and creek (J-3)
Cardinal River; after Sir George Simpson's Iroquois canoe-man. He was a member of the Southesk party in this region in 1859. (1925)

TOMBSTONE, mountain (9,700 feet) (M-4)
Named by Dr. G. M. Dawson, 1884, from a peculiar selection of pinnacle-like slabs near the summit resembling tombstones.

TONGUE, creek (M-4)
In Blackfoot, *matsin-awastam* (Nelson); *natsina*, meaning tongue (Palliser report). Steele says that the Old Man (of Indian legend) hunted a band of elk and killed them all but one doe. He hung up the tongues on a pole to dry. He then ran a race with the wolf, who beguiled him away so that the rest of the wolves could eat his meat, which they did, and the wolf ran up the pole and ate the tongues.

TONQUIN, hill (7,861 feet), pass and valley (J-2)
After the ship which carried the Astor expedition to the mouth of the Columbia River in 1810. (1916)

TOPLAND, locality (H-5)
From its situation on a ridge between the Athabasca and Freemen Rivers. (1914)

TORNADO, mountain (10,169 feet) and pass (N-5)
Cautley says: "Tornado Mountain is a storm centre of the locality . . . for days at a time dark thunder clouds, rent by vivid flashes of lightning, were seen to gather around the summit." (1915)

TORRENS, mount (7,400 feet) and river (H-1)
East fork of Narraway River; after Sir Robert Richard Torrens (1814-1884), Irish-Australian who introduced the Torrens system of land titles which became law in South Australia in 1858. (1922)

TORY, mount (9,287 feet) (J-2)
After Henry Marshall Tory (1864-1947). In 1905 he became the first president of McGill College in Vancouver (the forerunner of the University of B.C.). From 1908-1928 he was the first president of the University of Alberta and it was under his guidance that a solid academic foundation was built. In 1923 he became first chairman of the National Research Council and in 1928 its first full time president. In 1942 he was first president and chairman of the board of governors of Carlton College, Ottawa (later Carlton University) and held this post until his death.

TOTHILL, locality (N-8)
After Alfred Tothill, first postmaster. (1924)

TOWER OF BABEL, mountain (7,580 feet) (L-4)
East of Moraine Lake; named by Wilcox, 1899, from a fancied resemblance to the biblical edifice the Tower of Babel.

TOWERS, THE, mountain (9,337 feet) (M-4)
Descriptive. (1918)

TRAPPER, peak (9,790 feet) (L-3)
After Bill Peyto, a noted trapper and guide; see Peyto, lake. (1918)

TRIDENT, range (J-2)
From its shape. (1916)

TRISTRAM, locality (K-6)
After Tristram W. Fry, first postmaster. (1907)

TROCHU, town (K-6)
After Armand Trochu (1857-1930) who with a group of French Cavalry Officers incorporated the St. Ann Ranch Trading Company in 1905. The others were Joseph Devilder and Leon C. Eckenfelder. This marked the foundation of a settlement which became known as Trochu Valley. A number of French families came out at this time to settle in the area. In 1911 the settlement was incorporated as a village with the name shortened to Trochu. With the outbreak of World War I, most of the officers returned to France. After hostilities some returned to

Trochu; others were either killed or remained in France. Trochu himself remained in his valley but in 1917 he returned to France in failing health; he died in 1930. Trochu was the son of General Louis Jules Trochu (1815-1896), the defender of Paris, 1871.

TRUTCH, mountain (10,690 feet) (K-3)
After Sir Joseph Trutch (1826-1904). Trutch was a native of England and in 1849 came to California, lured by the gold rush. While there he practised his profession of civil engineering and later in Illinois. He arrived in B.C. in 1859 and for some time was engaged in contracts in construction of the Cariboo Road. From 1861-1863 he was a member of the House of Assembly for Vancouver Island and later was chief commissioner of lands and works for British Columbia. He was one of three delegates sent to Ottawa to negotiate terms of union between British Columbia and Canada. On Confederation (1871) he was appointed Lieutenant Governor of the new province. (1920)

TUDOR, locality (L-6)
After the English Royal House of Tudor. (1911)

TURBULENT, mount (9,000 feet) and creek (M-4)
After a destroyer engaged in the Battle of Jutland, 1916. (1916)

TURIN, hamlet (N-7)
After an imported Percheron stallion owned by a syndicate of farmers in the district. (1910)

TURNER, mount (9,230 feet) (M-4)
In honour of Lieutenant General Sir Richard E. W. Turner, V.C., K.C.M.G., C.B., D.S.O., commanding Canadian forces in the British Isles in World War I. (1918)

TURNER VALLEY, village and valley (M-5)
After Robert and James Turner, early settlers who homesteaded in the north end of the valley in 1886.

TURQUOISE, lake (L-3)
Bow River; descriptive of colour.

TURTLE, mountain (7,230 feet) (N-5)
Named by Louis O. Garnett, 1880, when on a trip from Pincher Creek, owing to resemblance to a turtle. It was the scene of the Frank Slide of 1903 when some 70 million tons of rock slid down the mountain side burying the mining town of Frank and taking seventy lives.

TUTTLE, locality (K-5)
After W. W. Tuttle, rancher. (1892)

TUZO, mount (10,648 feet) (L-4)
After Miss Henrietta L. Tuzo (later Mrs. J. A. Wilson, Ottawa), Warlingham, Surrey, England, who was the first to climb it in 1906. She was a charter member of the Alpine Club of Canada. This mount is No. 7 of the Ten Peaks, (q.v.). (1907)

TWEEDIE, locality (H-7)
After T. M. Tweedie, member of the Legislative Assembly for Calgary Centre, (1911-1917); later Justice of the Supreme Court of Alberta. (1917)

TWIN BUTTE, locality (O-5)
Named from two prominent hills facing each other. (1905)

TWINING, locality (L-6)
After General Geoffrey Twining (1862-1920). Although a graduate of the Royal Military College, Kingston, he spent most of his military life away from Canada, returning to Canada for six years (1893-1899) to teach military engineering at R.M.C. (1912)

TWINS, THE, peaks (12,085 feet and 11,675 feet) (K-3)
Named by Stutfield and Collie, 1898; a double-headed mountain.

TWO HILLS, town (I-7)
Named after two hills which are located southwest of the town. The first post office established in this area in 1908 was named Poserville but changed to Two Hills in 1913. The name is related to two distinct hills southwest of town—there is no information as to who did the naming. (H. D. Charchun, Municipal Secretary, letter, August, 1970).

TYRRELL, creek, mount (8,019 feet) (L-4) and lake (O-6)
After Joseph Burr Tyrrell (1858-1957) M.E., Geological Survey (1880-1897) who explored extensively in northwestern Canada. He was also an historian of note. James William Tyrrell (1863-1945), C.E., D.L.S., accompanied his brother Joseph Burr Tyrrell on a survey in 1893 between Lake Athabasca and Chesterfield Inlet and made surveys elsewhere in Canada. The feature listed is not always identified as being named after one or the other Tyrrell.

TYRWHITT, mount (9,428 feet) (M-4)
After Rear Admiral Sir R. Y. Tyrwhitt, leader of British destroyer flotillas during the First World War. (1918)

— U —

ULLIN, locality (K-4)
It was possibly named after the poem *Lord Ullin's Daughter* by Thomas Campbell. (1914)

UNCAS, locality (I-6)
After Uncas, Oklahoma which in turn is probably for the character in Fennimore Cooper's *Last of the Mohicans*. There is Uncasville, Connecticut which is named for a famous Mohican chief of the seventeenth century. (1909)

UNIPAUHAOS, Indian Reserve (I-8)
After chief of this name, successor to Puckeechkeeheewin (q.v.). The name means "standing erect"; the chief's English name was Stanley. (1879)

UNWIN, mount (10,723 feet) (J-3)
Maligne Lake; named by Mrs. M. Schäffer, after her second guide, Sidney Unwin. She notes "Opposite our camp rose a fine snow-capped mountain down whose sides swept a splendid glacier . . . we promptly named it 'Mount Unwin'." (1908)

UPPER KANANASKIS, lake and river   (M-5)
See Kananaskis, range, lake, etc.

UPPER ROWE, lake   (O-5)
After Lieutenant Rowe, R.E., surveyor, British Boundary Commission,
1872-76. (1960)

UPPER SPRAY, falls   (M-5)
See Spray, mountains. (1958)

UPRIGHT, mountain (9,700 feet) and pass (6,470 feet)   (J-2)
So named because the strata of the mountain have been tilted to an
almost vertical position.

USONA, locality   (J-5)
There is a place of the name in California; initial letters of United
States of North America. This name for the United States was never
seriously considered. Name suggested by Mrs. A. Osterland. (1905)

UTIKOOMAK LAKE, Indian Reserve   (F-4)
See Utikuma, lake.

UTIKUMA, lake and river   (F-4)
It is a Cree Indian name meaning "whitefish."

UTOPIA, mountain (8,538 feet) and creek   (J-2)
To the surveyors it was a refuge from flies. (1916)

— V —

VACHE, PRAIRIE DE LA, prairie   (J-2)
This level stretch of land halfway between the mouth of the Whirlpool
River and the town of Jasper is referred to by Edward Ermatinger in
his *York Factory Express Journal* as "Campt des Vaches", May 3,
1827. It was also known as Buffalo Prairie. Hector refers to it as "Prairie
des Vaches." The literal meaning is "cow prairie."

VAL SOUCY, locality   (I-6)
Until 1913 mail from this area had to be brought in from Cookville
nine miles away. In that year Joe Soucy established a post office in his
home and named it Val Soucy (Valley of the Soucys). (1917)

VALAD, peak (10,650 feet)   (J-3)
After a Metis guide who accompanied H. A. F. McLeod to Maligne
Lake in 1875. In 1872, Sandford Fleming sent him to W. Moberly with
a letter of introduction. (1923) See also Henry McLeod, mount.

VALE, settlement   (N-8)
After Vale, Oregon, former home of the postmaster, John Evers. (1913)

VALHALLA, lake and locality   (G-2)
In Norse mythology, the home of the Viking heroes after death. The
name was suggested by the Reverend H. N. Ronning, Lutheran pastor,
who founded the settlement, where a number of Scandinavians settled.
(1916)

VALHALLA CENTRE, hamlet (G-2)
See Valhalla, lake and locality. (1923)

VALLEYVIEW, town (G-3)
Probably a descriptive name.

VANRENA, locality (F-2)
Compound of the names of Van and Rooney, early settlers. (1914)

VAUXHALL, town (N-7)
After Vauxhall, London, England. The town grew up around a camp
of the Canadian Land and Irrigation Company. The townsite was first
surveyed in 1910 and named after its English namesake supposedly in
an attempt to attract capital.

The name is derived from *Faukeshale* (1279) which in turn appears
to have been derived from Falkes de Greaute who married the heiress
of the local manor in about 1220. Falkes is an old French name and
may originally have had German origins. The second part is the Old
English "heall" or "hall": literally, Falkes' hall, (Ekwall).

VAVASOUR, mount (9,300 feet) (M-4)
After Lieutenant M. Vavasour, R.E., who, with Lieutenant H. J. Warre,
aide-de-camp to the commander of forces in Canada, crossed the Rockies
in 1845 on a military mission. Vavasour died in 1866. (1918) See also
Warre, mount.

VEGREVILLE, town (I-7)
After Father Valentin Vegreville (d.1903). He arrived at St. Boniface in
1852 and two years later he established a mission at Cold Lake. Later
he was in charge at Ile à la Crosse, St. Peters on Caribou Lake and
was ultimately director at St. Boniface College. He was taken prisoner
by Riel at Batoche in 1885. Father Vegreville was an expert linguist in
Cree, Montagnais and Assiniboine languages. The town was first established by French settlers from Kansas and the post office was opened
in December, 1895. Later it became a centre for Ukrainian settlement.
Strangely enough, although it was named for Father Vegreville, he himself was never in the immediate district at any time.

VELDT, locality (K-7)
Boer name for plain; Botha (q.v.) which was named after General
Botha, the famous Boer general, is on the same line of the C.P.R. (1909)

VENICE, locality (H-7)
J. O. Billos, postmaster came from Venice, Italy, in 1902. (1916)

VERDANT VALLEY, locality (L-6)
Descriptive of a green valley. (1910)

VERDIGRIS, coulee and lake (O-7)
The name comes from a green crystalline substance found along the
banks of the coulee.

VERMILION, lakes (L-4)
Near Banff; there are ochre beds in the vicinity.

VERMILION, lakes and river   (I-7)-(I-8)
North Saskatchewan River; translation of Cree name, *wiyaman*. There
are ferrous beds in the vicinity of the lakes and at numerous points
along the valley of the river. Another Indian name is *kianiskkotiki*,
"chain of lakes joining each other."

VERMILION, pass (5,416 feet)   (L-4)
This pass on the Alberta-British Columbia boundary takes its name from
the iron oxide found in mineral springs some six miles southwest. The
deposits from them form ochre beds of yellow, orange and red near
the Vermilion River on its western side. Their historic interest lies
in the fact that they have in the past been the haunt of Indian tribes, the
Kootenay and the Blackfeet who came to gather the material for war
paint and other decorative purposes. Cautley, writing in 1917 notes extensive remains of old teepee poles in the vicinity of the springs indicating extensive visits by the Indians. "It is likely", he says "the Vermilion
River derived its name from them."

Sir James Hector crossed the pass in 1858, the first recorded
journey this way by Europeans. Hector descended the Vermilion River
to the Kootenay in his circuitous route to the Kicking Horse Pass
(q.v.). To-day Vermilion Pass is traversed by the Banff-Windermere
Highway.

VERMILION, town   (I-7)
The post office name until 1906 was Breage, after Breage, Cornwall,
England. "The town of Vermilion was named after the Vermilion River
on the south bank of which it is situated. The river was named such by
the Indians because of the red springs in this area. These springs are
red since there was iron in the water and as a result the area around
the springs became a reddish colour and the Indians were able to use
the reddish earth for war paint." (D. R. Mitchell, Secretary-Treasurer,
letter, August, 1970). (1905)

VERTEX, peak (9,700 feet)   (J-2)
The name is descriptive of the sharp triangular summit. (1916)

VETERAN, village   (K-7)
"According to long-term residents, the Village received its name following the crowning of an English King in the early 1900's (1911) at
which time many of the communities in this area received names
associated with this event, for instance, Coronation, Throne, Consort,
Federal, etc." (Mrs. E. A. Christianson, Secretary-Treasurer, letter,
August, 1970). (1911)

VICTOR, creek   (G-8)
After Victor Gay of Lloydminster, member of a survey party.

VICTORIA, mount (11,365 feet) and glacier   (L-4)
Named by J. J. McArthur, D. L. S., after Queen Victoria (1819-1901).

VICTORIA CROSS, range   (J-2)
A range in Jasper National Park in which the peaks have been named
after winners of the Victoria Cross since World War I. This range
includes Mounts Pattison, Kinros, McKean, Kerr and Zengel, (q.v.).
(1952)

VIKING, town (J-7)

It was probably a difference of opinion where the railway survey would take place that caused the location of two hamlets. Viking on land to north owned by A. Naslund and just east of the present hospital and Harland to the south. The railway was surveyed through low lying slough land between them. The railroad engineers staked out their new townsite and named it "Meighen." As a result all the buildings in the two existing hamlets had to be moved.

People of the hamlet, however, did not like the name "Meighen" as it was pronounced like "mean" and therefore competition arose for a new name. "Viking" was favoured by the Scandinavian settlers while "Harland" was the choice of the others. Ben Gray a leader in the community, favoured "Viking" and was not to be outdone. When the vote on the name came up and he felt it might go the other way, he enlisted the aid of several Norwegian ladies standing by and so got a majority. Several names were forwarded to the Post Office Department but the name "Viking" finally won out. (Secretary-Treasurer, Town of Viking, August, 1970).

VILLENEUVE, hamlet (I-5)

After F. Villeneuve, a Member of the North-West Territories Legislature.

VILNA, village (I-7)

The Vilna district was first opened up by homesteaders and squatters in 1918 and 1919. Mr. Z. W. Mikitka was one of the first settlers who arrived in the district early in 1919 from a homestead at Stry where he had settled in 1910. The first post office was located two miles east of the present village and a Mr. Southwell was the first postmaster and he named it Villett. The mail came in from Lamont and soon the post office was moved some two miles west. Mr. Mikitka built his general store here and the hamlet grew up. The location was known as Mile 90 and at the end of 1919 the Canadian National laid steel through the district and the hamlet was renamed Vilna after Vilna then in Poland and now part of the Lithuanian S.S.R. and known as Vilnius; this was a result of the adjustment of boundaries in that area of Europe following World War II.

VIMY, hamlet (I-6), peak (7,825 feet) and ridge (O-5)

Named in 1917 when the Canadians captured Vimy Ridge. (1917)

VISTA, peak (9,169 feet) and pass (6,834 feet) (J-2)

A descriptive name.

VOKES, lake (B-5)

After Lieutenant-Colonel Frederick Alexander Vokes, M.I.D., Calgary, killed in World War II. (1950)

VULCAN, town and county (M-6)

In Roman mythology, Vulcan was the God of Fire. Information available indicates that "the town of Vulcan was originally named by the C.P.R. townsite department and was presumably named after Vulcan the God of Fire." This is borne out by evidence that "the streets were similarly named after other mythical characters and celestial bodies such as Apollo, Minerva, Venus, Neptune, Juno and Jupiter. These street names have however, been changed to numbered streets." (H. K. Wallace, Secretary-Treasurer, letter, August, 1970). (1910)

— W —

WABAMUN, lake, hamlet, creek and Indian Reserve (I-5)
It appears as "White Lake" on Palliser map, 1865. The name is Cree for "mirror".

WABAMUN LAKE, provincial park (I-5)
See Wabamun, lake

WABASCA, lakes, river, hamlet and Indian Reserve (F-5)
A corruption of an Indian name *wapuskau,* meaning "grassy narrows."

WADLIN, lake (D-4)
After L. N. Wadlin, D.L.S. an assistant on a survey. (1914)

WAGNER, hamlet (G-5)
After a resident engineer of the Northern Alberta Railway during construction days. (1914)

WAHSATNOW, lake (I-7)
After an Indian farmer who lived near the lake.

WAHSTAO, locality (I-6)
A corruption of Cree *wahsato,* "spiritual light." The name was suggested by Peter Erasmus, (see Erasmus, mount). (1907)

WAINWRIGHT, town (J-7)
After William Wainwright (1840-1914), second vice-president of the Grand Trunk Pacific Railway; formerly known as Denwood Post Office, it was changed to Wainwright, June 1, 1908. William Wainwright was born in England and as a young man entered the service of the Manchester, Sheffield and Yorkshire Railway, as a clerk. In 1862 he came to Canada at the invitation of Sir E. Watkin to be chief clerk in the accountant's office of the Grand Trunk Railway. He rose steadily in the organization until, in 1911, he became senior vice-president of the railway and second vice-president of the Grand Trunk Pacific. (1908)

WAIPAROUS, creek (L-5)
North branch of Ghost River; it is on the Palliser map, 1865. It is a corruption of a Stoney Indian name meaning "Crow (Indian) scalp."

WALDIE, creek (M-5)
After a settler; "the Indian name is *ketoke* or prairie-chicken creek" (Stimson). It is possible that the settler was one E. F. Waldy, a remittance man who lived far up the Highwood River. He is described as a big cheerful Englishman who rode a large white Apaloosa horse. He was a great hunter and a keen shot and on one occasion was away hunting for so long that his remittances piled up at High River Post Office. At this time the Boer War broke out and he enlisted. He gave a great going away party in Calgary and it continued until the remittances were exhausted. He served throughout the war and may have returned to England for he was never again seen in the High River area. (*Leaves from the Medicine Tree.* High River Old Timers' Association, 1960). (1896)

WALKER, mount (10,835 feet) (K-3)
After Horace Walker, past president, Alpine Club, England. It appears on Collie's map, 1899. Collie mentions naming the mountain in August, 1897.

WALLACE, mount (4,130 feet) and river (G-4)
After James Nevin Wallace (1870-1941) who had a long experience as a surveyor in the Canadian West. He was a member of the British Columbia-Alberta Boundary Commission (1913-1924).

WALL OF JERICHO, mountain (9,500 feet) (L-4)
Slate Range; a descriptive name. (1960)

WALSH, hamlet (N-8)
After Superintendent James Morrow Walsh (1840-1905), of the North-West Mounted Police. From 1873 to 1883 he held the rank of Inspector. He was well known for his firmness in dealing with Sitting Bull and his followers who crossed into Canada following the Custer Massacre at Little Bighorn in 1876. For a short time he was in business but in 1897 he returned to the Force as a Superintendent and First Commissioner of the Yukon Territory at the difficult period of the Klondike Gold Rush. He retired in 1898. (1890)

WAPIABI, creek (K-3)
A Stoney Indian word signifying "grave"; from a grave on its banks. (1910)

WAPITI, river (H-1) - (G-2) locality (H-1) and mountain (9,936 feet) (L-4)
Indian name meaning "elk".

WAPUTIK, peak (8,977 feet), range, icefield (L-3)
A Stoney Indian name meaning "white goat." When the range was named by Dr. G. M. Dawson in 1884, it was a favourite haunt of the Rocky Mountain goat.

WARBURG, village (J-5)
The incorrect spelling of Warberg an ancient castle in Sweden. It was a Swedish settlement. (1916)

WARD, mount (8,300 feet) and creek (N-5)
After Captain A. C. Ward, R.E., secretary of the British Boundary Commission, Lake of the Woods to the Rockies. (1917)

WARDEN, creek (J-3)
Flows into Gregg River; it is crossed by a trail once used by Jasper Park wardens. (1925)

WARDLOW, locality (M-7)
After a daughter of J. R. Sutherland, a rancher in the area. (1922)

WARE, mount (6,700 feet) and creek (M-5)
After John Ware, well-known pioneer Negro cowboy and rancher. John Ware is believed to have been born in slavery but in 1882 he came to Alberta on a cattle drive and worked in the Highwood River country, first at the Bar-U Ranch and then at the Quorn. Finally he established his own ranch on the Red Deer River. He was widely known in the area and the stories of his fantastic feats of taming bronchos and of steer roping are legion. He died in 1905 as a result of a fall from his horse.

WARNER, village, county (O-7)
After A. L. Warner, resident and land agent, Alberta Railway and Irrigation Company. It was originally named Brunton but the name was changed. (1907)

WARRE, mount (9,000 feet) (M-4)
Two miles east of Whiteman Pass; after Lieutenant H. J. Warre (1819-1898), of Warre and Vavasour Expedition, 1845-46. The two officers were sent from Montreal to the mouth of the Columbia River to report on the practicability of establishing military posts and transporting troops across the western country. They crossed the Rockies by a pass "in about 50° 30′ N. lat." in 1845 and returned by Athabasca Pass, 1846. He subsequently became General Sir Henry Ware, K.C.B., having served in the Crimean War, and as Commander-in-Chief at Bombay. He was the author of *Sketches in Rocky Mountains and British Columbia* and *Sketches in the Crimea*. See also Vavasour, mount.

WARREN, mount (10,800 feet) (J-3)
Named by Mrs. M. Schäffer author of *Old Indian Trails*, 1911, after her head guide. (1911)

WARRENSVILLE, locality (F-3)
After E. Warren, first postmaster. (1921)

WARRIOR, mount (9,600 feet) (M-4)
After a British man-of-war which fought in the Battle of Jutland, May, 1916. (1918)

WARSPITE, mount, (9,250 feet) (M-4)
After H.M.S. *Warspite*, a British cruiser which was engaged at the Battle of Jutland, May, 1916. *Warspite* was one of the *Queen Elizabeth* class of battleship—a group which turned out to be some of the most successful battleships ever built for the British Navy. *Warspite* was probably the best known of the group although her reputation was gained in World War II. She was built in 1912 and served throughout both World Wars; in the second she served in many theatres of war and became affectionately known as "the Old Lady." After World War II she was ordered to be broken up. After her fittings had been removed she was under tow on the south coast of Britain en route to the breaker's yard when she sank as if she desired to avoid the ignominy of the scrap yard. (1922)

WARSPITE, village (I-6)
The village was built on the homestead of one Ralph Burns and was named "Frances" after his daughter. In 1920 it was named Warspite after the well-known British battleship (see Warspite, mount).

WARWICK, locality (I-7)
After one S. R. Warwick who settled here in 1899. (1904)

WARWICK, mount (9,535 feet) and creek (K-3)
A castellated mountain; so named from a fancied resemblance to Warwick Castle, England.

WASAGAMU, lakes (I-8)
A Cree Indian name meaning "clearwater"; descriptive name.

WASEL, locality (I-7)
After Wasel Hawreliak, first postmaster. (1911)

WASKAHIGAN, river (H-3)
Cree Indian for "House."

WASKASOO, creek (K-5)
Indian name meaning "red deer"; see Red Deer, river.

WASKATENAU, creek and village (I-6)
From an Indian name meaning "opening in the banks" referring to the cleft in the ridge through which the creek flows into the North Saskatchewan River. The village is at the north end of the draw leading down from the plain into the North Saskatchewan River valley. The first settlers came to the area in 1903 although it was not until 1919 that the first post office and the hamlet came into being.

WASTACH, pass (8,348 feet) (L-4)
Named by S. E. S. Allen and is on his map, 1896. It is a descriptive name; Stoney Indian for "beautiful."

WASTINA, locality (L-8)
A corruption of *miwasin*, Cree Indian for "pretty place." (1912)

WATCHTOWER, THE, mountain (9,157 feet) (J-2)
A descriptive name. (1916)

WATCHUSK, lake (F-8)
Cree Indian for "muskrat."

WATELET, lake (J-5)
Said to be named by a Belgian settler after himself. (1898)

WATERFOWL, lakes (K-3)
Many ducks were seen on them when they were named by Stutfield and Collie in 1898.

WATERGLEN, locality (J-6)
The name refers to lakes in the vicinity. (1908)

WATERTON, lakes, river and national park (O-5)
The Waterton Lakes were named by Lieutenant Thomas Blakiston of The Palliser Expedition after Charles Waterton (1782-1865), a naturalist who was the author of *Wanderings in South America, the North West of the United States and the Antilles in* 1812, 1816, 1820 and 1824. Although he ranged widely over the Northwestern United States, Waterton was never in Canada. While visiting South America he gained a measure of fame by riding an alligator. He wrote several books of which the above mentioned is his best known. He also established a bird sanctuary at his home near Wakefield, Yorkshire. The river and park take their name from the lakes.

WATINO, hamlet (F-3)
A word for "valley"; it was formerly named Smoky. (1925)

WAUGH, locality (I-6)
After W. J. Waugh, first postmaster. (1905)

WAVY, lake   (J-7)
So named from the snow geese (Waveys) that frequent it in spring.

WAYETENAW, lake   (H-7)
A Cree Indian name meaning "hollow."

WEALD, locality   (I-3)
The name comes from the Old English meaning wooded land. It is the
name of a district in southeast England lying between the North and
South Downs and covering much of Kent and Sussex, southern Surrey
and eastern Hampshire, (Ekwall).

WEASONE, creek   (H-4)
After Benjamin Weasone, a well-known Indian trapper. (1918)

WEBSTER, lake   (F-4)
After Squadron Leader A. E. Webster, D.F.C., Edmonton, killed in
World War II. (1947)

WEBSTER, locality   (G-2)
After George Webster (1875-   ), Member of the Legislative Assembly
for Calgary 1926-1935. He was a sub-contractor during construction
days; later an alderman for Calgary from 1920-1922, and Mayor from
1923-1926.

WEDGE, THE, mount (8,700 feet)   (M-4)
Descriptive of its summit.

WEDGE, THE, mount (8,700 feet;   (M-4)
Kananaskis River; the name describes the shape of the summit.

WEED, creek and WEED CREEK, locality   (J-5)
According to Sir George Simpson in his *Narrative of a Journey Round
the World*, 1847, he and his companions camped one night near "the
Atcheskapesequa seepee or Smoking Weed River."

WEED, mount (10,100 feet)   (K-3)
On Collie's map, 1903; after G. M. Weed, Appalachian Mountain Club,
Boston. He made a number of "first ascents" in the Canadian Rockies.

WELCH, creek   (K-5)
After Lance Corporal Dwight E. Welch, M.I.D., Erskine, Alberta, killed
in World War II. (1950)

WELLING, locality   (N-6)
After Horace Welling a farmer who settled in the area at the time. (1909)

WELLS, lake   (A-7)
After A. K. Wells, prominent igneous petrologist. (1958)

WELSTEAD, lake   (C-7)
Said to be named after a former reeve of Grantham township, Ontario.
(1917)

WEMBLEY, village   (G-2)
According to L. D. Chalmers, Secretary-Treasurer of the village in a
letter of August, 1970, "the original owner of the land where the village
of Wembley is situated was one Mr. Wadell who was born in Wembley,

England. He agreed to give up the land for the townsite with the stipulation that the new community be called Wembley after the place where he was born." The name Wembley first appears as *Wambeleg* in 1249 and is derived from *wamb,* womb, (Ekwall).

WENHAM VALLEY, locality (J-5)
After Mark Wenham, former postmaster. (1911)

WENKCHEMNA, peak (10,401 feet) pass, glacier (L-4)
Named by S. E. S. Allen, 1894. The word is Stoney Indian meaning "ten," as it is the tenth of the Ten Peaks, (q.v.).

WENTZEL, river and lake (B-5)-(C-5)
After Willard Ferdinand Wentzel (d. 1832), fur trader. Wentzel was born in Montreal and in 1799 entered the service of the North West Company. For a number of years he was a clerk in the Athabasca Department. He was "taken over" by the Hudson's Bay Company in 1821 at the Union of the two companies but he retired to Canada in 1825. In 1827 he re-entered the service of the Hudson's Bay Company and served two years as a clerk at Mingan on the lower St. Lawrence. He retired again in 1829 and died in 1832, a victim of a cholera epidemic.

WEST ARROWWOOD, creek (M-6)
Translation of Indian name; presumably the Indians obtained wood for arrows on the banks of this stream.

WESTERDALE, locality (L-5)
After Westerdale village in the North Riding of Yorkshire, England. It means "western valley", (Ekwall). (1910)

WESTLOCK, town (I-5)
The original settlement was four miles east of the present location and was named Edison after F. Edison an early pioneer of the district. Later it was moved to the site of the original homesteads of two settlers Westgate and Lockhart and was renamed Westlock. (1912)

WESTON, lake (N-7)
After T. C. Weston (1832-1911), of the Geological Survey of Canada.

WESTWARD HO, hamlet (L-5)
Named after Charles Kingsley's novel. The name was given by one Captain Thomas, a former British army officer who was an early settler. (1905)

WETASKIWIN, city (J-6)
Wetaskiwin is an adaptation of the Indian name *wi-ta-ski-oo cha-ka-tin-ow* or Peace Hills (q.v.) and when the townsite was laid out in 1892 the name was adopted. Wetaskiwin came into being with the coming of the Calgary and Edmonton Railway and became a city in 1906.

WHALEBACK, ridge (N-5)
The name describes the shape of the ridge.

WHEAT CENTRE, locality (M-7)
When the post office was named it had every prospect of being the centre of an extensive wheat growing area. (1910)

WHIRLPOOL, river   (J-2)
It is on the Palliser map, 1865. H. J. Moberly noted that there is a small whirlpool at the foot of a rapid in this river. The trail from the Athabasca River to the pass of the same name followed this river.

WHISTLER, mountain   (N-5)
Oldman River; probably after the *siffleur* or whistling marmot.

WHISTLERS, THE, mountain (8,085 feet) and pass (7,800 feet)   (J-2)
West of Athabasca River; there are colonies of the hoary marmot or whistler on the mountain. (1916)

WHITE, mount (9,040 feet)   (L-4)
Named by Dr. G. M. Dawson, 1884, after James White, assistant to Dr. Dawson in surveys of the southern Rocky Mountains in 1884; later technical adviser to the Minister of Justice. Mounts McConnell (q.v.), Tyrrell (q.v.) and White face each other across the valley.

WHITE EARTH, creek   (H-6)
It appears as White Earth Brook on David Thompson's map of 1814. It is a translation of the Cree Indian name *wapitanisk*.

WHITE MAN, pass (7,112 feet) and mount (9,768 feet)   (M-4)
The name of White Man Pass probably refers to an incident noted by Sir George Simpson in his account of his journey across the Rockies in 1841 (on his journey around the world). Simpson mentions that a party of emigrants came from the west that same year by way of Kootenay River and one of the passes through the mountains; this may quite well have been White Man Pass.

In 1845 Father Pierre-Jean De Smet (1801-1873), ascended the Kootenay River and crossed the Rockies by a pass that seems to have been White Man Pass. In his *book Oregon Missions and Travels over the Rocky Mountains in* 1845-46 he mentions the erection of a cross at a point where he crossed the height of land; he called it the "Cross of Peace."

A branch of the Cross River flowing southward from the summit of the pass to the Kootenay River is according to G. M. Dawson *tsha-kooap-te-ha-wap-ta* in reference to a story told by the Indians that some early traveller set up a cross in the pass near the summit; this was probably Father De Smet. Father De Smet notes in a letter written September 15, 1845 from the foot of the Cross of Peace: "After much fatigue, labor and admiration, on the 15th we traversed the high lands separating the waters of the Oregon (Columbia) from those of the south branch of the Saskatchewan or the ancient Bourbon River, so called before the Canadian conquest by the British. . . .

The Christian's standard the cross, has been reared at the source of these two rivers; may it be a sign of salvation and peace to all the scattered and itinerant tribes east and west of these gigantic and lurid mountains."

WHITEAVES, mount (10,300 feet)   (K-3)
After James Frederick Whiteaves (1835-1909). A native of England, he came to Canada in 1862 and settled in Montreal where for twelve years he was curator of the Museum of the Montreal Natural History

Society. In 1876 he was appointed to the staff of the Geological Survey of Canada as palaeontologist, in which capacity he carried out much important research. He was one of the original Fellows of the Royal Society of Canada and published 150 papers. His most important work was *Contributions to Canadian Palaeontology* which appeared in three volumes between 1885 and 1891. He was awarded an honourary LL.D. from McGill University. (1920)

WHITEBRUSH, lake (J-6)
A translation of the Indian name, *kawapetegok.*.

WHITECAP, mount (9,400 feet) (J-2)
It is descriptive of snow on its summit.

WHITECOURT, town (I-4)
The site of Whitecourt was known to the Cree Indians who named it *sak-de-wah,* "where even the waters come together" and today there is a slogan for the area "where even the waters meet". From 1905 to 1910 mail for Whitecourt was delivered to Green Court some 26 miles southeast. An individual named Walter White picked up the mail and delivered it to the settlers in the Whitecourt area. By 1910 the population growth warranted a post office for the settlement and the name "Whitecourt" appears to have been chosen by the postmaster at Green Court who was filling out the necessary papers for the establishment of a new post office. As the name was needed and there was not time to wait for one to be chosen he made up his own by taking the "court" as in Green Court and putting it behind "White", the name of the mail carrier, to make the name "Whitecourt."

WHITECROW, mountain (9,288 feet) (J-2)
White crows were seen on it when named.

WHITEFISH, lake (H-7)
There were many whitefish in the lake when the name was given.

WHITELAW, hamlet (F-2)
After a former car service accountant of the Edmonton, Dunvegan and British Columbia Railway.

WHITEMUD, creek (I-6)
It takes its name from a hill of the same name (now within the city limits of Edmonton) from which the Hudson's Bay Company obtained a white mud used as whitewash at their posts. (1961)

WHITFORD, lake creek and locality (I-6)
After the first family to settle near the lake. It was known in Cree, *munawanis,* "the place where the eggs are gathered." (1893)

WHITHAM, lake (G-1)
After Flight Lieutenant J. Whitham, D.F.C., Edmonton, killed in World War II. (1947)

WHITLA, locality (N-8)
After R. J. Whitla, a merchant of Winnipeg who visited the place when the narrow gauge railway ran through to Lethbridge.

WHYTE, mount (9,786 feet)   (L-4)
After Sir William Whyte (1835-1914), at one time second vice-president
of the Canadian Pacific Railway. A native of Scotland, Whyte came to
Canada in 1863 and entered the service of the Grand Trunk Railway.
In 1884 he went to the Canadian Pacific as superintendent of the Ontario
division. In 1901 he became assistant to the president of the railway and
in 1904 second vice-president. He retired from active business in 1911
and in that year was created a Knight Bachelor. He was known as
"smooth William!" White Avenue in Edmonton is also named after him.

WIDEWATER, hamlet   (G-4)
The reference is to the width of Lesser Slave Lake opposite the hamlet.
(1923)

WIGWAM, creek   (J-3)
Named for an Indian camp. (1918)

WILCOX, mount (9,463 feet), pass (7,700 feet) and peak   (K-3)
The pass was named by Collie in 1899, after Walter Dwight Wilcox,
author of *The Rockies of Canada,* 1906, probably the first white man
to traverse the pass.

WILDCAT, hills   (L-5)
Known in Blackfoot as *natayo-paghsin* (Nelson).

WILDCAT, locality   (L-5)
Name suggested by C.P.R., for trackage to a gas processing plant located
in the Wildcat Hills, (q.v.). The name is also used in oil and gas
terminology. (1961)

WILDER, creek   (F-1)
After one Wilder, who when constructing the telegraph line to Hudson's
Hope, used a pack trail along this stream. (1918)

WILD HORSE, locality, port of entry   (O-8)
Originally named Sage Creek in 1913, but re-named in 1926 to agree with
the name of the Customs port of entry.

WILDHORSE, creek   (K-4)
From reports of wild horses seen at the head of the creek. (1919)

WILDWOOD, village   (I-4)
"Mr. Horace Thompson in 1929 thought the name of Junkins was not
attractive and so suggested the name Cloverdale. A petition was taken
around and other suggestions as to a new name were asked. The name
Wildwood was suggested by Ruby Lord (now Mrs. George Carroll,
widowed) of Telkwa, British Columbia. Other names were on the list sent
but some had been already registered as town names and the name of
Wildwood was chosen by the government." (Mrs. Evelyn Hill,
Secretary-Treasurer, letter, August, 1970).

WILKIN, lake   (G-2)
After Squadron Leader R. P. Wilkin, Czech M.C., M.I.D., of Edmonton,
killed in 1943 during World War II.

WILLERVAL, mountain (10,420 feet)   (K-3)
After the village about five miles south of Lens, France, captured by
the Canadians, April 13, 1917.

WILLESDEN GREEN, locality   (J-5)
After Willesden Green, London, England. It was the former home of
George Wager, first postmaster. The name first appears in 1185 as
Wilesdune and means "Hill with a well;" (Old English *wiel*, meaning
well), (Ekwall).

WILLIAM BOOTH, mount (9,000 feet)   (K-4)
After General William Booth (1829-1912), founder of the Salvation
Army. It was named on the centenary of the founding of the Salvation
Army. (1965)

WILLIAM MCKENZIE, Indian Reserve   (F-3)
After an Indian who obtained severalty under Treaty 8.

WILLIAM SMITH, lake   (A-7)
After William Smith (1769-1839), English engineer, who became a self-
trained geologist. The father of stratigraphy, he made some of the first
detailed geological maps. (1958)

WILLIAMS, mount (9,000 feet)   (M-4)
After Major-General Victor W. Williams, C.E.F.; taken prisoner at Zillebeke, Flanders, June, 1916. (1918)

WILLINGDON, village   (I-7)
Formerly Agricola but renamed after the Governor General of Canada,
Lord Willingdon (1866-1941). "In 1927 the C.P.R. was building a railway from Lloydminster to Edmonton through the area lying close to the
Saskatchewan River south of it. Many areas through which the railway
ran had appropriate names. The area around where Willingdon now is
had no particular name since districts around were rather remote. It
is said that the C.P.R. officials in the Western Section of the C.P.R.
decided that the area should be named for the then Governor General
Lord Willingdon." (N. W. Svekla, Secretary, Village of Willingdon,
letter, August, 1970).

WILLMORE WILDERNESS, provincial park   (I-1)-(I-2)
After Hon. Norman A. Willmore (1909-1965), Alberta Minister of
Labour, 1953-1955 and Minister of Lands and Forests, 1955-1965.

WILLOW, creek   (I-5)
North Saskatchewan River. It takes its name from the willows lining
its banks.

WILLOW, creek   (N-5)
Oldman River. After the willow trees on its banks. It is known as
stiapiskan, "ghost hound", (Steele).

WILLSON, creek   (L-5)
After a veteran of the Riel Rebellion, South African War and World
War I. Colonel Willson went overseas in command of "D" Company,
49th Battalion, C.E.F., and served through operations at Messines,
Kemmel Hill and the Ypres Salient; died March 9, 1927, aged 77, (1908)

WILSON, creek   (H-7)
After Edward Wilson Berry, D.L.S. He served in World War I in
1917 and 1918. (1918)

WILSON, creek   (K-5)
After Pilot Officer R. Wilson, D.F.C., Stettler, Alberta, killed in World
War II. (1950)

WILSON, locality   (N-6)
After E. H. Wilson of the Alberta Railway and Irrigation Company.
(1912)

WILSON, mount (10,631 feet) and glacier   (K-3)
Named by Collie in 1898 after Tom Wilson, well-known guide of Banff.

WILSON, range   (O-5)
After Lieutenant C. W. Wilson, R.E., secretary to the British Boundary
Commission, Pacific to the Rockies, 1858-62. The name was originally
applied to a single peak by Lieutenant Blakiston of the Palliser
Expedition.

WIMBORNE, hamlet   (K-6)
Probably after Wimborne Minster, Dorset, England. The name Wim-
borne means meadow, the term "Minster" refers to a monastery that was
once there. The name first appeared about 844, (Ekwall).

WINAGAMI, lake   (G-3)
A Cree name, signifying "dirty-water lake."

WINAGAMI JUNCTION, locality   (G-3)
See Winagami, lake.

WINAGAMI LAKE, provincial park   (G-3)
See Winagami, lake.

WINDSOR, mountain (8,346 feet)   (O-5)
Named "Castle" by Blakiston, 1858; changed to Windsor 1915, to avoid
confusion with Castle Mountain (now Mount Eisenhower). The Cree
name is *o-mask-we-oo as-sin-wa-ti*, "queen mountain."

WINEFRED, lake and river   (G-8)-(F-8)
Named by one R. E. Young, D.L.S., after his wife.

WINFIELD, hamlet   (J-5)
After the Honourable Vernor Winfield Smith (1864-1932), Minister of
Railways in the United Farmers' government. A native of Prince Edward
Island he came to Alberta settling in the Camrose area where he farmed.
He was first elected to the Alberta Legislature in 1921 at which time
he was appointed Minister of Railways, a portfolio he held until his
death in 1932.

WINNIFRED, locality   (N-7)
Winnifred on 1888 map; after a relative of an English shareholder of the
Alberta Railway and Irrigation Company.

WINSTON CHURCHILL, provincial park   (H-7)
For origin see Winston Churchill, range.

WINSTON CHURCHILL, range   (K-3)
This range covering some 200 square miles is situated in Jasper National
Park and is just south of the Queen Elizabeth Ranges. It is bounded on
the east by the Sunwapta River, on the west by the Athabasca River and

on the south by the Columbia Icefield. Some of its peaks rise to a height of nearly 12,000 feet. The range was named in honour of Sir Winston Churchill (1874-1965) and was named in recognition of his distinguished services as wartime Prime Minister of Britain. In the dark days of 1940 he rallied the British people to the fight against the Nazis and led his people to victory. Defeated in 1945 he again became Prime Minister in 1951 and retired in 1954.

WINTERBURN, hamlet (I-6)

There are numerous Winterbornes and Winterbournes in England, most with a second name following. There is also one "Winterburn" in the West Riding of Yorkshire. It is probable that the Alberta hamlet was named by someone who hailed from one of the foregoing places. The name (however spelt) is derived from the Old English *winterburna* and means "a stream dry except in winter," (Ekwall). (1904). See Supplement.

WINTERING, hills (L-6)

Located south of the confluence of the Red Deer and Rosebud Rivers, they were selected as winter quarters by Metis because of the water, timber and winter grazing found here. In Blackfoot, *kikichep* "braced-up" hills.

WINTOUR, mount (8,800 feet) (M-5)

Opal Range (1922); After one Captain C. Wintour, killed in the naval Battle of Jutland, 1916.

WISTE, locality (L-7)

From the name of the Swedish father-in-law of C. Leaf, first postmaster. (1910)

WIZARD, lake (J-5)

According to Steele, the Indian name is *seksyawas sakigan* or Lizard Lake.

WOKING, hamlet (G-2)

After Woking, Surrey, England. The name "Woking" appears as *Wochinges* in Domesday Book, 1086. The meaning is uncertain. (1916)

WONDER, peak (9,300 feet) (M-4)

A descriptive name. (1913)

WOOD, lake (G-2)

After Regimental Sergeant-Major James Wood, D.C.M., Calgary, killed in World War II.

WOOD RIVER, locality (J-6)

There is no river of the name nearby. It is, however, named after Wood River, Hall County, Nebraska, from which I. J. Bulloch the first postmaster came. (1903)

WOODBEND, locality (I-6)

Woodbine was the name originally submitted, being that of a grade of flour milled here at the time. (1908)

WOODGLEN   (J-6)
Glenwood, after Glenwood, Minnesota, was the name first suggested
but as there were already Glenwood post offices in British Columbia,
New Brunswick, Nova Scotia, Ontario and Prince Edward Island, the
Post Office Department modified the name to Woodglen.

WOODHOUSE, locality   (N-6)
After W. E. Woodhouse, Calgary, former superintendent of motive power
of the Canadian Pacific Railway. (1909)

WOODS, creek   (E-8)
After one Joseph Woods, D.L.S. (1924)

WOOLCHESTER, locality   (N-8)
It was a sheep ranching centre when named.

WOOLLEY, mount (11,170 feet)   (K-3)
Named by Collie, 1898, after Herman Woolley of Caucasian and Alpine
mountaineering fame; a fellow climber.

WORTHINGTON, mount (9,600 feet)   (M-4)
On the Alberta-B.C. boundary. After Lieutenant-Colonel Donald Worthington of the B.C. Regiment who was killed in action in 1944. (1956)

WOSTOK, locality   (I-6)
A Russian word meaning "east." Russians from eastern Galicia were
the first settlers in 1896. (1899)

WRENTHAM, hamlet   (N-7)
After Wrentham, Suffolk, England. The name appears as *Wretham,
Uueretcham* in Domesday Book, 1086. It may be derived from "Wrenta's
ham" or "Wrenta's homestead", (Ekwall).

WRITING-ON-STONE, provincial park   (O-7)
In the valley of the Milk River, about 75 miles southeast of Lethbridge,
is a small area of sandstone cliffs on which are inscribed ancient
picture writing. The first known white man to see these pictographs
was James Doty in 1855. He wrote: "They (the sandstone rocks) are
worn by a thousand fantastic shapes, presenting in places smooth per-
pendicular surfaces, covered with rude hieroglyphics and representa-
tions of men, horses, guns, bows, shields, etc. in the usual Indian
style . . ." The Cree name for "writing-on-stone" is *masinasin*. See also
Masinasin, locality.

— Y —

YARROW, peak and creek   (O-5)
After Yarrow Water, Selkirk, Scotland.

YATES, locality   (I-4)
After a chief clerk in the treasurer's office at the Grand Trunk Pacific
Railway. (1911)

YELLOWHEAD, mountain (7,900 feet), pass (3,711 feet)   (J-2)
After François Decoigne, fur-trader in charge of Jasper House, Brulé
Lake, 1814; he was nicknamed "Tête-Jaune" or "Yellowhead", from the

colour of his hair. Cheadle says: "from being the spot chosen by an Iroquois trapper, known by the *sobriquet* of the Tête Jaune, or 'Yellow-Head,' to hide the furs he obtained on the western side." He also says the original "cache" was at the confluence of the Fraser and Robson Rivers. Sometimes called the Leather Pass, because the Hudson's Bay Company's posts in northern British Columbia obtained supplies of leather (dressed moose or caribou skins) by way of this pass. The Yellowhead Pass is the lowest pass in North America traversed by a railway. Originally intended as a route for the C.P.R. it was discarded but later became the route for the Grand Trunk Pacific and Canadian Northern Railways. When those two lines were merged to form the Canadian National one of the grades through the pass was abandoned. It later became part of the present highway that now crosses the pass.

YEOFORD, locality (J-5)
After Yeoford, Devonshire, England, the former home of Charles H. Marson, first postmaster. The word *yeo* is the Old English for "river". In this instance "river ford." (1909)

YOUNGSTOWN, village (L-7)
Youngstown was named after the homesteader (Joe Young) who home-steaded the land the village is now built on. (N. R. van Dam, Secretary of Village, letter, August, 1970).

— Z —

ZAMA, river and lake (B-2) (C-2)
After a Slave Indian chief whose trail followed the river. (1922)

ZAWALE, locality (I-6)
A Galician settlement; after a town in Galicia, now part of southeast Poland and the Ukraine. (1910)

ZEER, lake (H-7)
After Lance Bombadier Edwin Zeer, M.I.D., Calgary, killed in World War II. (1951)

ZENGEL, mount (8,400 feet) (J-2)
After Sergeant R. L. Zengel, V.C., M.M. of 45th Battalion of World War I, Rocky Mountain House, Alberta. He was born in Fairbautt, Minn. (1951)

ZIGADENUS, lake (L-3)
Named for the flowers of the white camas (*zygadenus elegans*) which are common around its shores. (1960)

A Note on Sources

Like the names portrayed here, the sources are many and varied. They range from letters from secretary-treasurers of villages to detailed reports of surveyors and explorers. There are periodical articles, monographs, newspaper articles and others. One source must be noted: the old work *Place-Names of Alberta* issued by the Geographical Board of Canada in 1928. In spite of its age it has proved most useful for although much of the information it contains is obsolete and some inaccurate there is much that is useful and the whole has served to point the way to further and newer material. We have freely used information from this publication but have added to it where necessary to illuminate the names and make them more interesting. The *Gazetteer of Canada—Alberta* has been most useful in pinpointing features. We have noted in brackets after most names the date the name became official.

Reports of explorers and surveyors have been most useful and only two will be used as examples. The first is the report of the exploration of Captain John Palliser and his party. Palliser, Hector and Blakiston were the main givers and recorders of names. The reports of the Geological Survey of Canada by G. M. Dawson and J. B. Tyrrell have proved invaluable. Tyrrell must be especially singled out for his careful listing of Cree and Stoney Indian names.

Records in the Provincial Library and the Provincial Archives have helped; particularly where biographical information has been required. Mention must be made of the booklet *Historic Sites of Alberta,* published by the former Alberta Department of Industry and Tourism and last reprinted in 1965. It contains most useful information concerning the events commemorated by the markers mentioned. The *Alberta Historical Review* has also been most helpful—various articles refer to naming of places even though the article may only have mentioned it incidentally.

Monographs and articles have been of great aid and those of which we have made frequent use are listed in the bibliography. These are many and are in some instances unusual. One work stands out—Eilert Ekwall's *Concise Oxford Dictionary of English Place-Names.* Many names in Alberta (Edmonton, Hythe, Vauxhall, etc.) are derived from ancient sources—Anglo-Saxon, Norman and Ekwall gives the derivation of such names, citing authorities such as Domesday Book, the first census by William I; the Close Rolls, Pipe Rolls and Book of Fees, those invaluable documents still to be seen in the Public Record Office, London. We have included these derivations where possible as a piece of added interest for those who wish to know more about the names of their locale.

Community histories have helped. These local histories, many written in 1967 the Centennial Year of Confederation, have provided much useful and new information. We have included them only within the body of the work as for the most part they are referred to but once. The Economic Surveys of Alberta cities, towns and villages published by the former Department of Industry and Tourism of the Alberta Government have furnished much useful information on early history, ethnic background of the settlers and former names, if any.

The reader may be surprised to find some unusual references. One is Richard Hough's *Dreadnought. A History of the Modern Battleship.* A number of mountains were named for battleships, prominent in World War I and this work supplied valuable data.

Finally, a word on maps. David Thompson's map, the maps of Aaron and John Arrowsmith, the cartographers and the Palliser map stand out as they indicate many features known to-day. The final accurate placing came later when the surveyors ultimately pinpointed them. The early mappers and cartographers did much however to point the way and due acknowledgment is made to them.

But after all the greatest source of information and that to which due credit must be given is to the Indians, the explorers, settlers, surveyors and others who named the features. They are the chief source; to them go our grateful thanks.

Select Bibliography

Alberta. Department of Municipal Affairs. Planning Branch. *Population—3. Unincorporated Communities.* Edmonton, 1970.

Canada. Geographic Board. *Place-Names of Alberta.* Ottawa, 1928.

Canada. Geological Survey. *Preliminary Report on the Physical and Geological Features of That Portion of the Rocky Mountains Between Latitudes 49° and 51° 31'* by G. M. Dawson. Ottawa, 1886.

Canada. Geological Survey. *Report on a Part of Northern Alberta and Portions of Adjacent Districts of Assiniboia and Saskatchewan . . .* by J. B. Tyrrell. Ottawa, 1887.

Canada. Office of the Surveyor General. *Report of the Commission Appointed to Delimit the Boundary between the Provinces of Alberta and British Columbia.* Part I, 1913-1916; Part II, 1917-1921; Part III, 1918-1924. Ottawa, 1917-1925.

Coleman, A. P., *The Canadian Rockies. New and Old Trails.* Toronto, Henry Frowde, 1911.

Ekwall, Eilert. *The Concise Oxford Dictionary of English Place-Names.* 4th edition. Oxford, Clarendon Press, 1960.

Ermatinger, Edward. York Factory Express Journal Being a Record of Journeys Made Between Fort Vancouver and Hudson's Bay in the Year, 1827-1828. *Transactions of the Royal Society of Canada,* 1912.

Fleming, Sandford. *Report in Surveys and Preliminary Operations on the Canadian Pacific Railway up to January, 1877.* Ottawa, 1877.

Footner, Hulbert. *New Rivers of the North.* London, T. Fisher Unwin, 1913.

Franchère, Gabriel. *Journal of a Voyage on the North West Coast of North America during the years 1811, 1812, 1813 and 1814* transcribed and translated by W. T. Lamb, edited with an introduction by W. K. Lamb. Toronto, Champlain Society, 1969.

Grant, George M., *Ocean to Ocean. Sandford Fleming's Expedition Through Canada in 1872.* Edmonton, Hurtig, 1967 (reprint).

Higinbotham, John D., *When the West Was Young.* Toronto, Ryerson, 1933.

Hough, Richard. *Dreadnought. A History of the Modern Battleship.* 2nd edition. London, Allen and Unwin, 1968.

Johnson, K. (ed.) *The Canadian Directory of Parliament, 1867-1967.* Ottawa, Queen's Printer, 1968.

Johnston, A., Place-Names of Southern Alberta. *Canadian Cattlemen,* August-October, 1957.

Kane, Paul. *Wanderings of an Artist Among the Indians of North America.* London, Longmans, 1859.

Lac Ste. Anne Historical Society. *West of the Fifth.* The Society, 1959.

Lacombe, Albert. *Grammaire de la Langue des Cris.* Montreal, 1874.

MacEwan, Grant. *Fifty Mighty Men.* Saskatoon, Modern Press, 1958.

MacGregor, J. G., *Peter Fidler: Canada's Forgotten Surveyor, 1769-1822.* Toronto, McClelland and Stewart, 1966.

MacGregor, J. G., *The Land of Twelve Foot Davis*. Edmonton, 1952.

Milton, William F. and Cheadle, W. B., *The Northwest Passage by Land*. London, Cassell, Petter and Galpin, 1865.

Palliser, John et al. *The Journals, Detailed Reports and Observations Relative to the Exploration of a Portion of British North America . . . During the Years 1857, 1858, 1859 and 1860*. London, H. M. Stationery Office, 1863.

Schäffer, Mary T. S., *Old Indian Trails*. New York, Putnam, 1911.

Southesk, James Carnegie, Earl of. *Saskatchewan and the Rocky Mountains*. Edinburgh, Edmonston and Douglas, 1875.

Stanley, George F. G., *Mapping the Frontier. Charles Wilson's Diary of the Survey of the 49th Parallel, 1858-1862, While Secretary of the British Boundary Commission*. London, Macmillan, 1970.

Steele, S. B., *Forty Years in Canada*. Toronto, McClelland, Goodchild and Stewart, 1915.

Stewart, George R., *American Place-Names*. New York, Oxford, 1970.

Stutfield, Hugh E. M. and Collie, J. Norman. *Climbs and Exploration in the Canadian Rockies*. London, Longmans, 1903.

Thompson, D W., *Men and Meridians*. 3 volumes. Ottawa, Queen's Printer, 1966-1969.

Thorington, J. M., *A Climber's Guide to the Rocky Mountains of Canada*. Revised edition. New York, American Alpine Club, 1953.

Wilcox, Walter D., *The Rockies of Canada*. New York, Putman, 1906.

Williams, M. B., *Jasper National Park*, 1949.

Williams, M. B., *Through the Heart of the Rockies and the Selkirks*. 3rd edition. Ottawa. 1924.

SUPPLEMENT

— A —

ABILENE, locality (H-7)

Formerly known as Clarksville after one Lewis G. Clark, an early post-master, it was probably named after one of several places in the United States named Abilene. The name may have been suggested by a pioneer from the U.S. Abilene was a tetrachy in ancient Syria and its capital was Abila. (1911).

AGATHA, locality (N-7)

Formerly the name of the C.P.R. station and called after one Agatha, Lady Hindlip. (1914).

ALBION RIDGE, locality (N-6)

"Albion" was the Roman name for Britain so it could have been a "British" settlement on a "Ridge." (1907)

AMBER VALLEY, locality

Originally known as Pine Creek this locality is a pioneer black settle-ment where settlers came from the southern United States around 1911. Apparently some found it difficult clearing the land and returned to Oklahoma or to larger centres in Alberta around 1914. According to Jeff Edwards, an old-timer in the area, who was interviewed on the Canadian Broadcasting Corporation, Edmonton programme "Hourglass" on April 13, 1973, the residents petitioned for a post office around 1932 and the local teacher suggested the name "Amber Valley" from the colour of the land.

ANNING, locality (I-7)

After a former postmaster, S. H. Anning. (1911)

ANSHAW, locality (H-7)

Derived from Angus Shaw of the North West Company who built a post on Moose Lake in 1789. It was also known as "Fort Lac d'Orignal" or "Shaw's House." In 1792 he built Fort George on the north bank of the North Saskatchewan River about 4½ miles above the mouth of Moose Creek.

ARDENVILLE, locality (N-6)

After an early settler from Ontario, one Arden Simpson. (1910)

ARVILLA, locality (I-5)

The first residents called the hamlet "Our Villa" and it was later con-tracted to its present form.

AZURE, locality (M-5)

Formerly the name of the C.P.R. station and probably descriptive of the skies at the time it was named. (1892-93)

— B —

BADGER LAKE, locality (M-7)

After a former small lake of the same name situated north of the original post office where badgers were once plentiful. (1913)

BALM, locality (I-4)

After the balsam poplar (*Populus balsamifera L.*) which were plentiful here at the time of its founding. The name Balm of Gilead is from the biblical Gilead, an area north of the Dead Sea, noted for its medicinal balm. (1914)

BANKHEAD, locality (L-4)

Formerly a C.P.R. station and named by Lord Strathcona (1820-1914), one of the directors of the C.P.R., after Bankhead, Banffshire, Scotland. (1905)

BANTRY, locality (M-7)

After Bantry Bay in the West of Ireland; formerly a C.P.R. station. (1884)

BARBARA, creek (I-2)

Wildhay River; named for Barbara Anne, daughter of T. C. Burrows (1890-   ). A native of Lancashire, England, he first came to Canada in 1910. He served in World War I, being wounded at the Somme in 1916. After the war he joined the Forest Service and became Forest Supervisor at Entrance. The creek was named on the occasion of his daughter's birth in 1922. (1945)

BARONS, village (N-6)

In 1907 Jack Warnock opened a store and post office just across the railway from where Barons is now. It was called Blayney. C. S. Noble (acting as agent for the C.P.R.) purchased land for the townsite in 1909. There were some businesses on the land nearby. When lots in the new townsite were offered for sale the name Baron was chosen after a railway official. The first bank called itself Baron's Bank and other firms soon added Baron's to their names but it was a few years before the C.P.R. changed its station name from Baron to Barons. (*Lethbridge Herald*, August 1, 1955).

BAXTER, lake (J-8)

Said to be named after a driver of a supply team for a survey party.

BEAUPRÉ, creek (L-5)

Bow River; after an early settler.

BEAVER, lake and creek (N-5—N-6)

Oldman River; translation of Blackfoot *kakghikstakiskway* "where the beaver cuts wood."

BEAVER MINES, locality (N-5)

Originally the home of the Beaver Coal Mines. (1912)

BEAVERDAM, creek and locality (H-8)

The creek wherein there were a number of beaver dams, flows into the Battle River and is on the Palliser map, 1865. The locality takes its name from the creek as does the former municipal district. (1913)

BEDSON, ridge (J-2)

After a former railway station nearby which in turn was probably named after an early Warden of Stony Mountain Penitentiary, Manitoba. (1916).

BELLEVUE, village (N-5)
French for "'good view"; said to be named after a mining camp where in 1910 a disaster took 31 lives. (1907)

BELLSHILL, locality and lake (J-7)
Named for Isobel, the wife of Archibald Brown, an early postmaster. (1907).

BIG PRAIRIE, hamlet (L-5)
Descriptive of the wide open country. (1909)

BINGVILLE, locality (M-8)
Taken from the comic section of the *Spokane Review* at the time the post office was named. (1914)

BIRCH, hills (F-2)
These hills near Wanham were for the fur traders at Dunvegan the principal source of birch bark for making and repairing canoes. The Journal of Fort Dunvegan kept by A. R. McLeod notes under date of June 15, 1806 that two men were sent off to the Birch Hills for bark and that they returned one week later with 2,000 barks (pieces of bark).

BIRDWOOD, mount (10,160 feet) (M-4)
In honour of Field Marshal Sir William R. Birdwood (1865-1951). He was in command of the Australian and New Zealand Army Corps at Gallipoli in 1915 both during the campaign and the evacuation. He was later in command of these same forces in France, 1916-1918 and of the 5th Army, France, 1918-1919.

BISSELL, locality (I-5)
Formerly the name of a C.N.R. station, it might have been named for a judge, H. P. Bissell of Buffalo, N. Y., who took part in speeches given at the centenary celebrations for peace along the Canadian-U.S. border in 1913.

BISTRE, mountain (7,757 feet) (J-2)
Descriptive of the brown pigment of the mountain. (1916)

BLACKTAIL, locality (N-6)
Originally the name of the post office which was on Blacktail Coulee which was possibly named after the blacktail deer. The name was changed from Willows to avoid duplication. (1913)

BLAKISTON, creek and mount (9,600 feet) (O-5)
Named for Lieut. Thomas Blakiston (1832-1891) who was attached to the Palliser Expedition. Blakiston was a lieutenant in the Royal Artillery (he later attained the rank of captain) and was appointed magnetic observer to the Expedition. He not only recorded magnetic observations but being interested in ornithology, he noted many species. He also named a number of geographic features. He differed with Palliser and this led to his leaving the Expedition; he later submitted a report on his own findings. Blakiston was a difficult person to work with although he was gifted. He was also a wanderer and saw service in many countries. (Creek, 1960)

BLOOMSBURY, locality (I-5)
Originally the name of the post office and school district it was suggested by former residents of the Bloomsbury school district in Manitoba. This in turn may have been taken from the Bloomsbury district in London, England. The Bloomsbury Cabin (still standing) was a watering place on the trail from Edmonton to the Klondike. The name itself first appears as *Blemondisberi* in 1281 and as *Blemundisbury* in 1335. It is said to derive from some member of the Blemund family resident in London; William de Blemunt in Tottenham, 1201, and William de Blemund, 1230. Blemont is a place in Vienne, France. (Ekwall)

BLUE RIDGE, hamlet (I-4)
The name describes the blue haze on the height of land in the area as viewed from a distance. Originally the name of the post office. (1927)

BOAG, lake (I-6)
After an early settler of the area, A. Boag.

BODO, hamlet (K-8)
Apparently named by local Norwegian farmers after a town located on the northern coast of Norway.

BOIAN, locality (I-7)
After a village in Bukovina; settlers in this district came from Boian. (1913)

BOILER, rapids (E-7)
The name is not descriptive of the rapids as might be expected but comes from an accident that occurred in 1886. Scows were taking the boiler and machinery of a steamboat to Fort McMurray. The scow carrying the boiler was wrecked in the rapids. Apparently the boiler is still there.

BONAR, locality (L-7)
It is believed to have been named after the First World War for the Hon. Andrew Bonar Law (1858-1923), Prime Minister of Great Britain, 1922-1923. Bonar Law was born at Rexton, New Brunswick and he was the only prime minister of Britain born outside that country. He was a life-long friend of Max Aitken, Lord Beaverbrook of New Brunswick.

BORDENAVE, locality (H-7)
After F. D. Bordenave, early postmaster.

BORRADAILE, locality (I-8)
Originally the name of the C.N.R. station, it is possibly named after Borrowdale, Cumberland, or Borrowdale, Westmorland, England or Borrodale, Inverness, Scotland which has an association with Bonnie Prince Charlie. The name of Borrowdale, Westmorland is said to be from the Old Norse *Borgardair* — "valley with a fort" or the valley of *Borgara,* i.e. "a stream by a fort." (Ekwall)

BOW CITY, locality (M-7)
Originally a village known as Eyremore (the combination of the names of W. T. P. Eyres and his wife, née Moore) it was located on the south side of the Bow River but was moved to its present location. Although

known as Bow City, the dream of a developer, the population was twelve in 1956 and four less ten years later. (1960)

BRAINARD, locality (G-1)
Named for the first postmaster, W. L. Brainard who with his wife came to the area in 1918 from the United States. At one time they had a large ranch and later established a well-known eating place on the Pouce Coupe trail in the Hythe district. "Ma Brainard's" as it was called became in time an institution and remained in operation until 1966; Mrs. Brainard died a year later. Her chicken dinners were a great gastronomic delight and no one ever passed this way without stopping for a meal. Among the famous visitors were: Sir Henry Thornton, one-time president of the C.N.R. and Lord Bessborough, Governor General of Canada, 1932-1936. (1919)

BRANDER, lake (C-8)
In honour of Dr. James F. Brander (1879-1963), a pioneer doctor of Edmonton. He was born at Northport, Nova Scotia and graduated from Queen's University in 1906. After he did postgraduate work in London, he came out to Ponoka where he practiced from 1909-1911. He then moved to Edmonton where he specialized in obstetrics. He was a keen amateur horticulturist and specialized in growing peonies; from 1923-1946 he had eight acres of land in the Silver Heights area of Edmonton. The Brander Gardens sub-division in Edmonton is also named for him. (1917)

BREDIN, locality (G-2)
After Fletcher Bredin, an early trader and rancher of the Peace River country. He was associated with J. K. Cornwall (see Cornwall, lake). (1915)

BREMNER, locality (I-6)
After James C. C. (Charlie) Bremner, (1867-1927), early settler. He came to Edmonton in 1891 and ultimately had a 500-acre farm near Clover Bar. The post office was originally called Hortonburg in 1896 but changed to Bremner in 1913.

BROKENLEG, lake (L-4)
Said to be a translation of an Indian name.

BROOKSLEY, locality (K-6)
Originally Brookfield and the original name of the school district; when the post office was opened the name was changed to avoid duplication. (1908)

BROXBURN, locality (N-6)
Probably after Broxburn, West Lothian, Scotland. (1909-1911)

BUCHANAN, creek (E-3)
After John Alexander Buchanan, D.L.S.

BUCK, lake and BUCK LAKE, hamlet (J-5)
"Bull' Lake on Arrowsmith map, 1859; in Cree *ya-pe-oo*, meaning "bull moose"; in Stoney, *tam-no-amna* (Tyrrell) Father Lacombe, in his Cree dictionary, gives *ayabe* as meaning "bull."

BUCKLAKE, creek (J-5)

Draining Buck Lake, called by David Thompson "Sturgeon" creek.

BULLS HEAD, butte and locality (O-8)
BULLSHEAD, creek

In Blackfoot, *in-e-oto-ka,* or "buffalo head" so named because of its shape (Dawson). The locality and the creek take their names from the butte.

BURBANK, locality (K-5)

Formerly the name of a C.N.R. station, it is thought that it is after Luther Burbank (1849-1926), the famous American horticulturist.

BURTONSVILLE, locality

After C. Burton, former postmaster. (1909)

BURY, ridge (J-2)

In honour of Major W. H. Bury, D.S.O., of Edmonton, killed in World War II.

BUSBY, hamlet (I-5)

The original post office was named Independence until 1915. The name was later changed to Busby, after a contractor working on construction of the E. D & B. C. Railway. There is a place of this name in England and it appeared in Domesday Book, 1086, as *Buschebi.* The name is derived from the old Scandinavian *Buski,* a shrub, (Ekwall). The well-known headgear of the Guards is known as a "busby".

BUTZE, locality (K-8)

Originally a C.N.R. station and named after A. Butze, a former purchasing agent with the Grand Trunk Pacific Railway.

— C —

CABIN LAKE, locality (L-8)

Name probably given after a former lake with an old cabin on its shore. (1923)

CAIRNGORM, mountain (8,564 feet) (J-2)

Gaelic for "yellow mountain." (1916)

CALAIS, hamlet (G-3)

The name was originally given to the post office for the Reverend Jules-Marie Calais, O.M.I. (1871-1944), the second priest in charge of the old mission on Sturgeon Lake.

CALDBECK, locality (L-5)

After Caldbeck, Wigton, Cumberland, England, the home of John Peel, a famous huntsman, immortalized in the well-known song. The song was written about 1820 by a friend of Peel's as they sat chatting before the fire at Caldbeck one winter evening. The name is first reported in 1060 as *Caldebek* (Ekwall) and means "cold brook."

CALUMET, peak (9,766) feet), creek and ridge   (1-2)
    Smokey River, the name was suggested in 1923 after the former name
    of the creek — Pipestone. The calumet was the peace pipe smoked by
    the Indians.

CAMPBELL, locality   (I-6)
    After Alex Campbell, one-time traffic manager, Edmonton, Dunvegan
    and British Columbia Railway; he later left to reside in Pocatello, Idaho.

CANNELL, locality   (I-5)
    After William Cannell (1867-1922), Edmonton contractor and formerly
    a president of the Acme Brick Company. (1913)

CANOE, pass   (K-2)
    Between the Whirlpool River and a branch of the Canoe River, B.C.
    After the Canoe River, B.C., a tributary of the Columbia River. David
    Thompson, in January 1811, ascended the Athabasca Pass to cross the
    mountains and descended the Wood River to the Columbia River at
    the mouth of the Canoe River. Here he remained until April, 1811,
    when he built a canoe in which he ascended the Columbia. Hence the
    name Canoe River and Pass.

CANYON CREEK, hamlet   (G-4)
    From a creek in the vicinity which probably takes its name from the
    shape of the river bed.

CAPITOL, mountain (8,000 feet)   (J-2)
    The Capitol was the Roman temple of Jupiter on one of the seven
    hills of Rome and no doubt this mountain has a fancied resemblance.

CARDINAL, lake   (F-3)
    Named about 1912 after one Louis Cardinal, an early settler.

CARSELAND, hamlet   (M-6)
    Formerly a village and originally called Griesbach; the present name
    was said to mean "river valley land," descriptive of the rich soil of
    the area. (1910)

CARUSO, locality   (L-6)
    Formerly named Cheadle. The present name was for the C.P.R. station
    and after Enrico Caruso (1873-1921), the famous Italian tenor who
    gained fame for his operatic roles. His voice was said to be unequalled
    in power and range. He was acclaimed in the major cities of the world.
    (1917)

CASKET, mountain (7,320 feet)   (I-1)
    Sheep Creek; from a fancied resemblance to a casket of a formation
    near its summit.

CASSILS, locality   (M-7)
    Originally a village and on the main line of the C.P.R., it was named
    after Charles Cassils, of Cassils, Cochrane and Company of Montreal.
    (1884)

CASTLE MOUNTAIN, locality   (L-4)
    Formerly a village and named after Castle Mountain now Mount
    Eisenhower (q.v.). (1883)

CASTLEGUARD, mountain (10,096 feet), river and glacier (K-3)
This magnificent mountain with its castellated appearance is set on the southern rim of the Columbia Ice Field and from its summit one of the finest views of the latter is to be had. There are no other peaks encroaching on its domain for many miles and the mountain rises as a guardian over the area. The river and glacier take their name from the mount.

CATACOMBS, mountain (10,600 feet) and creek (K-3)
The name describes the alcove formation of the mountain and was probably inspired by the underground burial places of the early Christians in Rome.

CATARACT, peak (10,935 feet) (L-4)
Head of the Pipestone River; after falls in the area. (1908)

CAUDRON, peak (8,355 feet) (N-5)
Livingstone Range; descriptive of the top which is said to resemble a cooking cauldron.

CAVE, mountain (8,697 feet) (M-4)
From a cave in the mountain. (1916)

CAVENDISH, locality (M-8)
Formerly Pancras. Named in honour of Victor Christian William Cavendish (1868-1938), Duke of Devonshire, Governor General of Canada, 1916-1921. (1917)

CECIL, locality (N-7)
For Mrs. J. M. Cameron, wife of a former general superintendent, C.P.R. Calgary. Formerly called Terrace. (After 1924)

CENTRE, peak (8,355 feet) (N-5)
This peak on the B.C.-Alberta border in the Livingstone Range is between the heads of two valleys.

CESSFORD, hamlet (L-7)
Formerly a village, the name was that of the post office and the name of the farm of the first postmistress, a Mrs. Anderson. (1910)

CHAILEY, locality (I-7)
After Chailey, Sussex, England, the former home of C. H. Brown who was the first postmaster. The name first appears in 1256 as *Chaglegh-Chag* meaning broom or gorse and *leah* meaning glade or clearing, (Ekwall). (1907)

CHAK, peak (9,114 feet) (J-2)
On the B.C.-Alberta border, the peak's name is the Indian word for "eagle." (1916)

CHARRON, locality (H-7)
Originally the name of the post office, it is after a Metis trapper. (1917)

CHEECHAM, locality (F-7)
Said to be named after an Indian. (1923)

CHERRY, coulee (N-7)
From Blackfoot name, *ami-onaskway,* signifying "berries up the hillside," (Nelson).

CHESTERWOLD, locality (J-6)

The former home of Peter A. Cooper, the first postmaster, was Chesterville, Nebraska. Chester comes from the old Roman word *castra* meaning a fortified camp and *wold* is Old English for open uncultivated rolling land. (1903)

CHETANG, ridge (J-2)

Stoney Indian word for "hawk" (1912)

CHEVIOT, mountain (8,925 feet) (J-3)

Possibly after the Cheviot hills which stretch along the border of England and Scotland. The origin of the name is obscure.

CHINOOK, village (L-8)

Named for the warm drying winds which early voyageurs named "chinook." These sudden warm winds which raise the temperatures as much as fifty degrees give southern Alberta a milder winter climate than the provinces to the east. The simplest explanation is that as a mass of warm Pacific air moves inland it is forced upwards by the Rockies and as it descends towards Alberta it increases in pressure and temperature. The chinook is characterized by a bright arch across the sky. These warm winds are experienced not only in Alberta but in Greenland and Switzerland where they are known as the "foehn."

An Indian legend states that Chinook was a beautiful maiden who wandered away and was lost in the mountains. Searches by the bravest warriors failed to find her until one day a soft warm wind blew from the West. The Indians whispered "It is the breath of our beautiful Chinook."

CLAIRMONT, hamlet (G-2)

Formerly a village and named after Claremont, Ontario, the birthplace of Walter McFarlane, who surveyed the townsite; the Alberta spelling is erroneous. (1916)

CLITHEROE, mountain (9,014 feet) (J-2)

After Clitheroe, Lancashire, England. The origin of the name is uncertain but may be from the Old Scandinavian *kliora* (song thrush) and Old Norse *haugr* (hill) — literally "song thrush hill." It appears in 1102 as *Cliderhou* (Ekwall).

CLOUSTON, creek (G-2)

For Noel Stewart Clouston, D.L.S., a member of a survey, 1920.

CLUNY, village (M-6)

It is uncertain how this community on the main line of the C.P.R. received its name. One version (*Place-names of Alberta*, 1928) states that it was after Cluny Parish, Aberdeenshire, Scotland. However, it may have been named after Cluny, France, which was in medieval times an important ecclesiastical centre of monastic reform. A third and more likely explanation (quoted by Leishman McNeill in *Tales of the Old Town*) is that it was named for Cluny McPherson Stades. (1884)

CODESA, locality (F-3)

Formerly Rahab, after a biblical character, a harlot of Jericho in the time of Joshua, it was changed in 1937 to its present name for E. *Collins*,

J. E. *De*akin and L. W. *Sa*unders, officials of the Northern Alberta Railway.

COLLEGE HEIGHTS, hamlet (K-5)
Named for the Seventh Day Adventist College situated on a height of land here.

COMREY, hamlet (O-8)
The initial letters of the names of the following early settlers were used for this derivation: (1) Columbus Larson, (2) Ole Roen, (3) Mons Roen, (4) R. Rolfson, (5) J. J. Evenson and (6) Ed. Yager. (*Warner Pioneers* — The Warner Old Timers' Association, 1962)

CONDOR, hamlet (K-5)
Formerly a village this hamlet takes its name after the gunboat H.M.S. *Condor* commanded by Captain Lord Charles Beresford, during the bombardment of Alexandria, Egypt, July 11, 1882. In April, 1882, there occurred an uprising in Alexandria headed by one Arabi Pasha and during the rioting that followed a number of Europeans were killed. The rebellion was put down by the British and in the course of this the British fleet bombarded Alexandria. (1914)

CONE, mountain (9,500 feet) (M-4)
Spray River; descriptive of the outline of the mountain.

CONKLIN, hamlet (G-7)
After John Conklin, the timekeeper for J. D. McArthur, a railway contractor. Formerly a village on the A. and G.W. Railway. (1916)

CORDONNIER, mount (9,910 feet) (M-5)
After a French general who distinguished himself in World War I. (1918)

CORK, locality (I-7)
Formerly the name of the post office and probably after County Cork in the southwest of Ireland. (1910)

CORNUCOPIA, locality (K-7)
Originally a post office name; horn of plenty — the name reflected the hopes of the early settlers. (1910)

CORNWALL, lake (A-B-7)
Named for J. K. Cornwall (1871-1955), who was born at Brantford, Ontario and was known as "Peace River Jim." At fourteen he left home and went to sea and before he was twenty-one he had travelled twice around the world, including a crossing of Russia. In 1896 he came to what is now Alberta and setttled in the Peace River area where he established himself as a trapper, trader and later he became interested in transportation, building boats and barges for the Peace and Athabasca Rivers. From 1908-1912 he was an M.L.A. for Peace River. He was a tireless advocate of the area both for settlement and for its natural resources — including the oil sands and he urged that roads and railways be built to make it accessible. During World War I he raised a battalion which went overseas at which time he received the rank of Colonel; in 1918 he received the D.S.O. On his return he continued to promote the Peace River area and later in World War II was a special consultant to the U.S. Army. He died in Calgary in 1955.

COUNTESS, locality (M-7)
Formerly a C.P.R. station and probably named after Countess Bassano or Countess Lathom; Bassano (q.v.), Lathom (q.v.) and Countess were adjacent railway stations. (1914)

COXHILL, hill (M-5)
Named by A. O. Wheeler, D.L.S. after an assistant named Cox. (1896)

CRAIGDHU, locality (L-5)
Originally the name of the C.P.R. station it is Gaelic for "black rock." (1912)

CRAIGEND, locality (H-7)
Originally the name of a school district and then given to the post office. (1925)

CRAIGMILLAR, locality (K-7)
William Penman, an early postmaster came from Craigmillar, Edinburgh, Scotland. (1913)

CRANDELL, mount (7,812 feet) and lake (O-5)
Named for Edward Henry Crandell (1859-1944) pioneer Calgary businessman. He also served on the city council and school board there. He was interested in the old Discovery oil well near Waterton which was to the west of the mountain. (1914)

CRIPPSDALE, locality (H-6)
The first postmaster was M. J. Cripps. (1912)

CULP, locality (F-3)
A station on the E.D. & B.C. Railway it was named after J. H. Culp, a former railway conductor. (1915)

CUMNOCK, mountain (8,071 feet) (J-2)
Named after Cumnock, Ayrshire, Scotland.

CURATOR, mountain (8,604 feet) (J-3)
From its position as custodian of Shovel Pass (7,500 feet) which forms a route to the Maligne Valley.

CURIA, mountain (9,300 feet) (J-2)
From a fancied resemblance to the Roman senate-house or curia. This mountain, Basilica Mountain and Rostrum Hill (q.v.) surround the valley known as The Forum in a fancied resemblance to the principal buildings of ancient Rome. (1916)

CURLEW, locality (K-6)
At one time the name of the post office, the name probably comes from the long-billed shore bird which could have been seen on small lakes in the area at the time of early settlement. (1906)

CYCLAMEN, ridge (7,403 feet) (N-5)
Probably named for the pink colour (similar to that of the flower) of the rock formation. (1914)

CYCLONE, mountain (10,006 feet) (L-4)
Apparently a storm was raging when the peak was named.

CYGNET, lake and locality (K-5)
This name was suggested by the proximity of this small lake to Swan (now Sylvan) Lake. There was a C.P.R. station here of the same name at one time and the locality takes its name from it.

— D —

DAIS, mountain (10,612 feet) (K-3)
The prominent raised forms give this mountain which dominates the Chaba Valley its name. It was originally named "Blackmonks" by Professor Jean Habel of Berlin who first explored the valley in 1901. (1912)

DALEHURST, locality (I-3)
Named for one Dale, a timekeeper or a merchant who had the main store here during construction days of the C.N. and G.T.P. Railways, around 1915. The local post office was Hinton until 1919. Ekwall mention *hyrst* (Old English) as "hill, wood, wooded hill."

DARDANELLES, stretch (O-5)
Between the Middle and Upper Waterton Lakes and named after the narrows leading from the Mediterranean Sea into the Black Sea.

DAVEY, lake (K-5)
Said to be named after an early settler. (1892)

DEBOLT, hamlet and creek (G-2)
Named for H. E. Debolt (1888-1969), the first postmaster who with his brother George Debolt (1884-1961) came to the Peace River area in 1919 from the State of Washington. The mail was originally picked up at George's house but when the post office was established H. E. Debolt became postmaster. H. E. Debolt was M.L.A. for the area from 1940-1950.

DELBURNE, village (K-6)
The origin of this name is uncertain but there are said to be two possible derivations. The first is that before the Grand Trunk Pacific Railway arrived in 1911, the original post office was known as Gaetz Valley Post Office and was located three miles east of the present village. When the railway came the post office was moved to the townsite and the station is said to have been named Delburn from *Del*la Mew*burn,* sister of Dr. (later Colonel) F. H. Mewburn (1858-1929), a pioneer medical practitioner.

The second possible origin of the name is that when the G. T. P. reached the location of the present village the railway officials gave a list of names to the owners of the land acquired for the townsite — M. J. Manning and W. C. Clendening — who discussed names with other settlers. The name Delburne (sometimes in the past spelt 'Delbourne') proved the most popular and so was chosen. (1912).

DELPH, locality (I-6)
Originally a post office; named for delft, the famous blue and white glazed earthware made at Delft in Holland. The spelling of the name is incorrect. (1913)

DESMARAIS, hamlet   (F-5)
Possibly after one F. Desmarais who built a road from Lesser Slave
Lake to Sturgeon Lake in 1902.

DEVENISH, locality   (G-7)
After Gwen Devenish, a friend of Mrs. Jack Judge, wife of an engineer
on the Alberta and Great Waterways Railway. Miss Devenish became
a nurse at the Johns Hopkins Hospital, Baltimore.

DEVONA, locality   (J-2)
The C.N.R. station was named in 1915 possibly after the Devonian
geological formations nearby. Williams in *Jasper National Park* (1928)
states "... those who are in no hurry ... will enjoy following the historic
trail along the west side of the Athabasca, past the site of Henry House
and Swift's plantation, and thence along the grassy flats bordering the
river to Devona ... "

DISASTER, point   (J-2)
On the Athabasca River near Pocahontas where Dr. E. G. Deville (1849-
1924) gave the name, jokingly, because Sandford Fleming's brandy flask
was broken on a rock here.

DIVERGENCE, peak (9,275) and creek   (K-2)
This peak is at an angle on the Alberta-British Columbia boundary line.
The creek takes its name from the mount. (peak, 1921)

DOG, island   (G-5)
This island two miles out in Lesser Slave Lake from the town of Slave
Lake was an old-time fishery where the fur traders used to put up fish
for dog feed.

DONNELLY, island   (C-4)
After Cecil B. C. Donnelly, D.L.S., P.L.S., M.L.S., born 1889.

DREAU, locality   (F-3)
After a priest who was very active in the district.

DUAGH, locality   (I-6)
After Duagh, County Kerry, Ireland. Originally the name of the post
office; later a village. (1900)

DUNGEON, peak (10,200 feet)   (J-2)
One of the Ramparts (Turret, Bastion, Redoubt). The term "dungeon"
usually thought to mean an underground cell also referred to a Norman
keep. (1916)

DUNN, locality   (J-8)
Formerly a village; the station was possibly named after a Grand Trunk
Pacific official — Samuel Dunn — in 1908. The post office name was
changed from Ribstone in 1914.

DYSON, mount (5.800 feet) and creek   (M-5)
Sheep River; after a rancher who probably lived nearby.

225

— E —

EDITH, lake (J-2)

This beautifully coloured lake northeast of Jasper townsite is named after the wife of H. A. McColl, general superintendent of the Grand Trunk Pacific Railway when he was in charge of construction.

ELKTON, locality (L-5)

From its proximity to the Red Deer River (q.v.) and originally the name of the post office. The early fur traders mistakenly referred to elk as "red deer."

ELSPETH, locality (K-5)

The station on the Canadian Northern branch line here was built or named in 1914 and possibly the name was given to honour the wife, daughter or sister of an early settler or railway official.

ENDIANG, hamlet (K-7)

The name was suggested by W. H. Foreman, early postmaster, and is Chippewa Indian for "my home." (1910)

ETHERINGTON, mount and creek (M-5)

In honour of Colonel Frederick Etherington, C.M.G., of Kingston, Ontario, who served during the First World War with the Canadian Army Medical Corps.

EVA, lake (B-4)

After the wife of J. N. Wallace, D.L.S.

EVARTS, locality (K-5)

After an early settler, Louis P. Evarts; originally the post office name. (1903)

EWING, locality (K-6)

Originally the name of a post office and lake; after John Ewing who settled on a lake once in the vicinity about 1898.

EXCELSIOR, locality (I-6)

A selected name originally given to the post office.

— F —

FALLIS, hamlet (I-5)

For W. S. Fallis a former president of the Sherwin Williams Company and later a vice-president of the Canadian Manufacturers' Association. (1911)

FENN, locality (K-6)

Formerly a village on the C.N.R. There are two derivations of this name. The first is that when the railroad was being built the weather was very hot. A local boy was employed to carry water to the workers; he was an efficient steady lad, took his job seriously and always had plenty of cold water for the thirsty men. His activity so impressed the men that it was decided to name the station in the vicinity after this efficient boy whose name was Fenn.

The second explanation is that among the earliest settlers was a man from the Fen district in England which is low lying and marshy. In the pioneer days around the Alberta Fenn district there was plenty of water and sloughs which reminded the early settler of his homeland. (1911)

FORT MACKAY, hamlet   (E-7)
Originally a post on the left bank of the Athabasca River below the mouth of the MacKay River it was named in honour of Dr. William Morrison MacKay (1836-1917), pioneer physician, surgeon and fur trader. A native of Scotland he received his medical education at Edinburgh where the famous Joseph Lister was lecturer at the time. In 1864 he joined the Hudson's Bay Company as surgeon and later became chief trader. He served at York Factory and Norway House but the greater part of his career was spent in the Mackenzie District and in what is now northern Alberta. He retired to Edmonton in 1898 and in 1902 was elected the first president of the Northern Alberta Medical Association, a forerunner of the Edmonton Academy of Medicine. (*Early Medicine in Alberta* — H. C. Jamieson, Edmonton, 1947)

FORTALICE, mountain (9,300 feet)   (J-2)
This outlying peak resembles a fortalice or a small fort. (1916)

FORUM, peak (7,922 feet)   (O-5)
This peak on the Alberta-British Columbia border is named for a small lake of the same name in B.C. It is not known how this lake came to be given this name but its shape may have been reminiscent of an ancient forum or Roman market place particularly the elliptical one at Jerash (now in Jordan).

FORUM, THE, valley   (J-2)
This alpine valley is surrounded by Curia Mountain, Basilica Mountain and Rostrum Hill (q.v.) as in the Forum in ancient Rome.

FOX, locality   (N-8)
After the early postmaster, James H. Fox. (1912)

— G —

GAGE, locality   (F-2)
After a locomotive engineer by the name of Gage formerly of the Edmonton, Dunvegan and British Columbia Railway.

GLORIA, mountain (9,500 feet) and lake   (M-4)
After the Latin *Gloria* meaning glory and probably described the feelings of whoever named it. (1917)

GOODFISH, lake and GOODFISH LAKE, locality   (H-7)
So named as it was well stocked with good fish. The locality takes its name from the lake.

GUNDY, locality   (G-1)
Named after Wood Gundy Ltd., well-known investment dealers originally of Toronto, owners of the nearby property known as Gundy Ranch when the station was named.

HEART, lake and river   (G-7)
From the shape of the lake; the river flows into the Owl River and is
named after the lake.

HEART, river   (F-3)
This river that empties into the Peace at the town of Peace River was
originally known as Heart Brook. To the voyageurs it was known as
"Riviere le Coeur." The English name Heart River prevailed.

HEATBURG, locality   (K-6)
Probably named by pioneers during an unusually hot spell during the
summer.

HIBERNIA, lake   (J-2)
This lake where the waters are reputed to be of a paddy green colour
is named after the Latin name for Ireland.

HIGHRIDGE, locality   (I-5)
From a high ridge in the area.

HOLCROFT, mount (8,800 feet)   (M-5)
After Herbert Spencer Holcroft, D.L.S., O.L.S., Surveyor General's staff,
surveys, 1904-1914.

HYLO, locality   (H-6)
Originally the name of a village on the A. & G.W. Railway. Hylo is a
term used in faro — a gambling game with cards, counters and other
equipment such as a shuffling box. The game was probably played by
railway construction workers in the early days. It originated in France
where it was much in vogue during the reign of Louis XIV and was
brought to North America. The game was popular in many gold rush
towns but fell out of favour owing to dishonest practices. It got its
name from Pharaoh, a picture of an Egyptian king appearing on a card
of the old French pack. (1914)

INKSTER, lake   (A-7)
After Oluff Inkster, D.L.S., A.L.S., International Boundary Commission.

JARROW, locality   (J-7)
Prior to 1909 this area was known as Jackson Coulee Post Office after
Edwin Jackson, postmaster and then prior to 1919 it was known as
Junkins Post Office. It was one of the stations listed in alphabetical
order by the Grand Trunk Pacific — Hawkins, Irma, Jarrow, Kinsella,
etc. The original station may have been named by someone from Jarrow,
County Durham, England. Although many names in this area of Britain
have Scandinavian origins, Jarrow is an exception. The name appears as

Gyruum ca. 730 (Bede), *Girwe* 1104-8, *Jarum* 1158, *Jarwe* 1228. The name is that of a tribe the *Gyrwe* or *Gyruii* who migrated from the fen country around Peterborough. The actual tribe name is derived from an old English name for mud or fen, i.e. marsh-dwellers, (Ekwall). It was in the monastery (built ca. 685) here that the Venerable Bede ca. 673-735 wrote his *Ecclesiastical History of the English People* which he finished in the year of his death.

JARVIE, hamlet (H-5)
Originally called Jarvis after a foreman or surveyor on the Edmonton, Dunvegan and British Columbia Railway. It was later changed to its present name by the Post Office Department probably to avoid confusion with another place of a similar name. (1914)

JEAN CÔTÉ, hamlet (F-3)
After the Hon. Jean Leon Côté (1867-1924), former Provincial Secretary, Province of Alberta and named by the Rev. C. Falher, O.M.I. J. L. Côté was the M.L.A. for Grouard Constituency from 1909-1923 and a member of the Alaska-Yukon Boundary Commission Survey, ca. 1903. He was, after the Gold Rush, joined in Dawson City, Y.T. by the two Cautley brothers (D.L.S.) in a survey partnership which was eventually dissolved when they moved to Edmonton. See also Côté, mount.

JIMMY SIMPSON, mount (9,700 feet) (L-3)
In honour of James ("Jimmy") Simpson (1878-1972) well-known guide and outfitter at Banff and Bow Lake. A native of England, he arrived in Canada in 1896 coming to Winnipeg and then Banff. A year later he first rode to the Bow Lake area and was impressed with the scenery. For a number of years he guided parties of hunters — in the early days — and climbers into the region. With the coming of the Banff-Jasper Highway he built a tourist lodge at Bow Lake. This lodge which is still in operation he named *Num-ti-jah*, the Indian for pine marten. The mountain overlooks Bow Lake and the lodge. (1973)

JOSEPHBURG, hamlet (I-6)
Named for a town in Galicia formerly part of the old Austro-Hungarian Empire. The first settlers hailed from two villages Brigidau and Josefsberg eight miles apart. From 1888 to 1890 many families left for Canada and took up homesteads near Medicine Hat, naming their settlement "Josefsburg." After two successive crop failures owing to drought they sought new land near Edmonton, arriving in 1891. One group took up land five miles east of Fort Saskatchewan and named the new settlement "Josefsberg." In December, 1893 "Josefsberg Public School District No. 296" was established and Gus Doze, the first secretary-treasurer began to spell the name of the district "Josephburg" which has been used ever since.

— K —

KEG, river and KEG RIVER, hamlet (D-3)
Peace River; the origin of the name is uncertain but it may have had something to do with an incident involving a keg of rum, salt pork or some other commodity from fur trade days.

KEITH, lake   (H-7)
    After V. B. C. Keith, Edmonton, owner of land in the township. (1915)

KERKESLIN, mountain (9,790 feet)   (J-2)
    South of Mount Hardisty and named by Hector in 1859 but the origin of the name is unknown at present.

— L —

LA GLACE, hamlet   (G-2)
    After Charles La Glace, Indian settler in Section 7, who was drowned in Valhalla Lake aged 62 years around 1909. Originally the name of the post office. (1917)

LABYRINTH, lake   (J-6)
    From its complicated shape. (1892)

LANES, lake   (K-7)
    After one John Lane, once a well-known rancher in the area.

LEAMAN, locality   (I-4)
    After a cousin of H. Philips, secretary, Grand Trunk Pacific Railway. Chip Lake Post Office until 1914. (1911)

LEYLAND, locality   (J-3)
    Originally the name of the C.N.R. station which was built or named in 1913 by the Mountain Park Coal Company under a contract with the G.T.P. Branch Lines Railway Company. It was named after F. W. Leyland of England, organizer and the first vice-president of the Mountain Park Coal Company and Railway.
    There is a Leyland in Lancashire and the name first appeared in Domesday Book as *Lailand,* in the Lancashire Pipe Rolls ca. 1160 as *Leilandia,* and in 1246 in the Assize Rolls as *Leyland;* it means "fallow or untilled land," (Ekwall).

LIPALIAN, mountain (8,900 feet)   (L-4)
    East of Lake Louise and named for the fossil shells found in the rock strata. (1959)

LITTLE GEM, locality   (L-8)
    The C.N. station was built in 1925 and named after Little Gem Post Office and school district. No doubt the first settlers thought that their area was a little gem!

LLOYDS HILL, locality   (K-8)
    After Mrs G. L. Lloyd, postmistress. (1915)

LOCHEARN, locality   (K-4)
    Formerly a C.P.R. and C.N.R. station and also the name of a former municipal district. The origin is uncertain. *Place-Names of Alberta,* 1928, makes the cryptic comment "Loch Ernie is near" but no feature of this name is recorded. There is a Loch Earn in Perthshire, Scotland. (C.P. 1914; C.N. 1918)

LONEBUTTE, locality (L-7)
From the only noticeable hill for miles around; originally the name of the post office and former municipal district. (1910)

LOOMA, locality (I-6)
Originally Looma Vista. This could be a descriptive name — 'loom' meaning a vague first appearance of land (at sea) and 'vista' indicating a long narrow view as between rows of trees. At one time the name applied to the village.

LUMPY, butte (O-6)
From the appearance of the butte.

LYMBURN, locality (G-1)
After John Farquhar Lymburn (1880-   ), a native of Scotland where he was educated, he came to Canada in 1911. He was elected to the Provincial Legislature in 1926 and again in 1930. He was appointed Attorney-General in 1926 in the United Farmers of Alberta Government and remained in that post until he was defeated at the general election in 1935.

— M —

MACKAY, locality (I-4)
After a contractor; originally the name of the C.N.R. station. (1911)

MACKAY, river (E-7)
For derivation see Fort MacKay.

MACKENZIE, mount (9,067 feet) (J-3)
South of Cardinal River and a local name reported in 1925.

MADDEN, hamlet (L-5)
After one Barney Madden, a prominent district rancher.

MAGOG, mount (10,050 feet) (M-4)
Probably after one of two legendary giants of early Celtic mythology, Gog and Magog. They were reputedly the last of a race of giants said to have descended from a race of demons who roamed Albion (Britain) until exterminated by one Brute and his companions, refugees from Troy. Gog and Magog were brought to London and chained to the palace of Brute where they served as porters.

MAJESTIC, locality (M-8)
To the early settlers this name probably described the area. (1914)

MANN, lakes (Upper and Lower) (H-7)
After Sir Donald Mann (1853-1934); see Mannville, village.

MEARNS, locality (I-5)
Originally St. Charles siding. Renamed Mearns by the Northern Alberta Railway probably after the place of the same name in Scotland. Originally an E.D. and B.C.R. station. (1912)

MOAT, lake and passage (6,939 feet) (J-2)
A moat was a ditch surrounding the ramparts of a castle and this lake is near The Ramparts.

MONITOR, hamlet (K-8)
The post office name was Sounding Lake until it was changed to Monitor, December 1, 1913. Originally a village, this hamlet is on the same line as Consort and Coronation which were named at the time of the Coronation of King George V in 1911. Perhaps in keeping with the names of the other stations and as a patriotic gesture the name of a shallow draught warship, a monitor — was chosen.

MORRIN, village (L-6)
The C.N. records state that this village could have been named after or for Joseph Morrin (1792-1861), a Scottish born physician and philanthropist who came to Canada at an early age. He was educated in Quebec and London and practised in Quebec City and gave a large sum of money to found Morrin College, a Presbyterian college there. He was the first president of the Medical Board of Lower Canada.

MOUNTAIN PARK, locality (J-3)
Partially descriptive as it was named after Mountain Park Coal Company who built stations along this line for the Grand Trunk Pacific Railway. (1913)

MURAL, glacier (K-2)
South of Gendarme Mountain, Smoky River; there is a great icewall at the head of it.

MUSKIKI, lake and creek (J-3)
Cardinal River; Cree Indian for "medicine."

— N —

NITON, hamlet (I-4)
Said to have been named for a railway construction contractor or the words "not in" reversed suggesting perhaps that the station agent was frequently absent! (1911)

NOJACK, locality (I-4)
When two entrepreneurs were building a service station and motel at this spot, they had no money and wished to name the establishment "Nojack." This idea did not meet with official approval but when the buildings were erected Nojack it became!

Other stories connected with this name relate that on one occasion some construction workers came looking for their pay and the timekeeper told them "No jack today boys!" Still another relates how a construction worker kept proposing to a local girl only to be told repeatedly 'No, Jack!"

NORAL, hamlet (H-6)
Originally a village on the Alberta and Great Waterways Railway; possibly short for "Northern Alberta." (1914)

NORFOLK, locality (L-5)

This name could have been given by a pioneer from the County of Norfolk in England or from Norfolk in Virginia or in Nebraska. "Norfolk" means northern people in contrast to "Suffolk" indicating people from the southern part of East Anglia, (Ekwall). (1914)

NOTIKEWIN, river and hamlet (E-3)

The Indian word for battle. The name was changed from Battle in 1915 to avoid duplication with the Battle River further south. The hamlet was formerly Battle River Prairie. The name Battle originated from a battle in which the Beaver Indians defeated the invading Crees.

— O —

OGRE, canyon and creek (J-2)

At one point in the gorge the rock resembles the outline of a grotesque head which, seen from a distance, appears to be holding a large rock in its mouth.

OKE, locality (J-3)

Originally the name of the C.N. station it could have been named after an early settler or there could have been an incident regarding the popular expression "O.K." for all right (and first spelled phonetically by a workman as "Ol Korrec.") (1912)

OLD FORT, point (J-2)

Site of an old post built by William Henry in 1812 as a cache for supplies and furs.

OPAL, locality (I-6)

A selected name originally given to the village, post office and later the former municipal district. (1912)

— P —

PATRICIA, lake (J-2)

This clear blue lake four miles north of the Jasper townsite is a sister lake of Pyramid and it is said that the waters have no visible inlet. It was named in honour of Princess Patricia of Connaught (Lady Patricia Ramsay, 1886-   ), daughter of H.R.H. the Duke of Connaught, Governor General of Canada, 1911-1916.

PENDANT D'OREILLE, locality (O-8)

The name of a former post office this locality south of Pakowki lake near the U.S. border means (in literal translation) "hanging ears." There is a river of a very similar name (Pend d'Oreille) flowing into southeastern British Columbia from the U.S. and its name is said to have been given by French Canadian voyageurs to a local tribe of Indians who wore shell ornaments hanging from their ears. The name of the Alberta locality may well have a similar origin. (1910)

PENDRYL, locality (J-5)

Originally the name of the post office it was possibly named by a pioneer from the area of Boscobel House, Shropshire, England. Boscobel House was originally a hunting lodge built about 1580 by the Giffards of Chillington under Richard Penderel. It was at Boscobel House that Charles II hid in the oak tree to escape detection. (1916)

PHARAOH, peaks (8,895 feet) (L-4)

From an imaginery resemblance to a row of Egyptian mummies.

PHOENIX, locality (K-4)

Possibly named by an early settler from one of the several places of this name in the United States. A phoenix is a mythological bird which was consumed by fire and from the ashes arose a new phoenix. The name was originally that of the post office. (1923)

PIERRE, creek (D-7)

Athabasca River; from a cliff of pipestone in the area which in French is 'pierre au calumet.'

PINE, creek (M-5)

Bow River; this name is shown on the Arrowsmith map, 1859 and possibly after pines nearby.

POCAHONTAS, locality (J-2)

Originally a coal mining village and named after Pocahontas, a coal mining town in Virginia, U.S.A. Pocahontas (1595-1617) whose real name was Matoaka was the daughter of Powhatan. According to legend she enabled many English settlers at Jamestown, Virginia, to escape the vengeance of her tribe. She is said to have thrown herself on Captain John Smith when he was about to be beaten to death by Powhatan's men. She married one John Rolfe in 1614 and in 1616 went to England where she was treated royally; she died in 1617 of smallpox and is buried in the church at Gravesend, Kent. (1911)

POSTILL, lake (K-6)

A local name reported in 1918 and said to be after a settler.

PRESTVILLE, locality (F-2)

Named for B. J. Prest (1884-1967). Born in England he received his education there, becoming a civil engineer. In 1906 he arrived in Canada and joined the Grand Trunk Pacific as a construction engineer and in 1912 went to the Edmonton, Dunvegan and British Columbia Railway as office engineer. It was he who was responsible at this time for the naming of a number of stations along this route. In 1931 he joined the Alberta Department of Lands and Mines and later transferred to the Main Highways Branch of the Department of Public Works. From there he went to the Department of Municipal Affairs and in 1938 again went to the Department of Public Works, this time with the Surveys Branch. In 1947 he became Director of Town Planning and retired in 1950. (1916)

PREVO, locality (J-5)

According to C.N. records it might have been the phonetic spelling of the French surname, Prevost. It could have been for a pioneer in the district or for one of the following prominent men: the Hon. François

J. B. Prevost (1870-   ) who was Minister of Colonization, Mines and Fisheries, 1905-1907 and who was counsel for the C.N.R. in Montreal or for a Senator Jules E. Prevost (1871-1943) who was a Member of Parliament. Formerly Norma.

PUNCHBOWL, falls and creek   (J-2)
Miss M. B. Williams in her book *Jasper National Park* (1928) describes the falls as follows: "A few minutes' walk from Pocahontas . . . tucked away in a narrow pocket of a valley which ends in a cul de sac, are the interesting Punchbowl falls. If the gods of the hills indulged in secret wassailing one could imagine no better place than this secluded and charming spot. The fall is formed by Punchbowl creek which, running along the rocky ledge above, apparently discoverd an opening and way of escape over the precipice. Tumbling down in a straight column, as if poured from a beaker, it falls into a rocky bowl, worn smooth and hollowed into lines graceful as a Grecian urn. Gathering here in a pool of jacinth, it spills over the rim and, reaching the valley, turns sharply at right angles to flow down to the Athabasca."

PYRIFORM, mountain (8,600 feet)   (M-5)
Sheep River; from its pear or pyramid shape. (1922)

— Q —

QUEENSTOWN, locality   (M-6)
Formerly a village the name was given to the district in 1888 by one Captain Dawson, the manager of the Canadian Pacific Colonization Company possibly in honor of Queen Victoria.

QUIGLEY, locality   (F-7)
Formerly the name of an A. & G.W.R. station it was for James M. Quigley, a railway contractor. (1917)

— R —

RED STAR, locality   (F-2)
Originally a school district name and then that of the post office. (1927)

REDLAND, locality   (L-6)
Probably descriptive of red soil in the area. Originally termed a village and on the C.N.R. (1914)

REDWILLOW, creek and RED WILLOW, locality   (K-6)
The name is probably from willows along the creek banks. Some accounts state that this was Old Wives Creek of the maps but Palliser refers to it as Beaver Dam Creek. The locality takes its name from the creek and was formerly a village with a post office. (1903)

REMUS, mount (8,800 feet)   (M-5)
For origin see Romulus, mount.

RICH VALLEY, hamlet (I-5)

The name was probably given by settlers who envisioned great prospects for the area from the rich soil.

ROMULUS, mount (M-5)

Probably after legendary founder and first king of Rome. Romulus and Remus were twin sons of Silvia and were set adrift on the Tiber in a trough which came to rest where Rome later stood. The two infants were suckled by a wolf and fed by a woodpecker. They were then brought up by a shepherd and later claimed the throne. Remus was later slain. Romulus then reigned alone. Mount Remus is adjacent.

ROSTRUM, hill (7,400 feet) (J-2)

The hill is said to resemble a pulpit or platform. The Rostrum of ancient Rome was a platform in the Forum adorned with the beaks of captured galleys. From it the orators and politicians harangued the crowds. (1916)

ROUND, lake (I-5)

Shown on the Palliser map, 1865, it is a descriptive name. Hector's itinerary reads on March 4th, 1859: "Cross high hills (between Round Lake and Pembina River) that form the watershed to the Saskatchewan, and halt on an island in Lac des Isles (Isle Lake), passing Lac Rond (Round Lake), three miles to our right."

— S —

SABINE, locality (K-6)

It is thought that this C.N.R. station was named for Sir Edward Sabine (1788-1883), soldier and explorer, who served in Canada during the U.S. War of 1812. He was born in Dublin, educated at the Royal Military Academy, Woolwich and served in the Royal Artillery. He was an astronomer on several voyages of discovery including Sir John Ross' first Arctic expedition in 1818 and on Sir William Edward Parry's expedition of 1819-20. His greatest service was in the field of terrestrial magnetism and he wrote a text on magnetic variation in many parts of the globe. He was elected a Fellow of the Royal Society in 1818, received the Copely Medal in 1821 and from 1861-1869 he was President of the Royal Society. (1903)

SADDLE, hills (G-2)

These hills between what was known as the Grande Prairie and the Spirit River Prairie are some 800 feet above the surrounding country and form a "saddle" between the two areas.

SCOTFORD, locality (I-6)

Originally the name given to the C.N.R. station it is after the Hon. Walter *Scott* (1867-1938), Premier of Saskatchewan and the Hon. A. C. Ruther*ford* (1857-1941), Premier of Alberta (see also Rutherford, mount).

SHAFTESBURY, settlement (F-3)

These flats which extend some 15 miles along the north bank of the Peace River above the modern town of Peace River have been the site of former Indian camps and trading posts. In 1879 the Rev. A. Garrioch arrived at the flats to select a site for an Anglican mission and farm. This effort did not prosper and was abandoned in 1881. In 1887 the Rev. J. Gough Brick started a new mission farm which was a success. These missionaries were probably sent out from England under the auspices of one of the missionary societies with funds possibly given by Anthony Ashley Cooper, 7th Earl of Shaftesbury, (1801-1885). A British parliamentarian he devoted much of his life to social reform and took a great interest in overseas missions.

SION, locality (I-5)
The name given to the post office originally, it is a biblical one sometimes spelt Zion. The holy hill of Zion referred to ancient Jerusalem but the name came to mean the Christian Church, the heavenly Jerusalem or kingdom of heaven and probably, at the time it was named, inspired high hopes. The name occurs frequently in the Bible as in *Isaiah* 40:5 "O Zion, that bringest good tidings, get thee up into the high mountain. . . ." (1904)

SITTINGSTONE, lake (K-6)
Probably a translation of the Indian name referring to a large stone in the lake.

SODA, lake and SODA LAKE, locality (I-7)
A shallow lake having soda content; a post office was established in 1903. (1893)

SPEDDEN, hamlet (H-7)
Formerly a village and originally spelt Speddin; Cache Lake Post Office until 1923. According to C.N. records the station was erected around 1920 and was named for R. Speddin who sent his yacht to the Arctic in search of Sir John Franklin (1786-1847) who died of scurvy with his crew. Many expeditions tried for years to locate the remains of the Franklin party, it was finally Captain (later Admiral) Francis L. McLintock (1819-1907) who discovered in 1857 the fate of Franklin. (See also Rae, mount).

SPURFIELD, hamlet (G-5)
From a spur line leading to the Canyon Creek Lumber Company of which a Mr. Field was manager. (1926)

SULPHUR, mountain (8,040 feet) (L-4)
This well-known feature south of Banff takes its name from the hot springs near the base. There is an observatory at the top of the mountain.

SWAN, hills, river and SWAN HILLS, town (G-4—H-4)
In Indian legend the hills — House Mountain, Deer Mountain and Wallace Mountain — are the home of thunder. In the hills are many huge birds and thunder is the sound of the flapping of their wings. The birds are said never to harm men but the Indians claim it would be unwise to visit their abode. Since they never leave their home no one has ever seen them. The river and the town take their name from the hills.

TAR, island and TAR ISLAND, hamlet (E-7)
So called from their proximity to the Athabasca Tar Sands which were first noted by the fur traders and even earlier by a Cree trader, Wa-pa-su, in 1719.

TECUMSEH, mount (8,364 feet) (N-5)
Named in honour of Tecumseh (Shooting Star) Shawnee, Indian chief (1768-1813). Born in the U.S. he became a champion of the Indians against the steady encroachment of white settlement on Indian lands. As a result of an American victory at Tippecanoe, Indiana, he and many of his tribe went over to the British in Canada. In the War of 1812 he was made Brigadier General and led his Indians against the Americans. He was killed at the Battle of Moraviantown, Upper Canada.

THRONE, locality (K-7)
Named in 1911 when King George V was crowned. Among adjacent stations on this C.P.R. line named at this time were Consort, Coronation, Loyalist and Veteran. Hamilton Lake was the name of the post office until 1912. A throne is not only the royal seat but the dais on which it stands as well.

TIELAND, locality (H-5)
At one time considerable ties and timber were taken from this area.

TOD CREEK, locality and TODD, creek (N-5)
The locality takes its name from the creek (Crowsnest River) which in turn was named for William Todd who settled in the area around 1886. The locality name is spelt erroneously. (1915)

TOLLAND, locality (J-8)
An early postmaster, O. H. Webber, came from Tolland, Massachusetts. (1913)

TOMAHAWK, hamlet (I-5)
Said to be named by early settlers who originally came from Tomahawk, Wisconsin. The word "tomahawk" which refers to the Indian hatchet, has become part of the English language. It is said to have originally referred to the shape of the weapon. (1907)

TOPLAND, locality (H-5)
From its situation on a ridge between the Athabasca and Freeman Rivers; originally the name of the post office. (1914)

TORLEA, locality (J-7)
Originally the name of the village. This could be a descriptive name — *Tor* meaning hill and *lea*, a tract of open grassland. Nestor Post Office until 1916. (1909)

TRIPOLI, mountain (8,629 feet) (J-3)
Cardinal River; a local name reported in 1922. Possibly a mountain with three peaks.

TWIN TREE, lake (J-2)
There were two lovely pines on an island in the middle of the lake at the time it was named.

TWO JACK, lake (L-4)
This lake in Banff National Park was named after Jack Stanley who at one time operated the boat concession on Lake Minnewanka, and Jack Watters who worked for the Bankhead Mines.

— W —

WABASSO, lakes (J-2)
Indian for "rabbit." This interesting chain of small lakes southeast of Jasper on Buffalo Prairie are not true lakes but have been formed by the damming up of numerous streams by beaver, (Williams).

WANDERING, river and WANDERING RIVER, locality (G-6)
Presumably from the numerous bends in the river.

WANHAM, village (F-2)
Said to be an Indian name meaning "warm winds" probably from the chinooks.

WASEL, locality (I-7)
The original post office was named for Wasel (William) Hawreliak (later spelt Hawrelak) (1880-1973), first postmaster and one of the first settlers in the area. He came to Canada at the age of 18 from his native Bukovina and reached his homestead by floating down the North Saskatchewan River on a raft. His arrival started the movement of hundreds of immigrants into the region. As his farm prospered he devoted much of his time to community activities such as organizing school districts and being a municipal councillor. He retired to Edmonton in 1946. His son, William, was mayor of Edmonton for a number of years. (1911)

WATERHOLE, locality (F-2)
See Fairview, town. (1912)

WEED, lake (M-6)
No doubt because of an extensive growth of weeds!

WESSEX, locality (L-5)
Originally a tribal name, 'the West Saxons'; it was one of the seven kingdoms formed by the Saxons in the west of England. Ekwall mentions *West Seaxe*, Anglo-Saxon Chronicle, 514. C.P.R. station originally. (1910-12)

WHISKY GAP, locality (O-6)
Named for an American whisky trading post that flourished in the area before 1874. The word whisky is from the Gaelic.

WHITERABBIT, creek (K-4)
North Saskatchewan River; a translation of a Stoney Indian name.

WINTERBURN, hamlet   (I-6)

Additional information is that a local tradition reports that the name could be derived from steam 'burning' off the muskeg in winter.

WOOD RIVER, locality   (J-6)

There is no river of the name nearby; I. L. Bulloch, an early postmaster came from Wood River, Hall county, Nebraska.

WOOLFORD, locality   (O-6)

After the first settler T. H. Woolford who came from Utah in the early 1900's. Originally the name of the post office. (1912)

WYND, locality   (J-2)

On the C.N. line west of Jasper; a "wynd" is said to be "an alley in a Scots town" and could have been named by a settler from that country.

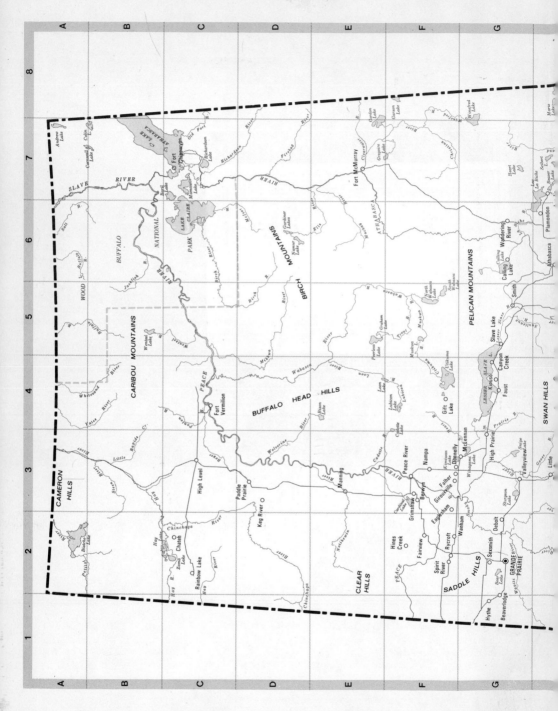